Motorcycle Journeys Through

NORTH AMERICA

Dale Coyner

Whitehorse Press
Center Conway, New Hampshire

Whitehorse Press books are also available at discounts in bulk quantity for
sales and promotional use. For details about special sales or for a catalog
of motorcycling books, videos, and gear write to the publisher:

Whitehorse Press
107 East Conway Road
Center Conway, New Hampshire 03813
603-356-6556 or 800-531-1133
CustomerService@WhitehorsePress.com
www.WhitehorsePress.com

ISBN 978-1-884313-93-6

5 4 3 2 1

Printed in China

Motorcycle Journeys Through North America is dedicated to the memory of Dan Bard, Bill Miller, and Dale "Stitch" Beetler, three exceptional human beings who enjoyed travel by two wheels. Their journeys ended far too soon.

Acknowledgements

A work of this depth can't rely on the wisdom of just one person. I've gathered help, insights, suggestions, and comments from dozens of riders around the world, many of whom have logged considerably more miles than I.

In particular, I'd like to thank the following folks for their willingness to review drafts, offer ideas, and for their encouragement. Bob Aylor, Dan Bard, John Bark, Jim Beachy, John Bourbon, Paul Cassel, Jean-Marc Demers, Gordon Dewald, Leslie Greenberg, Jim Guess, Robert Fennell, John Hammond, Michael Hammond, George Hooper, Keith Humphrey, Gene Mark, Brad Morgan, Dave Nelson, Rem Ricks, Joran Rudi, Ian Schmeisser, Dave Shipley, Jon Spittle, Duner Tor, Nick Vanoff, Henry Winokur, and Retired Jake.

I have years' worth of travel photos, thanks to the response to my request for pictures for this book. I've used as many photos as I could, and I thank you. I have to give special thanks to Claye Curtis who provided me with some incredible shots. Tim Mayhew at PashnitTours.com, Scott Cochran with USRiderNews.com and Ron Ayres at AyresAdventures.com also offered up some wonderful images of the roads they've covered. Plus, fellow Whitehorse authors Bruce Hansen and Ken Aiken chipped in photos from their areas as well. If you invite me over for a vacation slide show, be forewarned: I've got mine to show as well as pictures from a few hundred other folks!

And thanks once again to Lisa Dionne for her tireless efforts to make this a better book. Her eye for detail and passion for quality are evident on every page.

Dan and Judy Kennedy, thank you for the opportunity. Once again, it's a pleasure working with you and the folks at Whitehorse Press. You're a credit to motorcycling.

Sandy, this one's done. Thank you for you love, support, and patience. We can take a vacation now. I know just the place. Actually, I have a few ideas in mind . . .

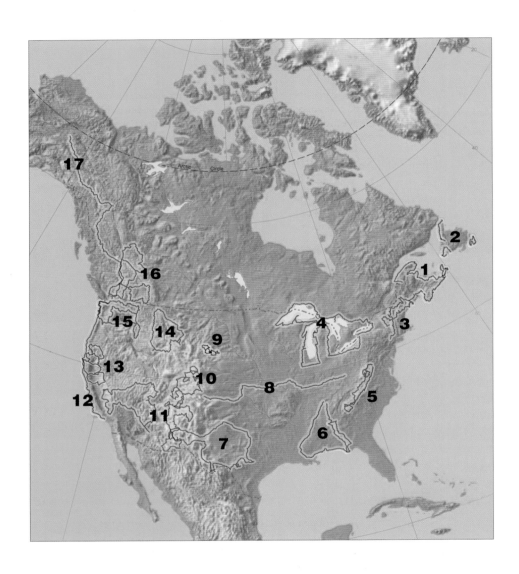

Motorcycle Journeys Through North America

CONTENTS

The official Route 66 has been decommissioned for decades but the spirit of the Mother Road lives on in communities from Chicago to Los Angeles.

INTRODUCTION

"No hour of life is wasted that is spent in the saddle." — Winston Churchill

Motorcyclists are a diverse lot. We are united by the thrill of the ride, a passion we share for two-wheeled travel and exploration. Beyond that, our common interests diverge quickly. Different professions. Different politics. Different positions on organic versus synthetic oil.

The same can be said of our journeys. What constitutes an unforgettable motorcycle trip? Opinions vary as widely as the continent.

For some, it's a long, contemplative ride through muted desert landscapes on an arrow-straight highway. For others, it's the thrill of chasing the apex for hours. Cruising the shoreline, enjoying a salt-tinged breeze. Crashing through the jungle on a path Indiana Jones might've trod. Scaling mountain peaks on trails blazed by mountain goats. At the height of summer. In the crisp fall air. Alone. With a partner. In a group. Following preplanned stops, organized to the last detail. Or counting on chance encounters guided by a strange twist of fate.

A memorable motorcycle journey takes you beyond your comfort zone. Makes you stretch your preparation and your riding skills. Introduces you to new cultures and different ways of life. A ride to remember brings you to the doorstep of those far-away places you've read about. Those roads that you've sworn you would ride. Some day. It's a ride that causes you to recognize the novelty of your experience in the moment. And whether to yourself or a companion, you feel compelled to shout over the roar of the open road "I can't believe I'm actually doing this."

Motorcycle Journeys Through North

America will help you find more of those moments. The routes contained within have been constructed to help you explore and enjoy the incredible diversity of geography, culture, flora, fauna, and riding with which North Americans are so richly blessed.

Winston Churchill may have been talking about a horse when he penned the words that began this chapter, but after seeing what this continent has to offer from the saddle of a bike, it doesn't really matter. Any time given to touring on a motorcycle is equally well spent.

Motorcycle Journeys: Continental Edition

Soon after the release of *Motorcycle Journeys Through the Appalachians,* I received a letter from a rider with an interesting question. He'd read the book and wanted to plan a long ride through the region. If he rode the length of Skyline Drive and the Blue

There's good riding to be found in any direction here in southeastern Oregon.

Ridge Parkway, how could he complete a loop without retracing his steps?

I replied with a suggested route that covered some of the best roads running parallel to the parkway and as I sent off that letter, I thought, "That's a great ride. I'll have to do it myself."

A similar query followed a few weeks later and I began to sense a trend. Riders were enjoying the day trips, but they were also looking for longer rides. And, they were asking for help in connecting routes between well-known riding destinations and the best roads to create multi-week trips. That makes sense. When I'm exploring a new region, that's how I like to ride, too. Give me a sampling of all the good stuff: the roads, the scenery, the food, things to do. Places to go and people to meet.

With that approach in mind, I took a fresh look at maps of the United States and Canada. I pulled out notes and pictures from past rides, borrowed ingredients from the excellent regional Motorcycle Journeys series, and seasoned each recipe with recommendations from other riders I know and trust. The result is a series of regional routes that tie together great roads, exciting rides, and interesting places, in a way that will help you make the best use of your time and money.

Who Needs This Book?

If you're new to the motorcycle traveling scene, welcome. You're standing at the doorway to a lifetime of great adventures. Where will you head to first? Every part of the continent holds something special for riders and *Motorcycle Journeys Through North America* will help you sample a wide range of its delectable treats.

When you're new to riding, one of the

The landscape at Craters of the Moon is so alien, NASA used it to train astronauts.

hardest things to gauge is how long you should plan to ride each day. *Motorcycle Journeys Through North America* lays out itineraries to help you enjoy the ride as well as what you'll find along the way. It includes an overview of tour planning as well as tips I've gathered from experienced riders, to ensure that your first tours are great ones.

And what of the grizzled old road veteran? You're the kind of rider who goes to sleep at night recalling past great rides and planning new ones. You dream in the gold- and pink-tinged tones of an oceanside sunset or the brilliant colors of a New England autumn. You wake at first light and immediately consider what out-of-the-way route you'll take to work today. The journeys offered in this book are built around many of the best rides on the continent that you've always wanted to ride. Have you checked them all off your bucket list?

Does it matter what or how you ride? Not in the least. Folks who enjoy touring at a gentle pace will find tour segments that offer you a chance to ride and relax between points. Riders who prefer a faster pace can stitch together segments as needed. Roads range from wide open and straight, to curvy, technical sections. Novice and veteran riders can enjoy them all, but at different speeds.

How This Book is Organized

The chapters contained in this book include well over 30 routes, circuits and one-day sub-loops. The rides described within are designed to be ridden over the course of one to three weeks. For each ride, you'll find the following information:

Introduction: Every region of the country offers the opportunity for enjoyable motorcycle touring. Each journey, however, focuses on something unique to that region, the topic *du jour* at the beginning of each journey. For example, in the American South tour, you'll enjoy down-home hospitality as you tour a string of small towns connected by quiet, easy-riding byways. Tours in the Pacific Northwest feature startling contrasts in terrain and hundreds of miles of technical roads that beg to be ridden hard. In the east you'll meander along the Atlantic coastline from Nova Scotia to Florida, while rides orig-

Countless thousands of miles of beautiful back roads and byways await your arrival.

inating in Texas, New Mexico, and Arizona introduce you to the desolate landscapes and primitive cultures of the Desert Southwest.

Notes From the Road: This section offers a vivid portrayal of the ride, broken out in a segmented basis that is designed to help you develop a realistic travel itinerary. You'll discover what you can expect to see and experience. What you'll learn. How it'll make you a different person. This is where you find out what makes this particular ride an unforgettable ride. No journey would be complete without those offbeat discoveries you'll find

along the way and this section will help you find them.

Route Details: Nearly every trip I've suggested offers a complete route plan, but you should consider it only as a starting point. With routes of the length suggested in this book, it's inevitable that portions may sometimes not be suitable for riding and will require you to detour. That means you'll still need to do some research and prepare for detours.

For example, portions of the Blue Ridge Parkway are routinely closed for repairs that may require a detour. In 2005, the Beartooth

Highway between Wyoming and Montana suffered major damage due to mudslides and was closed for an entire season. A road in the high Sierras might receive enough snow in July to shut it down.

Connections: Want to travel longer? Got an itch to stay on the road for months at a time? Every journey in this book is connected or adjacent to other routes, loops, or tours. This section will help you put them together to plan an ultimate journey lasting months. Ride northern California, then the Pacific Northwest, which connects to the Canadian Rockies, which leads to Alaska, or cross the Heartland or visit Atlantic Canada . . . you might never be seen again!

Eat and Sleep: As this book covers such a vast area, with such a vast range of choices for food and lodging, I did not attempt to offer a comprehensive list of suggestions. In a few instances, I mentioned restaurants or

inns that were notable, but in most areas you are left to your own resources—and those resources are plentiful these days. Practically all lodging houses are on the Internet and most restaurants are too. As you travel into more remote areas (Alaska, for instance), where lodging establishments are few and far between, you would do well to make reservations in advance, especially during periods of heavy tourist traffic.

The Journeys

There will never be a consensus of the "Best Rides in North America," but that doesn't matter. This book will help you hit the high-lights, whether you're planning to ride in a particular region or you have designs on a six-month tour of the continent. You'll see that this book focuses on fabulous rides in Canada and the United States. Yes, Mexico is part of North America and in Mexico are

Following quiet byways instead of busy interstates is the best way to relax and enjoy the journey. Don't worry about how many miles you'll log. Just enjoy being "in the moment."

Any journey along Utah 12 will be a memorable one. This great road cuts through an austere but stunningly beautiful landscape.

some superlative motorcycling roads. We are holding Mexico's motorcycling riches for another book, however.

Though the routes differ widely in topography and location, every ride through the Great White North is an opportunity to enjoy Canada's greatest asset: the warm, welcoming, and generous spirit of her people. Canadians know they're blessed with a wonderful country and they enjoy sharing it with others, especially those who seek out its pleasures via motorcycle.

When I put together the tours featured in this book, my primary goal was to lay out practical daily routes over a selection of the most exciting and scenic roads in each region. Some of these roads are well known among motorcyclists as destinations unto themselves, Bucket List entries famous for their remote beauty, unique history, one-of-a-kind vistas, or insane twistiness. Other equally memorable byways have managed to retain a lower profile, awaiting your discovery.

Of course, motorcycle journeys are more than just the ride: the chance encounters you'll have with locals, the dive that delivers a five-star meal, strange landmarks, and more. Each tour segment includes an admittedly abbreviated list of the most noteworthy aspects you'll find along the way, but there are many, many more than space would allow me to put into this book.

Appendix

If you're looking for more information to help you round out your travel plans, consult the Appendix for resources that will help you research and plan a great motorcycle adventure. I've included a condensed planning primer and detail some of my favorite resources, tools, and forums that include the most helpful advice.

Contact Me

I'd like to hear about your journeys, both those based on this book and ones you develop on your own. Which routes appealed to you most, and which didn't? What alternatives did you find that you favor?

Reach me through Whitehorse Press or via e-mail at dale@coyner.com. I'm usually updating adventures of my own at www.dalecoyner.com. Stop by when you get a chance.

Now, let's ride.

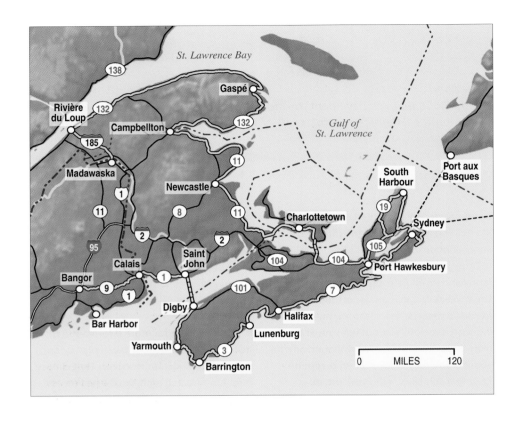

1 ATLANTIC CANADA

Quaint fishing villages perched on dramatic coastlines, extreme tides, whale sightings, and miles of open road are just a few of the pleasures that await you in the Atlantic provinces of New Brunswick, Nova Scotia, and Prince Edward Island. And, if time is no constraint, consider extending your fun to Newfoundland, via the ferry service from North Sydney, Nova Scotia. Charting nearly 3,000 miles of pavement, this tour launches from Bangor, Maine, following the Atlantic coast for much of its run, including the deservedly famous Cabot Trail.

Remember that giddy feeling you had when you first began touring by motorcycle? Pulling away from familiar surroundings, heading out to explore new roads and lands on your reliable mount? The prospect of days at a time alone with your thoughts? A chance to really clear your head? You'll recapture that feeling in Atlantic Canada.

Home to some of the earliest European settlements, this rugged and beautiful collection of provinces features some of the most scenic, fun-to-ride roads found anywhere on the east coast. Countless paths off the main road lead to land's end, where a collection of ramshackle fishing villages cling

to a rocky, ragged coastline. Here you'll discover seaside cafés, cliffside inns, and friendly, approachable locals who love to tell you about their home and their livelihood.

Few are at a loss for words to describe the natural beauty and a sense of harmony that binds people to the land. And in the northern portion of the tour that runs through Québec most likely they will be speaking French. Brush up on a few key phrases, especially for locating those essential services like food, shelter, and gas.

Roads through the northern Cape Breton Highlands and around the Gaspé Peninsula frequently rival or surpass better known

Picturesque villages like Lunenburg line the coast between Yarmouth and Halifax, Nova Scotia. Ride, stop, relax, repeat.

Hopewell Rocks, near Moncton, are visually stunning examples of erosion caused by tidal extremes.

coastal drives elsewhere in North America. Despite its long history of habitation, this area remains isolated, especially inland. Portions of the route will cover miles before you see the next sign of a settlement. Every curve holds the promise of another classic scene combining sheer cliffs and saltwater spray.

Maybe you've heard or read about these eastern Canadian treasures in conversation with friends, or read an article about them. They seem inviting, but so remote. Truth is, Atlantic Canada is not as far as you think. A ride from the U.S. mid-Atlantic to the Canadian border at Calais, Maine, is an achievable two-day slab run, an easy three days by non-interstate routes. Fly-and-ride programs are available, too.

The weather here can be cool and blustery at times. Air masses from the Arctic and the Atlantic clash often, creating winds that push thundering waves ashore. Pray for good weather but prepare for the worst. Don't let that deter you, as the weather is often beautiful, especially from April to October, the common travel season here. Summers remain cool, with temperatures av-

eraging in the 60s and 70s at the peak of the season. Wearing a fleece under your regular riding jacket should give you enough insulation and the flexibility to shed a layer should you encounter a warm spell.

The folks in Nova Scotia and surrounding regions have made a special effort to reach out to motorcyclists, and it appears their efforts are paying off. Every year a growing number of resources spring up to spread the word about this idyllic motorcycling paradise (www.motorcycletourguidens.com), which means you'll meet plenty of folks who share the same passion for adventure that you do.

Connections

After 3,000 miles in Atlantic Canada, you might just be getting good and warmed up for your next adventure. What do you say? Hop a ferry from North Sydney to one of the most remote spots on the eastern seaboard, the island of Newfoundland? Explore New England with The Nor'easter tour? Or head south to Appalachian Adventures? As the ancestors of the Cajuns might say *"Laissez les bons temps rouler!"* Let the good times roll.

Segment One

Bangor, Maine, to Yarmouth, Nova Scotia

The route to Nova Scotia used to go through Bar Harbor, Maine, by way of a ferry. After years of service the ferry was discontinued in

Route Details – 231 miles

➤ From Bangor, Maine, ride to Calais, Maine, on Rte 9. (95 mi.)

➤ Follow Provincial Hwy 1 to Saint John, New Brunswick. (70 mi.)

➤ Take the ferry to Digby, Nova Scotia (a 3-hour crossing).

➤ Ride Rte 101 west to Saint Bernard. (22 mi.)

➤ From Saint Bernard, follow Rte 1 to Yarmouth. (44 mi.)

Spring 2010 when budget cuts forced the Canadian government to drop their subsidy. Other solutions are being sought, so keep an eye out for this. If the ferry is reinstated, you could launch this trip out of Bar Harbor and begin your Canadian riding in Yarmouth, Nova Scotia.

Which is not to say the ride through New Brunswick will be a bust. It's quite the contrary, in fact. Maine Route 9 out of Bangor is considered one of the best in the state and leads you almost directly to the border crossing at Calais. Once into New Brunswick, follow Route 1 into Saint John.

You could spend a day following side roads off of Route 1 that lead to the water.

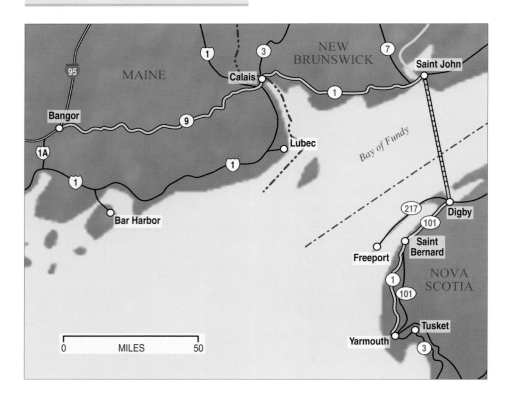

At low tide, Daniel's Flat is a vast plain between sea and land. As the tides change, it may be forty feet or more below water.

Route 172 is an especially inviting option, leading to the L'Etete ferry, a jumping off point that leads to a series of ferries between Deer Island and Campobello. Once on Campobello, you can loop around and re-enter the U.S. at Lubec.

All the roads and villages situated by the water are on the Bay of Fundy, where tides rise and drop more than anywhere on Earth. Elsewhere in North America normal tides range from a couple of feet in the Gulf of Mexico to several feet by the time you reach the upper mid-Atlantic. In the Bay of Fundy, tides regularly swing 25 to 30 feet about every 12 and a half hours with some areas seeing a change of 50 feet. Seasonal variations and the alignment of moon and sun can cause even higher swells. During the course of one tidal cycle, more water rushes in and out of Fundy Bay than is contained in the flow of all the world's freshwater rivers and streams. The extreme tides create unusual effects and sights. For example, as you pull into a harbor along the bay, it's common to see boats resting on the tidal flats, waiting to rise on the incoming tide. And in Saint John, New Brunswick, the tides rise to over-power the outflow of the Saint John River, creating a "reversing rapids" that flows in on flood tide and out on ebb tide.

Cross the bay on the ferry from Saint John to Digby and turn west on Route 1 toward Yarmouth (www.nfl-bay.com). Any road you take will be worth following. Interior roads are lined by vibrant green forests; perimeter roads are dotted with seaside homes and villages. For example, follow Route 217 straight out of Digby to its end in Freeport and you'll discover Lavena's Catch Café (look it up on www.tripadvisor.com), an out-of-the-way gem featuring seafood fresh off the boat, just the kind of place you hope to find on an excursion like this.

Anywhere along this part of the coast is a good spot for whale watching. In the spring finback and minkhe whales begin appearing, with humpbacks gathering throughout June. While you can frequently spot them from the shore, a whale-watching tour, available from many of the local harbors, offers you the best up-close look at these massive creatures (www.novascotiawhalewatching.ca). Finish the day's run in Yarmouth where you'll find ample lodging and dining options.

Segment Two
Yarmouth to Halifax, Nova Scotia

Depart Yarmouth on NS 3, a coast-hugging route that alternately joins then splits from the main route, 103. While Route 103 isn't a bad road, Route 3 will give you more of what you came for: open road and seaside views.

The entire segment from Yarmouth to Halifax is known as Nova Scotia's Lighthouse Route (www.novascotia.com/site/media/novascotia/lighthouse.pdf). Along the shore, wave-carved headlands and island-studded bays look much as they did when explorers like Champlain and du Mont first landed more than four centuries ago. They were lucky they made it. Foggy weather and sudden gales, when mixed with a broken landscape often led to broken ships which, in turn, led to the many lighthouses that mark the coast. More than 20 historic lighted landmarks are found between Yarmouth and

Route Details – 262 miles
➤ From Yarmouth, Nova Scotia, follow the Lighthouse Route (Rte 3) to Rte 333. (220 mi.)
➤ Turn south on Rte 333 to Peggy's Cove. (17 mi.)
➤ Continue on Rte 333 to Halifax. (25 mi.)

Halifax, many open for visits. Any of them make for a great photo opportunity.

In addition to the lighthouses, fishing villages and small towns strung along the coast, each with a unique story and character, stand ready to offer a break from the ride any time you choose. Tusket, for example, was settled in 1785 by refugees from the American Revolution, while the Pubnico region was settled by an Indian tribe of the

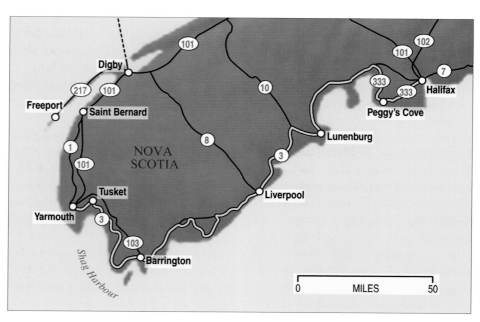

Peggy's Cove is a picturesque fishing village on the southern shore of the Nova Scotia mainland near Halifax.

same name around 1653. Pubnico remains a vibrant example of Acadian culture, including a living history museum that replicates an 1860s-era Acadian village (acadianvillage. museum.gov.ns.ca). Then there's Shag Harbor, where in 1967 a UFO was thought to have crash landed in the sea (no trace was found); Barrington, the self-proclaimed lobster capital of Canada; and Liverpool, a seaside community with a bawdy seafaring history that includes privateering and rum running. Route 3 also passes through Lunenburg, recognized as one of the best-preserved examples of a British colonial settlement. The port is frequently filled with tall ships and trawlers. The Fisheries Museum of the Atlantic is home to several historic vessels including the *Theresa E. Connor*, a traditional wooden schooner, and the *Bluenose II*, flagship of the Canadian tall-ship fleet.

As you near Halifax, look for Peggy's Cove Road, Route 333, and follow that to its namesake, a picturesque Atlantic coast fishing village. The village derives more of its income from tourism than fishing today, but locals still engage in the lobster trade, and strict building codes have preserved the town's rustic, undeveloped appearance. The red and white lighthouse perched on Peggy's Point provides the perfect backdrop for a picture of your journey along the coast.

Halifax is a busy, modern port city on the Atlantic coast, serving both the tourist trade and a productive North Atlantic fishing fleet.

Downtown Halifax is a varied mix of old and new facades and fun to explore by bike. Harborside shops and restaurants along Lower Water Street make a great spot to while away an afternoon or pick up a boat tour to see the rugged coast from a different perspective. Nearby is Alexander Keith's, one of North America's oldest breweries (www. keiths.ca). Begun in 1820, nearly a decade before U.S.-based Yeungling, Keith's produces traditional ales according to time-honored family recipes.

The Maritime Museum of the Atlantic is located here, too. The museum holds a collection of more than 30,000 artifacts and 70 small craft including the CSS *Acadia,* a steam-powered hydrographic survey ship. Displays showcase Nova Scotia's seafaring history, including small craft boatbuilding, sail and steam powered vessels, and its role in the story of the *Titanic* (museum.gov.ns.ca).

The museum also documents one of the more dramatic moments in the city's history, known as the Halifax Explosion, a genuine tragedy and a real truth-is-stranger-than-fiction story. Owing to its strategic location, Halifax was an important port during World War I, and its waterways were crowded. This led to a collision between a Belgian relief ship and a French munitions carrier. People naturally flock to a wreck, and the scene unfolding in the harbor drew a large crowd. Just after 9 a.m., December 6, 1917, the munitions ship exploded, generating a blast second only in man-made power to the bomb dropped on Hiroshima, killing 1,600 people

The lighthouse at Peggy's Cove is one of dozens along the Lighthouse Route on Nova Scotia's southern coast.

instantly and severely injuring thousands more. Windows were shattered 50 miles away and the shockwave was felt as far as Sydney, 250 miles distant. Aid poured in from neighboring provinces and the United States. Each Christmas, Nova Scotia sends a Christmas tree to Boston as a "thank you" for its compassionate response to the tragedy.

The waters of Halifax are much quieter to-day, of course. Working boats and touring craft fill the marinas now. On the south end of town, Fisherman's Cove (www.fishermanscove.ns.ca) is a working dock where you can watch fishermen come in with their daily catch. Or you can enjoy an afternoon exploring the local art gallery filled with the work of local residents. Restaurants throughout the city offer seafood right off the boat, specialty teas and coffees, and desserts.

Segment Three

Halifax to Port Hawkesbury, Nova Scotia

Halifax doesn't project into suburbs quite like Dallas or New York City, so after just a few miles, you could easily forget you were ever near an urban population center. Every turn along these coastal highways will push those concerns about work and home a little further from your mind.

A trip down Memory Lane will erase your last care, and you'll find it here along Route 7, literally. The Heritage Village in Lake Charlotte preserves a slice of Nova Scotian community life as it was in the 1940s and 50s. The village was created by residents of the area who wanted to preserve the time that felt most special to them, so a collective effort was launched to identify, relocate, and restore buildings that represented a typical village of the area. The collection of buildings, including stores, a clam factory, cookhouse, boatshop, gold mining complex, and more was laid out to accurately represent the local lifestyle as it was in the mid-

20th century. Local citizens carry out the routine activities that represented daily life in a simpler time.

The trip to the eastern shore of Nova Scotia is a relaxing ride that alternates between dense conifer forests, shoreline roads, and the occasional ferry crossing. Route 7 passes

Route Details – 266 miles

➤ Depart Halifax, Nova Scotia, on Rte 7 east to Sherbrooke. (125 mi.)

➤ Turn south on Rte 211, to Rte 316. (23 mi.)

➤ Follow Rte 316 to Rte 16. (44 mi.)

➤ Ride Rte 16 east to Canso. (11 mi.)

➤ Depart Canso on Rte 16, riding to Boylston. (26 mi.)

➤ Ride Rte 344 out of Boylston to Aulds Cove. (32 mi.)

➤ Ride Rte 104 to Port Hawkesbury. (5 mi.)

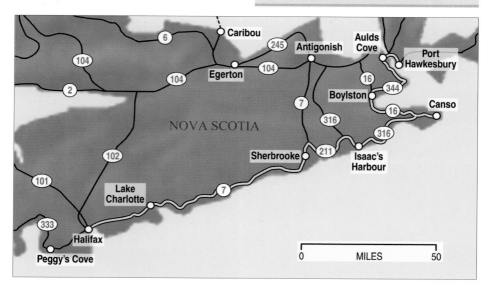

through Sherbrooke and presents another opportunity to go back in time, even further, to the dawn of the 20th century. It is home to the Sherbrooke Village, a preserved settlement depicting the life of coastal Nova Scotians from the mid-1800s to World War I.

At the junction with Route 211, turn right following Route 211 south to the coast. You'll cross Country Harbour on a cable-guided ferry. When Route 211 ends at Route 316, turn right again, following the road around Isaac's Harbour. Continue along Nova Scotia's rugged, pristine coast on Route 316 through a series of Acadian villages and fishing hamlets to the road's end on Route 16. Turn right to reach Canso, one of the earliest seaports in America. Originally settled by Basque fishermen from southern France in 1604, the area was often fought over by English and French forces for its access to rich fishing areas off the east coast.

Now let's say your interests in motorcycling combine with a penchant for camping and a taste for folk music. This is your tour and early July would be the time. Every year Canso, Nova Scotia, fills with internationally-recognized folk artists and songwriters for the annual Stan Rogers Folk Festival, affectionately known as "StanFest" (www.stanfest.com). Canso's normal population of 1,300 swells to thousands and area residents transform lawns and fields into makeshift campsites.

The cable ferry at Country Harbour connects Port Bickerton with Isaac's Harbour.

Departing Canso, follow Route 16 to Route 344. Turn right to continue along the coast with Chedabucto Bay to your right. Route 344 turns north to follow the Strait of Canso. Towns like Guysborough will tempt you to hop off the bike and take a stroll along the waterfront. Others, like Pirate Harbour, need offer nothing more than its name to conjure up an image of the region's colorful history. Route 344 ends on Route 104 near Aulds Cove. Turn right on Route 104 to cross the bridge to Port Hawkesbury.

Port Hawkesbury, located at the western end of Cape Breton Island, is Canada's second largest port measured by tonnage of goods shipped. You wouldn't know it as you ride into what seems to be just another small city by the sea. Settle in to one of the town's several motels or inns, then ride to the north end of Granville Street to find a perfect setting to take a picture with your bike at the Strait of Canso.

Route 7 winds along the southern coast of Nova Scotia, passing through dozens of small seaside villages, like Marie Joseph.

The reconstructed Fortress at Louisbourg will take you back in time to the center of French trade and military might in the New World.

Segment Four
Cape Breton Loop

If you had just a week to explore Atlantic Canada, I'd suggest that you spend at least half of it here on Cape Breton. Excepting Newfoundland, this portion of Nova Scotia is the most remote, most scenic, and offers the most rewarding rides. Green hillocks and ridges stand out along the eastern coast, creating scenes reminiscent of the North Sea. It probably looked that way to

many of those arriving from Europe, too. Beginning in the 1700s, Highland Scots, displaced by the arrival of English, migrated to Cape Breton, bringing their customs. For decades, Gaelic was the dominant language here, and from time to time you'll hear it in phrases and snippets from older residents.

Connected to the rest of the province by a rock-fill causeway, this spectacular 4000-

Signs and flyers like these are an open invitation to join in the fun. Music is one of the many languages spoken in Nova Scotia.

The MV Caribou *provides ferry service between North Sydney, Nova Scotia, and Port aux Basques, Newfoundland. It carries up to 336 cars and 1,200 passengers over the six-hour, 96-mile voyage.*

square mile island is nearly bisected by the intricate saltwater estuary of Bras d'Or Lake. The city of Sydney, always the focal point of commerce and industry for the region, has invested heavily in revitalizing its waterfront with pedestrian boardwalks, marinas, and cruise ship facilities, and is gaining recognition for its role in the unique cultural life of the area. With a nod to its deep musical roots, the world's largest ceilidh fiddle, at 56 feet, is a popular photo opportunity. Ask

around, as there is almost always a friendly festival in town.

The traditional gateway to the Cabot Trail, the more centrally located town of Baddeck, along the northern shore of Bras d'Or Lake, is also worth a stop, if not a stay. In addition to all the amenities a tourist might need, Baddeck is home to the former estate of Alexander Graham Bell, a Gaelic-speaking Scot who fell in love with the village. The lifelong work of Bell may have come to be eclipsed by his most popular invention, the telephone, but the full range of his talents and interests is showcased in a museum downtown that includes manned tetrahedral kites and a full-scale model of his hydrofoil.

This segment will loosely cover Cape Breton in two days, though there is much to see and do. If you have the time to continue onward to the farthest reaches of the eastern seaboard, your trip to Newfoundland will likely begin and end at the Marine Atlantic terminal in North Sydney, where ferries regularly run to Port aux Basques and Argentia during the season.

The Acadians in Chéticamp built St. Pierre Church from blocks of local sandstone which they transported by sled from an island in the harbor.

Segment Four, Day One

Port Hawkesbury to Sydney, Nova Scotia

You will want to spend at least a day exploring southeastern Cape Breton Island. After leaving Port Hawkesbury, exit Route 104 to take the Lennox Passage Bridge to Isle Madame, named for the wife of French King Louis XIV. A 28-mile road around the perimeter loops through charming Acadian fishing villages with neatly trimmed little homes clinging low to the rocky land.

Route 104 joins Route 4 near St. Peter's, a small incorporated village on the narrow isthmus that separates the southern end of Bras d'Or Lake from the Atlantic Ocean. One of the oldest European settlements in North America, St Peter's roots harken back to the 1630s, when French merchants established a fortified settlement at that location. Later, a garrison was built nearby to supply and sup-

port Fort Louisbourg. Like many small outposts in this part of the world, the history of the town is colored by the shifting winds of politics and fortune, but it does make for good stories, and every small hamlet seems to have its societies and museums which are happy to keep it all straight for the purpose of sharing it with someone who is curious, like you.

Route 4 continues along the southeastern shore of Bras d'Or Lake, home to a dazzling array of wildlife, including numerous nesting pairs of bald eagles. This spectacular inland sea, with its hundreds of islands and coves, was also the traditional home of the Mi'kmaq Indians, who still play a vital role in the culture of the region. The largest First Nations Community in eastern Canada

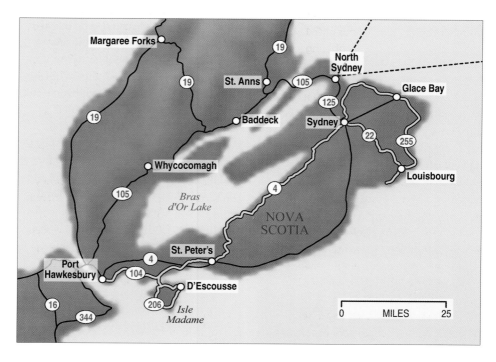

stretches out along the northern shore of East Bay.

As you move outward from Sydney and its surrounds, you will be heading into what was one of the largest coal mining and steel processing regions in the world. Production has since ceased, but numerous local museums and memorials all along this route stand as reminders of its former importance.

The reconstructed Fortress at Louisbourg takes you back in time to 1744, to the center of French trade and military might in the New World. Strategically located to face threats from the sea, the walled town was less well situated to repel overland attacks from the nearby hills. In 1745, Louisbourg was successfully besieged by British-backed troops from New England, only to be returned to France three years later. After the French capitulated to a second siege in 1758, British engineers systematically destroyed the fort. One-quarter of the original compound has been painstakingly recreated on site, totalling 50 buildings over 12 acres with costumed interpreters offering insight into the daily life of the period.

The octagonally-shaped lighthouse currently on the point to the south of the fort was built on the site of the original codfish-oil beacon that guided navigators into the bay in 1730, the first lighthouse in Canada and only the second in North America (www.lighthousesrus.org/Canada/NovaScotia.htm). Glace Bay, once known for its productive submarine coal mining is also home to the Marconi National Historic Site, where the first regular wireless communication began between the North American and European continents, the dawn of our current information age.

Your choice of where to stay tonight may be determined in part by how you plan to

1

Route Details – 195 miles

➤ From Port Hawkesbury, Nova Scotia, follow Rte 104 east to Rte 320. (15 mi.)

➤ Turn south, to Isle Madame, then east on Rte 320 to D'Escousse and Arichat. (15 mi.)

➤ At Arichat, continue west on Rte 206 through West Arichat and return north to rejoin Rte 104 on the mainland. (11 mi.)

➤ Continue east on Rte 104, joining Rte 4 near St. Peters. (10 mi.)

➤ Continue east on Rte 4 along the southern shore of Bras D'Or Lake to Sydney River and the intersection with Rte 125. (52 mi.)

➤ Follow Rte 125 south to the intersection with Rte 22. (3 mi.)

➤ Follow Rte 22 south through the village of Louisbourg and then to Fort Louisbourg. (25 mi.)

➤ From Fort Louisbourg, return through the village of Louisbourg, join Rte 255 heading north, and proceed to Glace Bay. (41 mi.)

➤ From Glace Bay, take Rte 28 west to Sydney. (23 mi.)

spend your remaining time in the Maritimes. Ferry service to Newfoundland (www.marine-atlantic.ca) leaves from North Sydney, and accommodations in this tourist-friendly city are typically pleasant and plentiful. If you have time at the end of the day and you want to be closer to the Cabot Trail for the next day's ride, you can continue on to Baddeck, a great launching point. Lodging is plentiful on the eastern end of the cape, with several charming inns near the Alexander Graham Bell Museum.

Segment Four, Day 2

Sydney to Port Hawkesbury, Nova Scotia

Plan on at least one full day to savor the Cabot Trail, rightfully considered by riders to be one of the top routes in the Canadian provinces, equal to the northern Rockies. The

Route Details – 274 miles

➤ From Sydney, Nova Scotia, follow Rte 125 north to Rte 105 in North Sydney. (16 mi.)

➤ Follow Rte 105 north to Rte 19, the start of the Cabot Trail. (22 mi.)

➤ Follow the Cabot Trail around Cape Breton back to the intersection with Rte 105. (172 mi.)

➤ Follow Rte 105 northeast to Baddeck to see the Bell Museum. (7 mi.)

➤ Follow Rte 105 southwest and return to Port Hawkesbury. (57 mi.)

road is named in tribute to explorer John Cabot, who may have first set foot here more than 500 years ago, in 1497—although most think his historic landfall actually happened in Newfoundland. Details, details . . .

The 185-mile scenic loop winds along the rugged eastern and northern coasts of Cape Breton Island and delivers spectacular views of the ocean as it meets the steep, densely wooded cliffs of the Highland plateau. A serpentine asphalt ribbon climbs and descends the undulating shoreline, leaving little doubt as to the superiority of two-wheeled travel! In fact, only one question remains: clockwise, or counter-clockwise? Riders who prefer the former believe the vistas to be more dramatic, while those in the latter camp cite the unobstructed views immediately beyond your throttle hand. And the best way to set-

The loop road around Cape Breton, the eastern half of Nova Scotia, is one of the world's best kept motorcycling secrets. Word is slowly getting out about this rider's paradise.

tle this question is . . . ? Ride it clockwise today, the other way, tomorrow.

The unique flavors of Nova Scotia have been distilled to their essences on this remote peninsula, with the influence of early Scottish settlers well represented on the Atlantic side, while Acadian settlements on the gulf side proudly retain the language and culture of their heritage. To the spoken sounds of French, English, Gaelic, and Mi'kmac, you should include the universal language of music. Rolicking gatherings of fiddle, bagpipe, and Celtic song and dance, known as "ceilidhs" (pronounced KAY-lees), abound, making it easy to join the fun.

If the amazing scenery, riding, and charm of Nova Scotia hasn't completely depleted all the superlatives in your vocabulary, consider a 17-mile side trip from Cape North to Meat Cove, the northernmost point accessible by road, even if the last three miles are unpaved. Named by the seagoing vessels which used to come ashore to restock their supplies with fresh venison and moose, today's community tallies fewer than one hundred year-round residents, most of whom sustain themselves by fishing for lobster and crab. Every kilometer will open up a new panorama made for the cover of a motorcycle touring magazine. The road ends at a campground on a sheer bluff overlooking the Bay of St. Lawrence. It just doesn't get any better.

The once-remote fishing settlement of Chéticamp, just outside the western entrance to Cape Breton Highlands National Park, also stands out as a thriving enclave of Acadian tradition. Take the time to stop at Les Trois Pignons, a source for visitor information and local history with the small, fascinating Museum of the Hooked Rug and Home Life. Displays of common artifacts from the earliest residents illuminate what their days must have been like, but be prepared to be stunned by the extraordinary craftsmanship of Chéticamp's rug hookers, who patiently turn humble materials into works of art to warm the hearth and home. Many of the most beautiful of Elizabeth LaForte's complex hooked portraits and large-scale renderings of Bible scenes and Old Master paintings is on permanent display in the gallery.

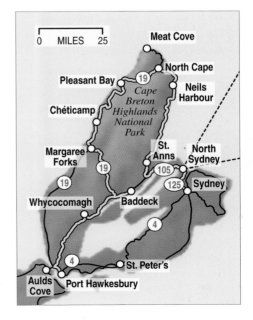

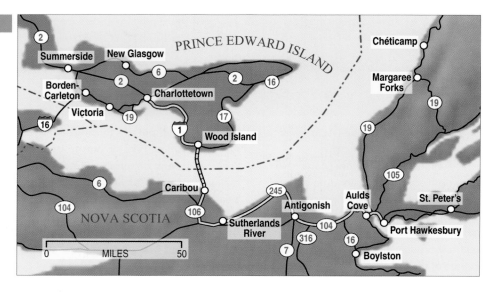

Segment Five

Port Hawkesbury, Nova Scotia, to Charlottetown, Prince Edward Island

Depart Port Hawkesbury on Route 104 to Antigonish. You're heading for the ferry at Caribou. The most direct route follows Route 104 to Route 106. A more leisurely approach departs Route 104 at Antigonish for Route 245, a coast-hugging trail that re-

Route Details – 138 miles

➤ From Port Hawkesbury, Nova Scotia, take Rte 104 west to Antigonish. (37 mi.)

➤ Follow Rte 245 to Sutherlands River. (40 mi.)

➤ Follow Rte 104 to Rte 106. (11 mi.)

➤ Ride Rte 106 north to the Caribou Ferry. (12 mi.)

➤ Take ferry to Wood Island, Prince Edward Island (75-min. crossing).

➤ Follow Rte 1 to Charlottetown. (38 mi.)

joins the main route near Sutherlands River. Signs on Route 104 indicate the Prince Edward Island (PEI) ferry exit onto Route 106. You'll make landfall at Woods Island. From here, follow Route 1 for a short 40-mile run to the provincial capital, Charlottetown.

Prince Edward Island is the smallest Canadian province in land area and population. Referred to as the "Garden of the Gulf," PEI is known for its pastoral scenery and rich agricultural lands. Charlottetown, the provincial capital, was the site where, in 1864, Canada held its equivalent of the U.S. Constitutional Congress. Three years later, Canada became a nation of its own.

PEI is a popular riding destination, made evident by a website dedicated to two-wheeling around the island (www.motorcyclepei.com). Plan to spend two or three days here if you want to see everything the island offers. Head east to discover the red sandstone cliffs and beaches, unexpected forests, and lush green fields stretching from the inland horizon to the coast. The Points East Coastal Drive includes 300 miles of scenic byways through the eastern portion of Prince Edward Island (www.pointseastcoastaldrive.com).

A western ride around the island on Route 19 leads to a panoramic view of Charlottetown Harbour. Continue west through farm country, passing through Victoria-by-the-Sea and Summerside, a popular destination. Summerside's boardwalk beckons you to abandon your bike and enjoy this attractive seaside city by foot. Water sparkles in the protected harbor and there is a picturesque downtown area, filled with Victorian homes that are as well-kept as the city's spotless waterfront.

The boardwalk leads to Spinnaker's Landing, a marketplace situated within a reconstructed fishing village. The larger downtown Summerside area is filled with entertainment and dining options. Riding east on Route 6 leads to the home of author

The Hector *brought the first Scottish settlers to Nova Scotia in 1773. A beautifully made replica floats in the harbor near Pictou, Nova Scotia, where the original ship landed.*

L.M. Montgomery, which inspired the popular novel *Anne of Green Gables,* now preserved by Parks Canada. Riders frequently stop in at the restaurant in New Glasgow whose name is its menu—New Glasgow Lobster Suppers (www.peilobstersuppers.com). What do you think you'll have?

Coastlines around the region display evidence of high tides and water erosion that leave behind strange shapes and windows like this one on Prince Edward Island.

Segment Six

Charlottetown, Prince Edward Island, to Campbellton, New Brunswick

The ride to Campbellton begins by following the Confederation Bridge connecting Borden-Carleton, PEI, with Cape Jourimain, New Brunswick. At eight miles, it's the longest bridge in the world crossing ice-covered waters and it remains a unique achievement in Canadian history. After crossing Route 1 to New Brunswick, turn north on Route 15 at Port Elgin toward Shediac. This connects you with Route 11, the route you'll follow for most of this segment.

Route 11 traverses the Acadian Coastal region. The first European settlers arrived here from France in the 1600s, establishing a province of New France called Acadia and living largely undisturbed for nearly a century. Although control of Acadia was ceded to Britain in 1710, Acadians continued to live peacefully for the next 40 years. In 1755, Britain began stirring up trouble, inviting the French-speaking colonists to leave and forcibly removing those who did not. Many of the displaced Acadians made their way to the French colony in Louisiana where they could find fellow countrymen and assimilate more easily. As they established their roots in the bayous and backwaters near the Gulf of Mexico, they took on the name we know them by today, the Cajuns.

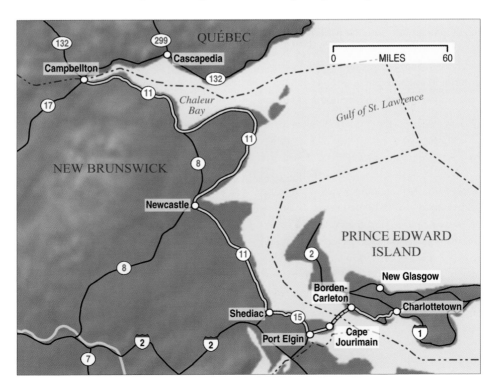

Charlottetown, the capital of Prince Edward Island, is where, in 1864, Canada's provinces organized as a country. Delegates arriving by ship were rowed to shore by the PEI delegate because all the dockhands were at the circus.

You won't go far in this part of the world without stumbling across tales that recount the struggles of seafaring life and the ghosts that haunt the region. Chaleur Bay, which lies between the provinces of New Brunswick and Québec, is home to a widely reported ghostly tale: the legend of a blazing ship. Throughout the years, sightings of a three-masted, fully-rigged ship ablaze a few miles off shore have been reported. Accounts of its origin vary. Some say the ship was a Spanish galleon loaded with human cargo, others say it was a pirate ship chased up the bay by a British man-o-war. Keep a lookout as you follow the coast. What you see may be an illusion, or maybe not. The phantom ship has been seen for hundreds of years and there's no doubt it'll make its presence known again.

Campbellton is the stopover for this segment. Being situated where it is,

Campbellton is a cultural estuary, a point where separate ethnicities overlap and influence one another, yet retain their identity (new-brunswick.net/new-brunswick/tourism.html). Separate schools in town serve either French-speaking or English-speaking students. Campbellton is known for its Atlantic salmon fishing and the springtime hunt for fiddleheads, the unfurled fronds of ferns considered a local delicacy.

Route Details – 343 miles

➤ From Charlottetown, Prince Edward Island, take Rte 1 west to Borden-Carleton. (35 mi.)

➤ Cross the Confederation Bridge to Port Elgin, New Brunswick. (25 mi.)

➤ Follow Rte 15 north to Rte 11 near Shediac. (30 mi.)

➤ Ride Rte 11 to Campbellton. (253 mi.)

Cap Bon-Ami in Forillon National Park has a dramatic view of the northeastern terminus of the Appalachian Mountains.

Segment Seven

Campbellton, New Brunswick, to Gaspé, Québec

This part of the journey returns to a familiar mountain range, the Appalachians. Route 132 follows the coast between the mountains and the sea, creating a ride and a view on par with the Cabot Trail. For its beauty, the Gaspé Peninsula is growing as a destination for summer travelers but it still remains relatively unknown, especially for riders. I'm willing to bet that this will be one of your favorite rides in eastern North America.

To find a drive elsewhere that combines the land and sea like this, you'd have to venture to the other end of the continent, to the California and Oregon coast. The relative lack of traffic and sparse population here makes me think this is the better ride. Stops that

Fishing is still an important part of coastal life in the Atlantic Canadian provinces.

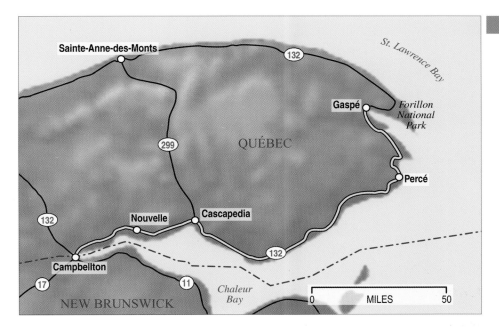

capture your interest along the way are numerous. Stops for filling up your bike, less so. Better to top off a few times than find yourself close to empty with the next station twenty miles distant. That's an unpleasant ride.

The focus for most folks is the tip of the peninsula and Forillon National Park (www. pc.gc.ca/pn-np/qc/forillon). The Appalachian Mountains come to a shuddering halt at the head of St. Lawrence Bay, marking the northeastern boundary of this ancient range. Repeat what I've just told you in a group, and some smarty-pants will tell you the Appalachians end over on Newfoundland. Technically, that's true. Practically, who gives a hoot? When you've ridden this far, I think you can honestly say you've ridden to this end of the earth.

When planning your trip to the Gaspé, it's a good idea to determine where you'll be staying ahead of time. If you're up for something unique, Parks Canada offers yurt

Route Details – 194 miles

➤ From Campbellton, New Brunswick, follow Rte 132 east to Gaspé, Québec. (194 mi.)

camping at Forillon. A yurt is like a cabin with fabric walls, or a big tent built on a wooden frame. The yurts at the Petit-Gaspé campground have wood floors, windows, beds, and running water. For more traditional accommodations, the village of Percé on the southeastern end of the peninsula has plenty of lodging, in part a reflection of the popularity of Percé Rock. On the north side, Sainte-Anne-des-Monts has a few motels and inns (www.infogaspesie.com). Aside from these options, lodging around Gaspé is scattered. The ride to Sainte-Anne is 150 miles forward, the run to Percé is 50 miles back in the direction you just came, so it's worth thinking about how you'll tackle this segment before you reach it.

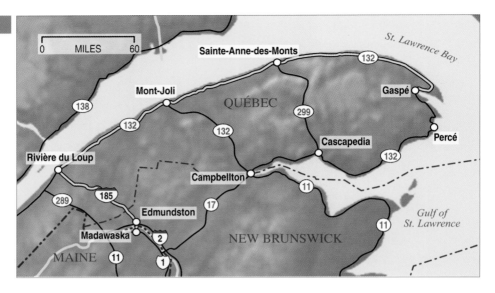

Segment Eight
Gaspé, Québec, to Madawaska, Maine

You know the last section of this route through the Haute-Gaspésie region will be unique when you see signs that warn you of the possibility of waves crashing onto the highway. For long sections, the road runs right along the narrow shoreline or hugs the cliffs. In truth, most of the wave crashing occurs in the winter when vicious winds whip up the water, piling it against the seawalls and onto the road. Expect to see moose or deer throughout your peninsula ride, especially in these largely uninhabited areas.

Your arrival in Sainte-Anne-des-Monts marks the end of the remote portion of the journey and it represents a good stopping point for exploring the St. Lawrence River. Like the Bay of Fundy, St. Lawrence Bay is another popular whale-watching destination. Here at the dock in Sainte-Anne-des-Monts, the Exploramer features an aquarium, museum and sea excursions (www.exploramer.qc.ca).

Route Details – 393 miles

➤ From Gaspé, Québec, take Rte 132 west to Rivière du Loupe. (318 mi.)

➤ Take Rte 185 (becomes Rte 2 in New Brunswick) to Edmundston, New Brunswick. (73 mi.)

➤ Follow Rte 120 south to Madawaska, Maine. (2 mi.)

The last leg of this journey turns south toward Maine. Riding through Rivière du Loup, stick with Route 132 until you reach downtown, then turn south on Rue Lafontaine. Signs for Edmundston will begin to appear, leading you through this attractive French-styled *petite ville.*

Route 185 is an easy run across Québec and New Brunswick, entering the U.S. at Madawaska, Maine.

Water-powered mills were once located in villages throughout the Atlantic provinces, creating goods from locally-sourced materials.

Road Tip – The Paperwork Kit

Perhaps the greatest on-the-road inconvenience is what to do about a stolen or lost wallet. You probably no longer carry a wad of cash, but it's still a hassle to cancel and replace cards, especially when you can't remember what was in your wallet. Make a "paperwork packet" that includes a list of cards, vehicle registration numbers, photocopies of everything and a duplicate license. Store this in a secure spot on your bike and if your wallet goes missing, you'll have all the info you need at hand to quickly cancel and replace everything. By the way, take the time to clean out your wallet before you leave so that you bring only the barest essentials like a couple of credit cards, your medical insurance card, and your drivers license.

Fort Kent Mills marks the beginning, or end, of US Route 1 on the East Coast. Madawaska, a few miles east, is the official northeastern rally point for the Four Corners tour.

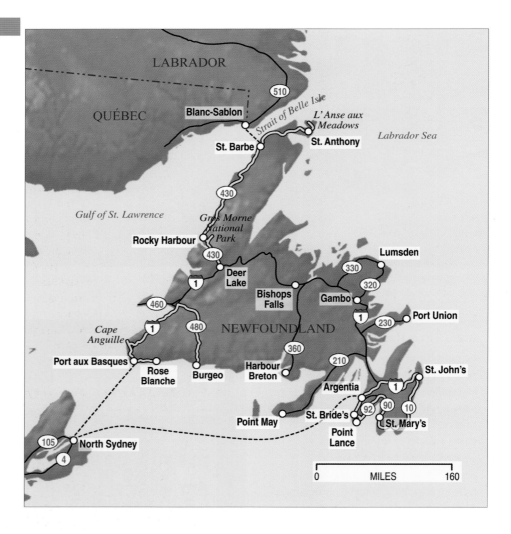

2 DISCOVERING NEWFOUNDLAND

Because it is so remotely located from most of the population of North America, exploring Newfoundland requires a bit of a commitment—but anyone who has spent time on The Rock will be quick to convince you that it's worth it!

Newfoundland's rough and tumble landscape boasts hundreds of miles of paved and easily passable dirt roads drizzled over a fractured terrain that is often unlike anything you've ever seen. Innumerable coves dot the island's ragged coastline, sheltering outport settlements that were, until fairly recently, connected only by sea. Such long-standing isolation means that cultural pockets up and down the coastlines still reflect the distinct fishing communities from whence their original inhabitants hailed: France, Basque Spain, Portugal, Acadia, England, Ireland, Scotland, and Wales.

Perched on the edge of the Grand Banks, much of Newfoundland's history has been dominated by the quest for cod, which when dried and salted became a durable staple in the diets of western Europeans. Factory fishing, introduced in the 1950s had a devastating effect on fish populations. Overfishing led to a moratorium on cod fishing in the early 1990s—still a touchy subject, by the way. Decades later, the stocks still have not recovered, but you can still spot wooden drying racks, known as "flakes," bleaching silver in the sunshine up and down the coast.

To make one's living in such a risky and uncertain profession requires resilience and a sense of humor, and today's residents have these characteristics in spades, often poking fun at themselves with a quirky and colorful twist of phrase. You may have to start the conversation, however. The weather is always a good topic, since it's known for changing quickly between extremes. Fog can be especially dense, as the cold air of the Labrador Current meets the moist, warm air of the Gulf Stream.

In fact, weather should figure prominently

The mountains of Gros Morne National Park are an outlying remnant of the Appalachian mountain chain.

Newfoundland's Caribou Barrens is aptly named. One of the largest eastern herds of caribou roam the flat grasslands.

in your plans. Brisk northern waters, where the average summer water temperature reaches only 54 degrees, means correspondingly cool land temps as well. July is the warmest month, with daily highs in the mid-60s. That's comparable to early April in the mid-Atlantic. Weather conditions also can be fickle. Hope for clear skies and a crisp breeze, but steel yourself for the possibility of a wet, blustery ride. You can easily start in one and end in the other.

Although it is not an "extreme" trip, Newfoundland is made for riders seeking a higher degree of adventure than the average journey. But the experiences you'll enjoy—whether you wander the island's roller-coaster highways, make new friends of folks cut from seafaring stock, or watch whales toss and play in choppy seas studded with icebergs—everything you find here in this still-wild land will convince you. It was well worth the effort.

Planning Your Trip

So how does one go about laying a plan to explore Newfoundland's 42,000 square miles? Good question. Travel facilities,

though adequate, aren't found at every crossroad, requiring a bit more forethought than a casual jaunt on the mainland. Note that the wooded interior of the island, which is still largely undeveloped, is home to a thriving population of moose and caribou. These big antlered ungulates are often seen by the road, licking salty run-off or browsing tender vegetation near the sun-warmed asphalt. Riding at night is a definite no and general caution is always advised, especially when visibility is limited.

Getting to Newfoundland and back requires a seagoing adventure. Ferry service from North Sydney, Nova Scotia, reaches two points on Newfoundland and neither crossing qualifies as a hop, skip, or a jump (www.marine-atlantic.ca). The shortest traverse, to Port aux Basques, is a six-hour float with frequent daily crossings during the short riding season. The voyage to Argentia stretches to fourteen hours and runs only a few times a week. Reservations are strongly recommended. Your itinerary will be guided, at least in part, by what you can see and do before your scheduled ferry is set to return.

In plotting your itinerary upon landfall,

consider your port of arrival and departure and your time budget, and then have a few Plan B options, just in case . . . It helps to allow some flexibility for both the weather and the unforeseen delights you are sure to discover along the way.

Arriving at Port aux Basques

If you have been bitten by the urge to visit Newfoundland but only have a couple of days, your time is best spent if you arrive and depart from the same port and use the days between to explore the coastline around you. For example, the diving, climbing, swooping insanity of Route 470 out of Port aux Basques leads to a series of tiny fishing villages perched precariously on the island's shoulders along the southwestern coast. Rose Blanche, an archetypical Newfoundland fishing village stands at the road's end. Be sure to check out the lighthouse, built from locally quarried granite. Total round-trip length is about 53 miles.

Or head north on the Trans-Canada to Route 407 and turn toward Cape Anguille, a narrow strip of flat land 600 feet above sea level on the westernmost point of Newfoundland. Two of the lightkeeper buildings have been refurbished into a bright and cozy

inn that gets high marks from other travelers. This 75-mile round-trip from Port aux Basques follows the fertile Codroy Valley between the Anguille and Long mountain ranges, leading to an area prized for its large salmon runs.

Ranging farther from port, Route 480 to Burgeo, known as the Caribou Trail is a fascinating, varied, 93-mile ride through pristine terrain. As the heavily forested heights of the Long Mountains recede into your rear view mirror you'll be dropping into the rolling foothills of the Caribou Barrens, home to a large herd of migratory caribou. The final segment crosses a moonscape of glacial boulders before the ride ends at the picturesque village of Burgeo, where the views of the deep harbor, and an extremely rare complement of beautiful beaches and sand dunes is ringed by a panorama of mountains. You could easily spend a day or two exploring narrow, winding village streets, or hop a ride on the ferry to the nearby island of Ramea.

Don't let the short riding distances in these suggestions fool you. You can spend the better part of a day wandering through the area's villages and absorbing the view. Don't hurry. What're the chances you'll ever come this way again?

Each year, hundreds of chunks of ice "calve" from the Greenland ice sheet, creating icebergs. Air that was trapped during formation is released as it melts, creating a fizzing sound you can hear.

This monument to Marconi marks the spot where the first trans-Atlantic wireless transmission was received from a station 2,200 miles east in Poldhu, Cornwall.

Arriving at Argentia

The ferry ride from North Sydney to the Avalon Peninsula requires a bigger time investment. The payoff? An area laced with alluring roads and weeks' worth of surprising things to see and do. Once the closest ports to the fishing grounds of the Grand Banks, crenellated coastline remains an unparalleled hub for viewing icebergs, nesting seabirds, and humpback whales.

Just off the ferry in Argentia, follow Route 100 south to St. Bride's to reach Newfoundland's Irish Coast. Roads from here to St. John's roam the hills and coves settled by some of the earliest migrants to the region, hailing from Celtic lands. As you pass through brightly-painted villages, chat with the townspeople, and enjoy the local food and traditional music, you can't help but feel a centuries-old connection to the Emerald Isle. Heading east from St. Bride's, you'll find dozens of potential stopping points along the way.

Standing well above Saint John's, Signal Hill was fortified by the mid-1600s.

Located on Newfoundland's Avalon Peninsula, Saint John's is the island's largest population area and the oldest English-founded town in North America.

A short detour from Route 100 leads to Point Lance, one of the most isolated spots on the Avalon Peninsula. Telephone service did not reach this outport community until the early 70s. Since Newfoundland's entry into the Canadian Confederation in 1949, government pressure to consolidate isolated coastal settlements have resulted in the abandonment of more than 700 small villages like this one. Fortunately for you, the folks of Point Lance have resisted the enticements that would separate them from the place their families have called home for so many generations. In such a remote spot, you can expect your visit will be noted as a special event.

Patch together a ride on Routes 92, 91, 90, and 10 and you can navigate the entire Irish Coast. After rounding St. Mary's Bay the undulating Route 90 leads to Cape St. Mary's Park Preserve, one of the most spectacular seabird rookeries anywhere. During the season, 30,000 nesting pairs of gannets, black-legged kittiwakes, cormorants, gulls, murres, razor-billed auks, and black guille-

mots cover the sheer cliffs and 100-meter sea stack known as Bird Rock.

At the far eastern end of the peninsula lies St. John's, the continent's oldest English settlement and the island's current center for commerce and government. Today, offshore drilling for oil has taken up some of the economic slack brought on by the collapse of the cod fishing industry in the 1990s. Downtown, Water Street and Duckworth Street are lined with brightly colored heritage shops and cafés favored by local residents.

Along the waterfront, slightly seedy seaport watering holes make much of their authenticity by offering tourists a traditional "screeching in" to commemorate their visit. The ritual involves a shot of alcohol whose pedigree is descended from the vile sugary sludge found in much re-used casks of rum, followed by kissing a fish on the lips, and repeating some innocent phrases that, nevertheless, sound vaguely salacious. For all this you will receive a certificate declaring you an honorary Newfoundlander. On the northeast

Hundreds of years before Christopher Columbus sailed the ocean blue, Norse explorers established settlements on the eastern shores of Newfoundland.

side of town, check out Signal Hill. Located on a strategic bluff, fortifications have been placed here since the mid-1700s. It's also a good spot to pick up a radio signal. Owing to its height and proximity to Europe, Guglielmo Marconi received the first trans-Atlantic wireless transmission here on December 12, 1901.

Farther North

The Great Northern Peninsula of Newfoundland is justly famed for its historical significance, variety of wildlife, and its natural beauty. If you elect to launch a campaign up the Viking Trail, give yourself a week. That will allow you to make a comfortable ride from Port aux Basques to the starting point at Deer Lake, taking in the western shore along the way. It's only 270 miles from Deer Lake to St. Anthony, but if you stop at even a fraction of the intriguing spots along the way, you'll consume three or four days.

Named for what were likely the first European settlers in the New World, the Viking Trail out of Deer Lake follows Route 430 along the northernmost ramparts of the Appalachian mountain chain to the Strait of Belle Isle, a narrow passage that separates

the island of Newfoundland from the southeastern edge of Labrador. You may meet up with other dual-sport and adventure riders who are beginning their tour of The Rock from this point, after having traversed the Trans-Labrador Highway from Québec, 650 miles of loose gravel roads with few services.

Towns and villages all along the northern peninsula offer many opportunities for seafaring activities, such as whale watching or looking for icebergs, great sculpted monoliths calved from glaciers in western Greenland. The northeastern coast of Newfoundland, known as Iceberg Alley, sees its greatest activity in early summer. (www.newfoundlandlabrador.com/ThingsToDo/IcebergViewing). In addition, two special sites deserve a visit when you head this way:

Gros Morne National Park is a short ride out of Deer Lake. Designated a UNESCO World Heritage Site in 1987 (whc.unesco.org/en/list/419), Gros Morne's rugged landscape offers new and surprising geological wonders at every turn, in a rare display of the process of continental drift. The barren hillocks of Tablelands, located between Trout River and Woody Point, reveal ancient ocean mantle forced upward by the collision of continental plates, while the rocks of Green Garden appeared as the result of a continental split and volcanic rupture, and the pink quartzite mountaintops at Bonne Bay display the remnants of sandy beaches and tropical reefs, evidence of a time when the climate was very different than now.

Western Brook Pond, a landlocked fjord within the park, can be reached via a 0.2 mile boardwalk through coastal bogs. Specially-certified, minimal-impact boats can take you out on the water, which rates among the purest in the world. Its sources include Stag Brook on the eastern end, and the myriad waterfalls tumbling off the green velvet cliffs, such as the ironically named 1150-foot Pissing Mare Falls.

No venture up Route 430 to the tip of the peninsula would be complete without a stop at L'Anse aux Meadows National Historic Site (whc.unesco.org/en/list/4) where the remnants of an 11th-century Viking village marks the first known European settlement in North America. Some of this history is actually recorded in the Norse sagas of Erik the Red, who discovered and explored a land west of Greenland known as Vinland. A reconstructed sod house flanks the archeological site, which includes the remains of both an iron smithy and a carpentry shop.

History may give them low marks on the civility scale for their tendency to raid and pillage, but these untamed travelers were serious explorers. You can't help but notice how very small their open, shallow-draft boats were, and appreciate the seamanship and courage it must have taken to navigate into the unknown. We get a little out of sorts when a dinner doesn't measure up to our expectations or a bed's a little too hard. Imagine the average Norseman's experience, floating over two thousand miles in cold, rough seas to arrive in a strange land that provided little encouragement.

If these guys wore patches on their tunics, you know the largest one would have read "Row Hard or Stay Home." And if the Vikings made it to Newfoundland in creaky wooden boats, a thousand years ago, surely, you can, too.

The Tablelands are a portion of ancient ocean floor mantle, a part of Earth's crust that is rarely exposed. A lack of nutrients and a high concentration of heavy metals preserve its barren appearance.

3

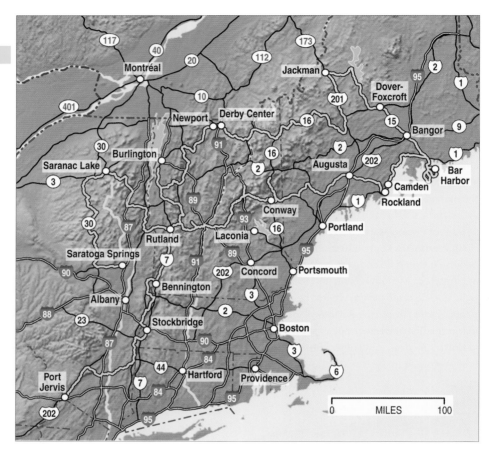

3 THE NOR'EASTER

This 1,750-mile tour explores the rich history, culture, scenic vistas, and byways of the Northeast region. Beginning in Saratoga Springs, New York, this route meanders through the vast lake country of the Adirondacks, then turns east to wander along pastoral byways in Vermont and New Hampshire. A visit to New England isn't complete without a trip to the shore, so the next portion turns to the rugged and memorable coast, passing first through the heart of Maine's deep woods. A return path through quiet New England towns and villages completes the tour. The route is broken into seven easy segments, but you could easily dink around here for a couple of weeks. This route runs in relative proximity to the Atlantic Canada and Great Lakes trips for a combined run of eight weeks or more.

Much of what makes the character of the United States unique can be traced to the history and culture of its Northeast colonies, from a strong work ethic to the ideas of self determination and town hall democracy. The folks who left oppressive societies in the 1600s to settle this portion of an unknown and sometimes savage land had to be an especially hearty breed to endure the weather and wrest a living from fickle seas and rocky soil. We remember from history, of course, the important role early American colonists

Ride to the end of nearly any road along Maine's coast and you'll find a deserted, rocky shore like this one at Pemaquid Point.

< Be sure to visit Acadia Park on your way along the east coast. At certain times of the year, the sun rises here first in the U.S.

played in building a new identity in these strange lands, competing with the French for territory and resources, chafing under the yoke of the British Crown, and ultimately, throwing over the whole mess. New England struck the match that lit the American Revolution. And we know from postcards that it's a pretty place to visit in the fall.

But you were just looking for a good ride, right? Isn't the Northeast so densely populated, there's nowhere to ride? *Pshaw!* It's true that much of the East Coast, in general, got an early start building its towns and cities outward from the oceans that connected them to the rest of the known world. Drift inland, however, and you find a landscape pleated north to south by steeply rugged and parallel mountain chains. Roads can be tight, twisty, narrow affairs that retain the character of their origins as game trails, cowpaths, and overland trade routes threading through deep woods and over broken hills punctuated by villages and family farms.

Global connectivity is wearing away regional differences everywhere, but here in the Northeast you may still encounter backcountry remnants of the archetypal Yankee character: practical, independent, and frugal of words. If you hail from a more talkative part of the country, you could easily misunderstand the reserve that characterizes good manners around here—but unfriendly it is not. Conversations are easily joined, and you may just find yourself appreciating the nuanced undercurrent of true wit that's required for saying a great deal with few words.

The region is home to several large

motorcycle events. Each June, the world's largest gathering of motorcycling tourists takes over the area surrounding Lake George, New York, for Americade (www.americade.com). What began as a small event thirty years ago now draws riders of all marques from around the world. Americade is followed closely by the rally held in Laconia, New Hampshire, an event that originated from motorcycle races organized here in the early 1920s.

New England summers are mild and short. Touring season is in full swing by mid-May when daytime temperatures warm enough to make riding comfortable, though local riders and other cold-loving travelers are out much earlier. Nights are cool, regardless of the time of year. Fall is a popular touring season, the time when autumn colors create a brilliant backdrop for covered bridges, steepled white churches, and traditional village scenes arranged around a town square. Summers are generally dry, though humid days will occasionally spawn an afternoon thundershower.

Road Tip – Mail Drops

If you plan to be on the road for weeks or months, you can still receive mail along the way. Have mail sent in your name via "General Delivery" to a specific post office and your package will be held for you for up to 30 days. If there are multiple post offices in an area, the postmaster can tell you which facility is designated for general delivery shipments.

Covered bridges like this one in Newfield, New York, are found throughout the Northeast. Bridges built of wood were covered to protect them from the elements and help them last longer. This one has been in service since 1853.

The Maine Acadian Culture site documents the history and heritage of Acadian culture in the northeastern U.S. This school is one of many examples of culture that are expertly preserved and presented.

Leonard Harrison State Park in north-central Pennsylvania offers views of Pine Creek Gorge, more widely known as the Grand Canyon of Pennsylvania.

Connections

From Ellsworth, Maine, follow US Route 1 north to Whiting and Route 189 to Lubec, on the U.S.-Canada border. From here you can island-hop your way across the Bay of Fundy and land in New Brunswick to take up the Atlantic Canada and Newfoundland tours.

Mostly rural, US Route 6 crosses a scenic part of northern Pennsylvania that includes the regionally-known "Grand Canyon" near Wellsboro. This puts you in close proximity to the Great Lakes Loop. One final note: to avoid congestion on US 6 around Scranton, follow Route 107 at Jermyn. This road reconnects with US 6 seventeen miles later at Factoryville, Pennsylvania.

Segment One

Saratoga Springs, New York, to Rutland, Vermont

As a gateway to the Adirondacks, Saratoga Springs makes the perfect launching point for a tour. Visitors have been flocking there for centuries to enjoy waters with reputed healing properties. Over time, the region became equally well known for horse racing, and as a home for artists. Saratoga's vibrant downtown is filled with museums, galleries, and cafés that reward the casual traveler, so take a little time to explore. Publicly-accessible mineral springs are found throughout

the area, many covered by small pavilions or denoted with a plaque. Feel free to bottle some water for the road.

Follow Route 29 west out of Saratoga Springs, a gentle ride through central New York state. An occasional break in the trees offers a glimpse of the southern Adirondack Mountains, a welcome portent. For many, the name "New York" first conjures visions of skyscrapers and crowded sidewalks. A ride through the Adirondacks (visitadirondacks.

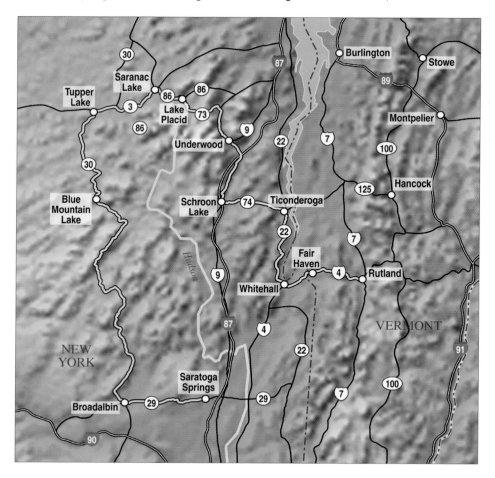

com) will change that. More than six million acres, a region larger than the neighboring state of Vermont, is designated as a wilderness area. Although some portions of the park are privately owned, development is managed by a park agency and accounts for less than one percent of the park's area.

The Adirondack Mountains stand apart from their nearby cousins, the Appalachians, but the once-towering peaks of both ranges have been humbled over the eons to more intimate heights by natural erosion and the movement of glaciers. The Adirondacks are studded with lakes and ponds, many of which were formed when mammoth chunks of ice broke from retreating glaciers, leaving pools and ponds in their wake.

Don't miss the Adirondack Museum (www.adkmuseum.org) on your way past Blue Mountain Lake. The museum's extensive collections, displays, and events explain the relationship between people and the

Route Details – 283 miles

➤ From Saratoga Springs, New York, take Rte 29 west to Broadalbin. (24 mi.)

➤ Turn north on Rte 30 to the Adirondack Museum. (79 mi.)

➤ Continue on Rte 30 to Tupper Lake. (32 mi.)

➤ Ride east on Rte 3 toward Saranac Lake. (21 mi.)

➤ Follow Rte 73 east to Lake Placid. (10 mi.)

➤ Continue on Rte 73 east; join US 9 south, on to Schroon Lake. (46 mi.)

➤ At Schroon Lake, turn east on Rte 74 to Ticonderoga. (19 mi.)

➤ Follow Rte 22 south to Whitehall. (26 mi.)

➤ In Whitehall, pick up US Rte 4 heading east to Rutland, Vermont. (26 mi.)

3

It's easy to while away time wandering the sidewalks of scenic towns like Saranac Lake. The Adirondacks offer an attractive mix of small town life and outdoor activities like canoeing, hiking, and moose tipping.

Strategically situated at the narrows between Lake Champlain and Lake George, Fort Ticonderoga was a target of frequent attacks during the colonial period.

3

Adirondack wilderness. Wonderfully detailed and interpreted exhibits explore any facet of Adirondack life you can name, from the impact of logging and the importance of railroads to the development of Adirondack furniture, crafts, and folk art.

Beyond the museum you'll find countless villages and hamlets along the way that look so inviting you'll find yourself getting more exercise climbing on and off the bike than usual. At Tupper Lake, take a right on Route 3 toward Saranac Lake, then follow Route 86 east to Lake Placid.

Lake Placid, two-time home to the winter Olympics, is situated near the southern end of its namesake body of water and in close proximity to Whiteface Mountain (www. lakeplacid.com). You might remember this, too, as the location of the famous Miracle on Ice, the semi-final ice hockey game in 1980

in which the scrappy U.S. team upset the Soviet Union, resulting in a gold medal.

Route 73 begins a graceful exit from the wilderness, escorting you on a series of wide, long sweepers to the eastern end of the park. Route 73 ends on US Route 9 near Underwood. Thanks to nearby I-87, Route 9 is largely empty, making it a great ride through eastern New York. Continue south on US 9 to Schroon Lake, turning east on Route 74. More unhurried touring awaits.

Your route will take you through Ticonderoga, a name that should harken back to elementary school history (a trip that's much longer for some than others). At a strategic portage between Lakes George and Champlain, the French built Fort Carillon in 1755 to protect French settlements from British encroachment. The fort eventually fell into British hands, as did a vast expanse of territory to the north. During the American Revolution, the fort changed hands again just three weeks after opening salvos at Lexington and Concord, Massachusetts. The capture of Fort Ticonderoga represented the first American "victory" of the Revolutionary War.

Out of Ticonderoga, follow Route 22 south into Whitehall. This tour uses only a small part of Route 22, a largely rural road that runs nearly the entire length of the state's eastern border. In Whitehall, turn east on US Route 4, passing through Fair Haven just prior to arriving in Rutland, Vermont.

Kayaking is a popular way to explore the thousands of lakes in the Northeast, much as motorcycling is a great way to explore the great roads.

Segment Two
Rutland to Derby Center, Vermont

Compared to the western parts of North America, the East has a more complex road system. Riding in the big western states, it's not uncommon to pick a road and ride a hundred miles without thinking about your next turn. In New England, however, your road choices might be more abundant, but less obvious. The side roads that twist out of sight, inviting exploration, however, may not always connect to your intended destination—or anything else for that matter. But if you have plenty of daylight (and know how to use the trackback feature on your GPS receiver) you'll likely enjoy the adventure. The sensibility of the Green Mountain State embraces a rural, outdoor ethic that supports grassroots environmentalism and great locally-sourced restaurants. Since 1968, billboards have been banned in Ver-

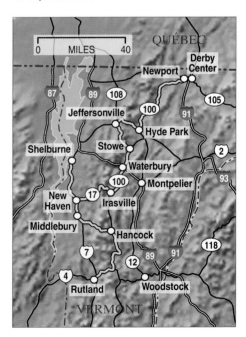

mont, leaving your enjoyment of the rolling fields and mountains unobscured.

This segment highlights just a few of Vermont's great roads, hitting the tight mountain gaps better known around these parts as "notches." Start the ride out of Rutland on Route 4 to Vermont Route 100 heading north. Route 100 is a great ride all the way up the state, but a few east-west detours will make it even more fun. For example, at Hancock, turn left on Route 125, following the road through Bread Loaf and over Middlebury Gap (okay, this one's a gap) into Middlebury. Turn north on US 7 and ride to the junction with Route 17. Decision time.

The Shelburne Museum (www. shellburnemuseum.org), famed for its collection of paintings, folk art, quilts, and textiles is twenty miles north. The museum's 150,000 works are housed in a collection of historic structures relocated from around the region to include houses, barns, a meeting house, schoolhouse, lighthouse, a jail . . . and a steamboat—the 220-foot *Ticonderoga*—for good measure. It's worth a visit, as is Burlington, a vibrant, funky college town just north of Shelburne with a pedestrian-only main drag lined with food vendors, retail shops, bicycle racks, street performers, and restaurants. On the other hand, more great riding awaits to the east. Perhaps the best decision is to choose both.

Following your visit to Shelburne, return via Route 7 to Route 17, then turn east, passing through Bristol. An increase in curves signals your arrival at the doorstep of Camel's Hump State Park. (Named "Camel's Rump" on a 1798 historical map by Ira Allen, you have to wonder if the name was subsequently changed accidentally, or sanitized because it was too scandalous.) Route 17 is a great ride, bringing you back to Route 100 at Irasville.

Turn north again to pass through Waterbury. North of the Interstate, Route 100 passes a factory whose products some find irresistible. It may be the only factory in the world that features a cow viewing area, a peace pole, and a flavor graveyard. Or a collection of giant pint lids, poised for photo opportunities. If you haven't already guessed, you've arrived at Ben & Jerry's world famous Waterbury ice cream factory (www.benjerry.com).

Take the tour and you'll learn how founders Ben Cohen and Jerry Greenfield turned a five-dollar correspondence course on ice cream making into a world brand. Take your purchase from The Scoop Shop (you know you're going there), and plunk down on one of the Adirondack chairs outside to enjoy a view of the Worcester Mountains. And the cows.

Follow Route 100 north to Stowe and turn northwest again, this time following Route 108 over Smuggler's Notch. The gap took its name from a route blazed by smugglers to ferret illicit goods from Canada during the colonial period. Runners used caves along the trail to cache their goods, a practice that was revived during Prohibition. Near the top of the notch, the road narrows to one lane and is bounded by large glacial boulders known as erratics. There's little room for erratic riding here, and oncoming traffic may not share your concern for lane control, so pay special attention on this part of the ride.

At Jeffersonville, turn right on Vermont Route 15, returning to Route 100. The road threads narrow valleys running parallel to the mountains, a pastoral ride that features

Route Details – 224 miles

- ► From Rutland, Vermont, follow Rte 4 east to Rte 100. (11 mi.)
- ► Ride Rte 100 to Hancock. (24 mi.)
- ► Turn left on Rte 125 and follow to Middlebury. (16 mi.)
- ► Ride north on US Rte 7 in Middlebury to the intersection with Rte 17. (8 mi.)
- ► At the intersection with Rte 17, continue north to Sherbrooke Museum. (20 mi.)
- ► Return to Rte 17. (20 mi.)
- ► Continue east on Rte 17 to Irasville. (25 mi.)
- ► Turn north on Rte 100, continuing to the Ben and Jerry's factory. (15 mi.)
- ► Continue north on Rte 100 to Stowe. (9 mi.)
- ► Head west on Rte 108 over Smuggler's Notch to Jeffersonville. (25 mi.)
- ► Follow Rte 15 east to Rte 100. (13 mi.)
- ► Turn north on Rte 100 and follow it to its end on Rte 105. (33 mi.)
- ► Ride east on Rte 105 into Newport. (5 mi.)

the hundreds of small dairy farms that occupy a large portion of Vermont's countryside. Route 100 ends just outside Newport, Vermont. Follow Route 105 into Newport. Between here and Derby Center, you'll find plenty of choices for lodging and restaurants.

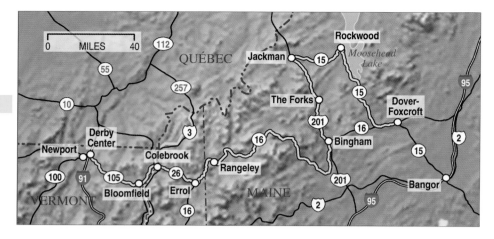

Segment Three

Newport, Vermont, to Dover-Foxcroft, Maine

New Englanders enjoy their outdoors, and there's a lot to love. The wilderness area of the Adirondacks may get more press in the wider world, but Vermont, New Hampshire, and Maine are home to hundreds of miles of trails, thousands of lakes, and millions of acres of woods. Maine's forest covers 90% of its land area, making it the most heavily forested state in the nation, and the ubiquitous lakes and rivers of the region historically provided both transportation for harvested lumber and power for milling and dressing it. So let's take a ride through the big woods.

From Newport, head east on Route 105 and finish your run across the top of Vermont. The casual curves along this route allow you to give more attention to the rolling hills and panoramic views. At Bloomfield, turn north on Route 102, following the Connecticut River north to Colebrook, New Hampshire.

Colebrook offers one of the better-known bike blessing events, occurring annually near the end of June. The event takes place at Our

Lady of Grace, about a mile south of town, where you'll also find a shrine to motorcyclists.

Riders up here could use the extra protection. Colebrook is near the southern end of

Route Details – 323 miles

➤ From Newport, Vermont, follow Rte 105 east to Bloomfield, Vermont. (41 mi.)

➤ Turn left on Rte 102 and follow to Colebrook, New Hampshire. (13 mi.)

➤ From Colebrook, ride east on Rte 26 through Dixville Notch. (11 mi.)

➤ Continue on Rte 26 to Errol, New Hampshire. (11 mi.)

➤ At Errol, follow Rte 16 north to US 201 in Bingham, Maine. (116 mi.)

➤ Ride north on US 201 to Jackman. (49 mi.)

➤ From Jackman, follow Rte 15 east and south to Dover-Foxcroft. (82 mi.)

Moose Alley, a region with a large, active moose population. If you're up for a side trip, make the forty-mile run from here to the Canadian border and back. Route 3 is a quiet two-laner all the way to the border, and the chances are better than average that you'll see a few moose, though they are most active early in the morning and near dusk. If one happens to be standing in the middle of the road, a common occurrence, stop well back. Moose are unpredictable, so be patient, keep your thumb off the horn, and let them figure out their next move. They'll move when they're good and ready.

From Colebrook, follow Route 26 east through Dixville Notch to Errol. Home to

The blueberry is a native plant found in Maine's many bogs. A quarter of the nation's packaged blueberries come from Maine.

Located in central Maine, Moosehead Lake is a regionally popular tourist destination that is only slowly becoming known to outsiders.

fewer than a hundred residents, Dixville makes news every four years, corresponding to the presidential election cycle. In a tradition that dates back to 1960, all eligible voters in Dixville gather at midnight preceding Election Day in the ballroom of the Balsam Grand Resort (thebalsams.com) and cast their ballots. The polls are closed minutes later, the votes tabulated, and the first results in the nation are reported.

A short distance beyond Dixville, Route 26 meanders into Errol, New Hampshire. Lacking any gear for your trek into the Big Woods? Stop by L.L. Cote (www.llcote.com), outfitters to northern New Hampshire, and beyond. Hardware, camping gear, boats, fishing tackle, ammo . . . you name it, it's here. Cote's claim to fame—aside from a massive firearms selection—is its extensive display of taxidermy, including a large stuffed white moose that stands watch over shoppers in the 50,000-square-foot store.

Fully fed and provisioned, you're now ready to ride into Maine. From Errol, follow Route 16 north and east. A small blue sign doesn't herald your arrival in Maine. It's more of an understated acknowledgement of the obvious, in keeping with the area. "Ayuh, you're in Maine. Nah watch y'self."

By the time you reach Maine's Rangeley Lakes region, you'll be at that point in the tour where your mind is ready to release your everyday cares, allowing you to relax and enjoy the full measure of your ride. The steady hum of the motor, a heavily pine-scented breeze, and the simplicity of Maine's

New England hosts a growing moose population. Most collisions occur between dusk and dawn. If you must ride at night, do so with extreme caution.

beauty, renewed at every turn, combine to form an intoxicating riding experience along the northern edge of Mooselookmeguntic Lake, as it is joined by the Rangeley and Kennebego Rivers. The name translates from the Abenaki for "moose feeding place." This is all prime natural habitat for brook trout and wetland wildlife of all varieties.

At Bingham, turn due north on US Route 201 heading to Jackman, Maine, home of Sky Lodge, a sportsman's paradise in the Kennebec and Moose River Valleys. The lodge is constructed of prime spruce, harvested from nearby Burnt Jacket Mountain and floated across Big Wood Lake to the site.

A few hours into Maine it's hard to believe that you've made only the smallest incursion into the state. Anywhere else 'round here you'd have crossed a state border by now. Or two. In area, Maine nearly equals all other New England states combined, but the vast majority of its population is settled along the coast. Portions of the state are so sparsely settled and lacking in formal political organization they still meet the definition of "frontier." A large part of Aroostook County in northern Maine counted twenty-seven residents in the 2000 census, one for every hundred square miles.

Route 15 from Jackman to Dover-Foxcroft skirts the shore of Moosehead Lake, an island-studded, sparkling blue lake framed by mountains and dense woodland. Once known only to locals and avid sportsmen, Moosehead is gaining a reputation outside the region. A log cabin rental on the

This statue of Paul Bunyan in Bangor reflects the region's legacy of timber harvesting. The mast of many a tall ship was harvested from the Maine woods.

lakeshore might just make the perfect stopover (www.mooseheadhills.com) where you can watch bald eagles soar over the lake, catch a glimpse of moose crashing through the dense undergrowth, or listen to the haunting sound of loons bidding the day to draw to a quiet close. A broader range of accommodations and restaurants are available a short distance farther in Dover-Foxcroft.

Segment Four
Dover-Foxcroft to Rockland, Maine

When someone mentions Maine in casual conversation, what comes to mind? Probably not the remote wilderness you've ridden through, especially if you're a "from-away." In their mind's eye, most potential visitors see Maine's rugged, rocky coastline filled with fishing boats clustered in deep water ports and lighthouses standing watch over a pounding surf. Or if they're hungry, Maine lobster. To plot today's route, we'll be heading "down east," a direction that dates to the days of folks sailing with the prevailing winds up the coast from the more westerly port of Boston.

Ride Route 15 south and east out of Dover-Foxcroft and into Bangor. The easiest way through town is to just ride straight ahead. Stay with Route 15 as it crosses under I-95, becoming Broadway. Crossing US 2 near the center of town, Broadway becomes Oak Street, then State Street, which intersects with US 1A on the south side of town; that's the road you'll want to follow to Ellsworth.

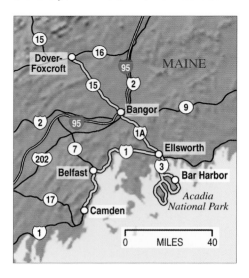

The stretch of US 1 along the coast is where you'll find the largest concentration of lobster pounds in Maine. Turn down any of the side roads here and toward the end, you'll usually find a cedar-shingled shack with an awning, picnic tables, billowing smokestack, and a takeout window. Until the 1800s lobster was considered an inferior food and fit only for peasants, widows, and orphans. A law forbade feeding prisoners lobster more than once a week because anything more than that was considered cruel and unusual punishment. So when you start feeling a bit famished, pull into the closest shack, order up a lobster by the pound, then take your seat at the table outside and start taking your punishment. Bad biker! Bad!

At Ellsworth, turn onto Route 3 and follow it into Bar Harbor. This area is a popular tourist destination and it'll be crowded during July and August, but if you're interested in visiting Acadia National Park, there's really only one way in. A convenient ferry service between Bar Harbor and Yarmouth, Nova Scotia was suspended in 2010, but if you have plans to visit Nova Scotia, check again. Plans have been discussed to resume service on a limited basis.

Acadia National Park encompasses most of Mount Desert Island and several other islands off the shores of Maine. The broken coastline has drawn visitors for centuries to watch the tides crash and fall where land meets sea, observe whales migrate through the bay, and catch the first glimpse of sun in the continental U.S. Originally, Mount Desert was one of several large summer colonies along the east coast. "Summer colony" is another term for "vacation area for the wealthy." A massive fire in 1947 burned many of the mansions that once populated the island and most owners never returned. Today, the area depends on a tourist trade fueled by folks like us. Judging by the number of people here, I'd say we're doing our part.

The ride from Ellsworth follows US Route 1 along the Atlantic coast into Camden (www.camdenmaineexperience.com). You can easily while a way a day in Camden alone. Camden Harbor is home to a large number of schooners and tall ships, many of which offer daily sailing trips. Regular ferry service makes it easy to explore the islands of Penobscott Bay. Waterfront and downtown are perfect for a late afternoon stroll and casual dining. Maybe you need to work off those lobster rolls you had for lunch. (How many did you eat? Three?!) Take a kayak tour of the harbor or rent a bicycle to cruise the town's side streets, lined with neatly-kept cottages and seaside homes. Many of these homes sport a "widow's walk," an up-

Route Details – 203 miles

➤ From Dover-Foxcroft, Maine, follow Rte 15 into Bangor. (37 mi.)

➤ Continue through Bangor on Broadway, Oak, and State Streets. (6 mi.)

➤ Join US 1A and continue to Ellsworth. (20 mi.)

➤ Follow Rte 3 south to Acadia National Park entrance. (10 mi.)

➤ Complete Park Loop Road. (58 mi.)

➤ Take Rte 3 south to Bar Harbor, Maine. (3 mi.)

➤ Return to Ellsworth via Rte 3 north. (13 mi.)

➤ Follow US 1 south to Camden. (56 mi.)

3

per story or rooftop overlook with a view to ships entering the harbor. Or maybe you just need to lie down and take a nap. A range of inns and guesthouses are prepared to accommodate you.

Bar Harbor, Maine, enjoys a vibrant nightlife during the high summer. With dozens of family-run restaurants and shops, it makes a fun place to spend some time on your journey through The Pine Tree State.

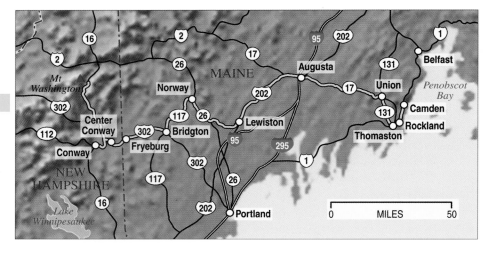

Segment Five
Camden, Maine, to Conway, New Hampshire

Before turning inland, ride south from Camden to Rockland where you'll want to check

Route Details – 200 miles

- ➤ From Camden, Maine, follow US 1 to Thomaston. (13 mi.)
- ➤ Follow Rte 131 to Route 17 in Union. (13 mi.)
- ➤ Follow Rte 17 to Augusta. (29 mi.)
- ➤ Turn south on US 202 to Lewiston. (31 mi.)
- ➤ Ride west on Rte 121 to Rte 26. (14 mi.)
- ➤ Follow Rte 26 north and west to Rte 117 in Norway. (9 mi.)
- ➤ Ride Rte 117 south to US 302 in Bridgton, Maine. (15 mi.)
- ➤ Follow US 302 west to Conway, New Hampshire. (24 mi.)
- ➤ Take Rte 16 north to Mount Washington Auto Road. (26 mi.)
- ➤ Return to Conway, New Hampshire. (26 mi.)

out the Farnsworth Art Museum (www.farnsworthmuseum.org). The Farnsworth collection celebrates Maine's role in American art with more than 10,000 pieces in its collection from some of America's greatest artists, including three generations of Wyeths. Or if you prefer a more mobile form of expression, the Owl's Head Transportation Museum (www.ohtm.org) has more than 100 pioneer-era aircraft, automobiles, bicycles, carriages, and engines on permanent display. If you are in the area in September, their Vintage Motorcycle Meet and Antique Aeroplane Show is a much anticipated yearly event, attracting hundreds of rare, old, and infinitely interesting machines.

From Thomaston, a series of roads will cut through the more heavily developed areas of southern Maine. At Thomaston, follow Route 131 to Route 17 at Union. Take 17 through Augusta to US 202, which leads to Route 121, followed by Route 26 to Norway. Out of Norway, Maine, Route 117 leads to

Even if you've never been to Maine, you've held a picture of it in your hand. Pemaquid Point Light appears on the state's commemorative quarter.

Bridgton and US Route 302 and this, to Conway, New Hampshire. Independent-minded to its core, the beautiful state of New Hampshire supports its provocative motto of "Live Free or Die" without a hint of irony or apology, and it extends that philosophy to its preference for limited government and minimal personal regulation. Heck, they don't even have sales or income tax!

As you work your way across the state, note how the glaciers that carved and eroded this region left behind telltale boulders and scree, giving evidence to the hardiness of the original settlers who attempted to turn a plow during the short growing season. The daily and never ending chore of sorting rocks to the edges of a cultivated field resulted in the many classic New England stone walls that still edge the landscape. You might also spot an example or two of connected farmsteads. These are homes built in the English tradition, connecting the main home with kitchen, stables, and barn. Homes were designed this way to allow folks to tend to the animals during harsh northeast winters without the need to go outdoors.

Conway, New Hampshire, is located at the lower end of the Presidential Range and is the gateway to the White Mountain recreational area. Follow Route 16 north out of Conway to the entrance to the Mount Washington Auto Road. Like Pikes Peak in Colorado, ascending the road to the summit of Mount Washington is a rewarding achievement and good fun, too. Running north on Route 16, the entrance is well marked. Mount Washington claims to be the home to the world's worst weather and they aren't kidding (www.mountwashington.org).

Standing at 6,288 feet, the pinnacle is located at the north end of the Presidential Mountain Range. Its unique position catches the worst of weather systems that converge from three points: cross-continental fronts, systems from the Gulf of Mexico, and weather off the Atlantic. Colliding systems frequently create weather extremes, especially at that altitude. Until recently the summit held the record for the highest recorded surface wind gust on earth, measured directly at 231 mph in 1934. Approximately one day in three features hurricane-force winds or higher, and a temperature drop of 30 degrees from the base to the summit is common. It has never topped 72 degrees at the summit.

The Mount Washington Auto Road is open only when conditions are safe for travel (mtwashingtonautoroad.com). While the road is mostly paved, it does become narrow above treeline. There's little between you and a sheer drop, so you'll want to stay focused until you get to the top. Views are going to be best on a clear day with low humidity. That means it'll be downright cold at the summit. But with little moisture in the air, you can see 130 miles into New York state to the west and spot the Atlantic Ocean 60 miles to the east. If you prefer not to ride to the top, take one of the Auto Road's guided tours. A cog railway will take

Seaside Camden is a great overnight spot, with trails to hike, parks to explore, charter boats, island visits, and more.

Riders prepare to ascend Mount Washington en masse on a special bike-only day. Mount Washington is home to some of the world's most extreme weather.

you to the summit, too, but its base station is on the west side of the mountain.

If you need to check "covered bridge" off your To Do list, you will pass by a perfect opportunity at the end of your descent from Pinkham Notch, at the small and picturesque hamlet of Jackson. As you return to Conway for the evening (where accommodations and restaurants are abundant), also note that the nearby village of Center Conway is home to Whitehorse Press and Whitehorse Gear (www.whitehorsegear.com), purveyors of motorcycling gear and, oh yeah, books! They welcome visitors to their warehouse store and are easily convinced to share a few of the less well-known local riding gems with folks who can appreciate them. Feel free to stop by and tell 'em Dale sent you.

Segment Six
Conway, New Hampshire, to Bennington, Vermont

Conway is the eastern terminus of Route 112, better known as the Kancamagus Highway. For fifty-odd miles the "Kanc," as it's known locally, meanders along the tumbling Swift River, then over the southern end of the White Mountains, connecting to the center of the state. The Kanc is a classic scenic byway, but its popularity extends to four-wheeled visitors and seasonal leaf peepers, and the local constabulary does take some interest in preserving a safe experience for all. If a clear line beckons and you

choose to attack the curves, stay honest, and keep an eye out for moose along the lower, boggier stretches. Several cars pulled haphazardly to the shoulder can indicate a positive sighting. A couple of pullouts near the summit overlook the raggedy peaks and protected hardwoods of the Pemigewasset Wilderness, providing a great backdrop for some "me and my motorcycle" pics.

At the point where Route 112 crosses US 3, turn north to make the run up to Franconia Notch State Park (www.

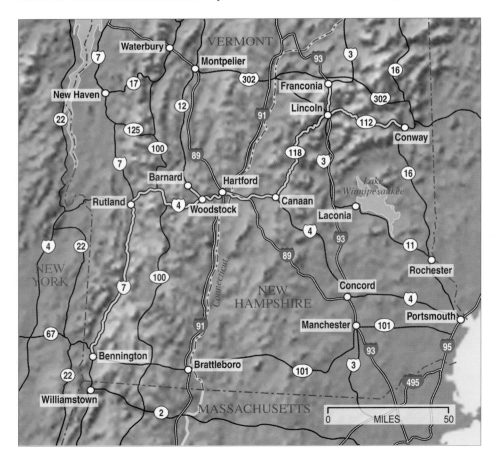

nhstateparks.org). Franconia Notch is the point where a granite formation discovered in 1805 came to be known as the Old Man of the Mountain. New Hampshire adopted his profile as a symbol of the Granite State. He appears on license plates, state route signs, and New Hampshire's commemorative quarter. You probably have one in your pocket. Inevitably, and despite the best efforts preservationists could muster, the Old Man succumbed to the forces of erosion. He slid quietly during the night of May 3rd in 2003, much to the dismay of his patron state.

There's more to the park than a memorial to the Old Man. An aerial tram whisks riders upward on a scenic eight-minute ride in one of two enclosed cable cars, rising to the 4,200-foot summit of Cannon Mountain. Or visit the Flume, a natural gorge extending 800 feet at the base of Mt. Liberty. The

Route Details – 238 miles

➤ From Conway, New Hampshire, take Rte 112 west to US 3. (35 mi.)

➤ Follow US 3 north to Franconia Notch State Park. (13 mi.)

➤ Return to Rte 112 in Lincoln. (9 mi.)

➤ Continue west on Rte 112 to Rte 118 (the Sawyer Hwy). (2.5 mi.)

➤ Follow the Sawyer Hwy to Canaan, New Hampshire. (37 mi.)

➤ Take US 4 west to Woodstock, Vermont. (33 mi.)

➤ Venture north on Rte 12 to Barnard and return. (22 mi.)

➤ Continue on US 4 to Rutland. (31 mi.)

➤ Turn south on US 7 to Bennington. (55 mi.)

Pastoral scenes like the Jenne Farm, a few miles south of Woodstock, Vermont, provide a pretty surprise around every bend.

Flume was first discovered in 1808 by "Aunt" Jess Guernsey who stumbled upon the formation while fishing. She had a hard time convincing others of her find but eventually persuaded folks to see it for themselves. Perhaps they thought Jess was seeing things. She was, after all, 93 at the time.

Return to the intersection with Route 112 and continue west. About 2.5 miles past the Interstate, follow Route 118 to the left as it splits off from Route 112. This is known as the Sawyer Highway, a section of rolling, climbing, twisting highway similar to the Kanc that is prized by local riders, though the asphalt may show more evidence of winter wear and tear than its more heavily trafficked cousin. As always, watch for moose.

Route 118 ends at US Route 4 in Canaan, New Hampshire. Pick up US 4 heading west. Your ride passes through Woodstock, Vermont, an iconic New England village de-

scribed by *National Geographic* magazine as one of the prettiest towns in America. You will be tempted to deploy the sidestand and stroll along Woodstock's inviting town green flanked by stately well-kept homes in the Georgian and Federal styles, sometimes with uniquely ornae details adorning the classical columns and pediments.

While you're this close, make a short detour north on Route 12 for another slice of real New England. The general store in Barnard has operated continuously since its establishment in 1832 (www.yelp.com/biz/barnard-general-store-barnard). Riders who stop in here rave about the hearty breakfast and lunch menus. And there's plenty to look at while you're waiting for your meal. Shelves groan from the weight of merchandise stacked and restacked over the decades. The wooden floor creaks beneath your feet as you stand around the woodstove at the

The aerial tram at Franconia Notch State Park rises to the 4,080-foot summit of Cannon Mountain in under 10 minutes. On a clear day, you can see into Canada.

center of the store. This ain't no Cracker Barrel. This is the real deal.

From Woodstock, continue your ride westward to Rutland, then turn onto US 7 heading south to Bennington. A warm summer evening spent in Bennington offers you the perfect opportunity to take in a movie at Hathaway's Drive-In (www.hathawaysdrive-in.com). First opened in 1948, Hathaway's runs a double feature every night from late April through early September. Hathaway's is just over the New York border near Hoosick Falls, New York. Head west on Route 67. From the New York border, the theater is about 3.5 miles ahead on the left.

Segment Seven
Bennington, Vermont, to Port Jervis, New York

The serenity and beauty of rural New England has inspired countless artists over the centuries, many of whom called this area home. On the way to Port Jervis, we'll see the works of a few. One of the nation's best known folk artists lived just over the border near Eagle Bridge, New York: Anna Mary Moses. You know her better as Grandma Moses, famed not only for her work, but also for beginning her painting career in her 70s when arthritis prevented her from continuing embroidery, her earlier form of handiwork.

Her genuine, simple paintings of family and country life sold for $2 or $3 at the drugstore in nearby Hoosick Falls. In 1938, a collector driving through town discovered her paintings, purchasing all the store had, as well as paintings she kept at home. Within a few years, her work was sought after internationally. Her tradition of folk art painting lives on through Will Moses, a fourth-generation family member (www.willmoses.com). Will maintains a studio at the family home in Mount Nebo, just down the road from the drive-in.

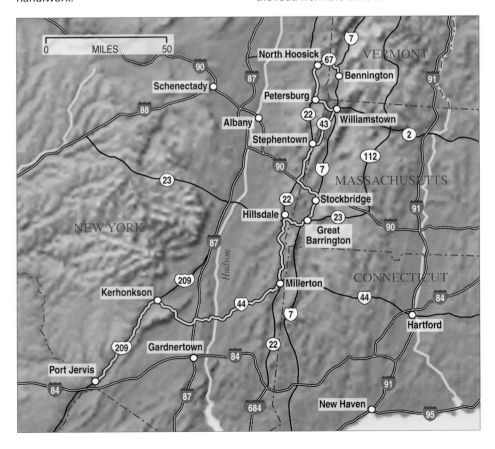

From Moses' studio, follow Route 22 south to Petersburgh, then turn east on Route 2 to Williamstown, Massachusetts. Route 2 follows the Mohawk Trail, originally a native trade route linking the Atlantic region with New York. It was used by both Metacomet (better known to history as "King Phillip") and Benedict Arnold during their respective armed conflicts. Although many old roads follow footpaths in theory, you can still hike part of the original Mohawk Trail. Stop off at the Mohawk Trail State Forest between Charlemont and Drury.

Williamstown is home to the Sterling and Francine Clark Art Institute, a museum and research center that exhibits Impressionist and Old Masters paintings from Europe and America. What makes the Clark unique goes beyond its impressive collection. Located in the western Berkshire mountains, the Clark's galleries incorporate the outside world as a part of the setting for its works. The collection features more than paintings. It is also home to exhibits of decorative arts, prints and drawings, and a growing collection of early photographs (www.clarkart.edu).

Continue south out of Williamstown on Route 43, a quieter alternative to US Route 7. Route 43 intersects once again with Route 22 at Stephentown, New York. Follow Route 22 south to Route 102, which leads you into Stockbridge, Massachusetts, the final stop on our fine arts tour.

Stockbridge is home to the Norman Rockwell Museum. Norman Rockwell produced more than 4,000 works during a long, prolific career. He first came to the nation's attention through the covers he created for the *Saturday Evening Post*. His illustrations, dismissed by some critics as idealistic, nevertheless touched readers as genuinely felt portrayals of American life. Rockwell helped

Route Details – 208 miles

- ➤ Out of North Bennington, Vermont, take Rte 67 to North Hoosick, New York. (6 mi.)
- ➤ Follow Rte 22 south to Petersburgh, New York. (14 mi.)
- ➤ Turn east on Rte 2 to Williamstown, Massachusetts. (12 mi.)
- ➤ Ride south on Rte 43 to Rte 22 at Stephentown, New York. (17 mi.)
- ➤ Continue on Rte 22 to Rte 102. (16 mi.)
- ➤ Follow Rte 102 into Stockbridge, Massachusetts. (7 mi.)
- ➤ Take US Rte 7 south out of Stockbridge to Great Barrington. (8 mi.)
- ➤ Ride Rte 23 to Rte 22 in Hillsdale, New York. (11 mi.)
- ➤ Continue on Rte 22 south to Millerton. (17 mi.)
- ➤ Follow US Rte 44 to Kerhonkson. (62 mi.)
- ➤ Take US Rte 209 south to Port Jervis. (38 mi.)

establish the museum in Stockbridge so that we can continue to enjoy his contributions to art and recognize his influence on popular culture and social commentary.

From Stockbridge, follow Route 7 south to Great Barrington, Massachusetts. Pick up Route 23 and turn west to New York Route 22. The run down rural Route 22 brings this segment and tour to a close, but the good riding isn't over yet. If you're headed west, follow US Route 44 after it joins Route 22 in Millerton, New York. Route 44 leads to US Route 209 at Kerhonkson, New York. Route 209 runs south to Port Jervis, New York and the junction with US Route 6.

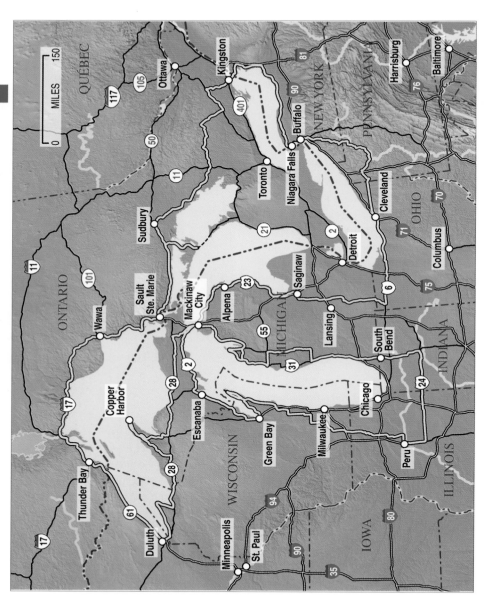

4 GREAT LAKES LOOP

This 4,400-mile route tours the five Great Lakes in the United States and Canada. It follows shoreline roads when practical but avoids most large metropolitan areas. The segments in this tour connect logical stopping points, but not all segments feature a full day's riding. If you like to cover a lot of miles you might choose to combine segments. Including a few non-riding days in your itinerary, figure about three weeks to complete this full tour.

Quick: Name the state in the Lower 48 with the longest shoreline. What did you come up with? Florida? California? Texas? By some measures, the answer is Michigan. According to the folks in the Wolverine State, when you account for the amount of Michigan lakefront, including its many islands, the answer is somewhere north of 3,288 miles, more than any state except Alaska.

(Actually, Maine claims 3,478 miles of shoreline. I don't know who's right, so we'll let the two of 'em duke it out.) Altogether, including connecting waterways, there are more than 10,000 miles of shore around the lakes between the U.S. and Canada. However you measure it, that's a lot of waterfront.

Every year, Americans and Canadians head

Traveling US 41 will take you across the Portage Lake Bridge, the only connection between the lower and upper portions of the Keweenaw Peninsula. It's the heaviest lift bridge in the world and the only one of its kind in Michigan.

Just one of the Thousand Islands that dot the waterway of the Saint Lawrence River between the U.S. and Canada. Not much to worry about in the way of yard upkeep, eh?

4

to the shores and islands of Michigan, Wisconsin, Ohio, and the other states and provinces of the Great Lakes region for fun, recreation, and relaxation. Boating, camping, fishing, waterskiing, sailing—all the classic watersports and outdoor pursuits can be found here. There is a lot of good riding to be found here, too. Hundreds of miles of hushed two-lane byways circle the Great Lakes, some passing through areas that seem as remote as the ride to Alaska.

The Great Lakes were formed in depressions created by glaciers carving out valleys. As the glaciers pushed south, they scooped up dirt and rock, depositing it at the southern end, creating moraines that cut off the flow of meltwater. As the glaciers melted in retreat, the water collected in the depressions. In essence then, the Great Lakes are

five very big water puddles. Collectively, the lakes contain a fifth of the world's surface fresh water.

When you tour the Great Lakes region you'll discover differences in food, art, language, and religion influenced by tastes and preferences of descendants of settlers from the Scandinavian countries. Offers of acres of land for homesteading drew thousands of immigrants arriving from Europe, many from Nordic countries.

The Great Lakes Circle Tour, established by the Great Lakes Commission in 1988, is a designated road system, marked by green and white signs, that closely follows the shoreline of all the Great Lakes. Where urban development is most concentrated, the route described here deviates from the designated Circle Tour. I'm sure you'd rather

Kayakers enjoy the waters around the Apostle Islands off the Wisconsin shore.

spend your time riding than paddling through traffic on a heavy and hot bike. If you have the itch to do the complete signed route, an alternate version of the route has been created for this, too, and is posted at dalecoyner.com.

If you don't mind a chill in the air, April and May feature fair but cold weather. Likewise, September and October offer cool touring temperatures to go along with bold autumn colors. High season runs from June through August.

Connections

The Great Lakes Loop can be combined with the The Nor'easter tour as well as the Atlantic Canada and Crossing the Heartland tours.

Minnesota's Route 61 is a remote, relaxed ride around the western border of Lake Superior. Who knew there were so many hills in the midwest?

Observers scour the cliffs for signs of the pot o' gold lurking at the end of the rainbow.

Segment One

Buffalo, New York, to Cleveland, Ohio

You can start anywhere you like on the loop, but this segment begins in Buffalo, where Lake Erie flows into Lake Ontario over Niagara Falls (en.wikipedia.org/wiki/Niagara_falls), one of the major features of the Great Lakes. As the lakes filled with water from retreating glaciers, water eventually found an escape path along the Niagara escarpment, form-

ing the falls. Over four million gallons of water pour over the falls every minute, making it easily the most powerful waterfall in North America and a treat to see (www.niagara-usa.com).

While you're in Buffalo, stop by Frank and Teressa's Anchor Bar (www.anchorbar.com), the original home of the Buffalo Chicken

The Rock and Roll Hall of Fame in Cleveland is more than a collection of props. It's a "working" museum with a regular schedule of concerts.

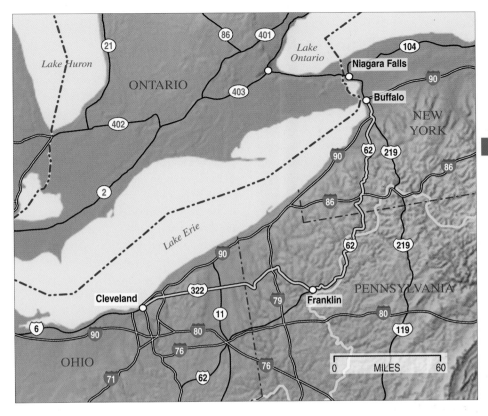

Wing. As a rider, the first thing that strikes you is not the aroma of the wings, but the collection of bikes hanging from the ceiling. The bikes belong to executive chef Ivano Toscani who directs the kitchen staff at the restaurant. Looks like a lot of perfectly good iron that should be on the road if you ask me!

Speaking of riding, the loop tour begins by heading south out of Buffalo on US 62. The farther south you ride on US 62, the prettier it gets. Heading into Pennsylvania puts you on a course to encounter the western slopes of the Appalachians. For most of

Route Details – 259 miles

➤ Depart Buffalo, New York on US 62 heading south to Franklin, Pennsylvania. (144 mi.)

➤ Take US 322 west to Cleveland, Ohio. (115 mi.)

its run, Route 62 follows the edge of small valleys and traces the course of rivers through the hills. A long stretch of the road follows the Alleghany River all the way to Franklin, where you'll pick up US 322 headed west.

Segment Two
Cleveland, Ohio, to Jackson, Michigan

Cleveland doesn't get much respect from folks in other parts of the country, but that's just because they haven't spent any time here. There's a lot to do and see in Browns Town, and much of it is located right downtown. During most of the riding season, you can enjoy baseball in a classic venue (Indians.com) at Progressive Field (still referred to locally as "The Jake," from when it was Jacobs Field). Make sure you try one of their hot dogs slathered with Bertman's Original Ballpark Mustard. Throw some kraut on it too. That's good eatin', even by the standards of an old southern raised-on-homecookin' boy like me.

It was here in Cleveland in 1951 that disc

jockey Alan Freed used the term "rock and roll" on-air to describe a mix of rhythm, blues, and progressive country he played for a multiracial audience. Freed's role, and the larger history of rock music is on display for your eyes and ears at the Rock and Roll Hall of Fame, right on the shore of Lake Erie.

Before you leave, pay a visit to Ralphie's home on "Cleveland Street," the setting for the classic holiday film *A Christmas Story* (achristmasstoryhouse.com). Although Jean Sheperd's classic story of boyhood was set in Indiana, the film was shot in locations around Cleveland. The film performed so-so at the box office when it debuted in 1983, but it became a cult classic when it came out on home video. Today, the original home has been restored to its appearance in the movie, including dad's famous "Major Award" which stands in the window.

The issue of pollution in the lake, and waterways in general, gained international attention when the Cuyahoga River, which

Route Details – 230 miles

➤ From Cleveland, Ohio, follow US 6 west to Bryan, Ohio. (166 mi.)

➤ Ride US 127 north to Jackson, Michigan. (64 mi.)

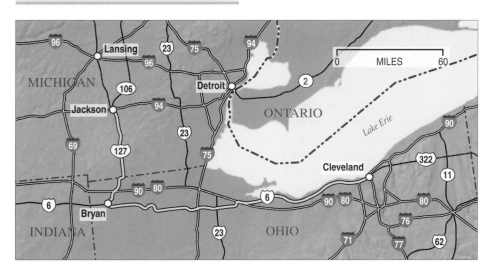

Motorcycle Journeys Through North America

flows through the center of Cleveland, caught fire in 1969. The embarrassment caused by this episode helped spur the environmental movement in the late 1960s, which led in turn to the passage of the Clean Water Act, a landmark piece of legislation that has helped us clean and protect rivers and lakes in the decades since. The fact that you're taking a tour of the lakes is proof of the benefits of clean waters.

This portion of our trip exits Cleveland on US 6 around the southern shores of Lake Erie, the shallowest of the Great Lakes. At Bryan, Ohio, turn north on US 127 toward Jackson, Michigan. Roads like US 6 and 127 won't appeal to thrill riders; they're just too straight. But they are perfect tonic for riders who seek the kind of easy riding that allows

your mind to disengage just a bit. Route 127 rolls through some of the world's most productive farm country. Endless fields blessed with rich midwestern soil are thick with rich, green crops, punctuated only by the occasional family farm.

Pass this way in early August and you'll find the road lined with yard sales and flea markets, one after the next. That would be the world's longest yard sale. Started originally by folks in Tennessee as a promotion of rural US highways, the infinite yard sale began stretching north and south. It now occupies the US 127 corridor for 675 miles, from Hudson, Michigan, to Gadsden, Alabama (www.127sale.com). It begins each year on the first Thursday in August and concludes three days later on the following Sunday.

Segment Three
Jackson to Alpena, Michigan

If you've spent the last day or two on this route, you've no doubt noticed there's been precious little waterside riding to show for it. What's up with that? The southern portions of the Lakes region are highly industrialized, but just a few miles out of the city, the roads return to a rural, agricultural environment. On this segment, you'll reach the shore.

Route 52 covers most of the run between

Jackson and Saginaw, where Routes 46 and 13 eventually lead to US 23 and the shores of Lake Huron. The general path of Route 23 was first laid out in 1820, and in 1926 it was added as one of the original US numbered highways, running between Jacksonville, Florida, and Mackinaw City, Michigan. As northern cities began to industrialize, thousands of folks migrated from the coalfields in southwestern Virginia and Kentucky along this route. Dwight Yoakam immortalized that search for the good life in his song "Readin', Writin', Route 23" describing the hope that many had for a better way of life as they were educated in the "three R's"—reading, writing, and roads to the North.

The majority of the ride on Route 23 closely follows the western shore of Lake Huron all the way to Alpena. The city is home to the Thunder Bay National Marine Sanctuary (thunderbay.noaa.gov) which is dedicated to researching the history of commercial shipping in the Lakes region and preserving historic remains of shipwrecks in the area. On a calm day, the waters of Lake Huron look placid and unthreatening, but the region is

Route Details – 246 miles

➤ From Jackson, Michigan, take Rte 106 east to Rte 52. (20 mi.)

➤ Ride north on Rte 52 to Rte 46. (71 mi.)

➤ Follow Rte 46 east to Rte 13 in Saginaw. (10 mi.)

➤ Ride Rte 13 north to US 23 near Standish. (41 mi.)

➤ Follow US 23 north to Alpena. (104 mi.)

Naturally, sailing is a popular pastime in the Great Lakes. As you travel around the lakes, you'll find many options to charter a boat.

well known for epic storms that build momentum over the Great Plains and sweep across the lakes. The cold fresh water of Lake Huron has preserved the remains of hundreds of wrecks, many of which remain undiscovered. The Great Lakes Maritime Heritage Center is adjacent to the sanctuary headquarters.

Segment Four
Alpena to Manistee, Michigan

This segment visits the upper portion of Michigan's "mitt" and begins a southerly return along the shores of Lake Michigan. This is the first portion of the route that features long stretches of undeveloped areas. You'll catch glimpses of Lake Huron through stands of pines, but frequently the lake is hidden from sight.

4

Route Details – 343 (279) miles

➤ Depart Alpena on US 23 north to Mackinaw City, Michigan. (95 mi.)

➤ Follow US 31 south to Traverse City. (102 mi.)

➤ Take Rte 22 north to follow the shore counter-clockwise to Empire. (88 mi.)

➤ (Alternate) From Traverse City, follow Rte 72 to Empire. (24 mi.)

➤ From Empire, ride Rte 22 south to Manistee. (58 mi.)

Near the top of the route is Mackinaw City, located at the Straits of Mackinac. This is the point where Lake Michigan flows into Lake Huron and it is spanned by the longest suspension bridge in the Americas. The bridge totals five miles between anchor points. Visit the Old Mackinac Point Lighthouse and climb the tower for one of the best views of the Straits and the bridge (www.mackinacparks.com).

In Traverse City, turn north on Route 22 and follow the loop around the peninsula to

What do you get when gigatons of ice push up billions of cubic yards of sand over eons of time? Impressive cliffs and dunes, such as those at Sleeping Bear Dunes along the shores of Lake Michigan.

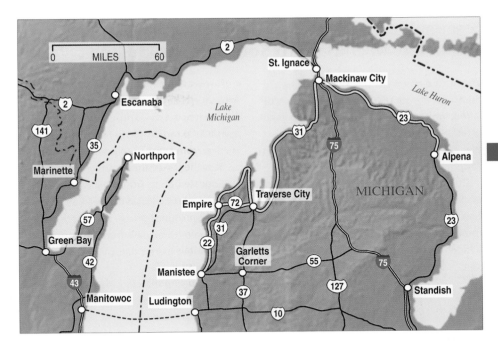

the Sleeping Bear Dunes National Lakeshore (www.nps.gov/slbe). The Dunes are an excellent example of what the forces of glaciation followed by erosion can accomplish. As mile-thick glaciers pushed south, they scraped up a mixture of dirt, sand, and rock like a continental bulldozer, frequently depositing piles of debris called moraines. The shoreline here along Lake Michigan represents one of those moraines. Waves and winds then cut away at the banks, loosening the sand to be blown by constant winds over top of the cliffs, forming dunes. A healthy 3.5-mile round-trip hike will take you to the top of the dunes and a spectacular view of Lake Michigan. It's all sand, so it takes effort to make the climb. A shorter hike leads to views of Glen Lake.

A shorter path to Empire and the Sleeping Bear Dunes National Lakeshore is to leave Traverse City on Route 72 heading west.

The next four segments return to the

The Mackinac Bridge connects Michigan's lower peninsula to the Yoopers. More than one and a half miles of the bridge are suspended, making it the longest of its kind in the Western Hemisphere.

south to make the run around Lake Michigan. If you prefer, you can skip those segments and cross into Michigan's upper peninsula on US 2 at Mackinaw City, avoiding the swing through the industrial areas of Gary, Indiana, and Chicago, Illinois.

Segment Five
Manistee, Michigan, to South Bend, Indiana

The most direct route from Manistee to South Bend is via US 31, most of which is divided, limited-access highway. This segment attempts to skirt as much of that as possible, following state routes through southern Michigan.

Unless you feel compelled to make a complete circuit around all the lakes, there are two ferry options along this portion of the route that are worth considering. The SS *Badger* departs from Ludington, Michigan,

and arrives three hours later in Manitowoc, Wisconsin (www.ssbadger.com). The Lake Express (www.lake-express.com) ferry departs a little farther south from Muskegon, Michigan, and sails to Milwaukee, Wisconsin. Advance reservations are recommended for both ferry lines. Figure that two passengers and a bike will run between $150 and $200. That sounds pricey, but you're trimming two or three days from the ride, a saving in travel expense that can more than offset the fare.

If you stick to the road, your ride passes through South Haven, home to the Michigan Flywheeler's Museum (www.michiganflywheelers.org). If you've ever been to a county fair and been fascinated by steam-powered mills and tractors, the Michigan Flywheeler's Museum is a must-see. The best time to visit is during a special event

Route Details – 243 miles

➤ From Manistee, follow Rte 55 to Garletts Corner, Michigan. (28 mi.)

➤ Take Rte 37 south to Casnovia. (74 mi.)

➤ Follow Rte 46 west to Muskegon. (23 mi.)

➤ Take US 31 south to South Haven. (65 mi.)

➤ Follow Rte 140 to Rte 31 Business (Old US 31). (40 mi.)

➤ Follow Rte 31 Business to Main Street, Niles, Michigan. (2 mi.)

➤ Follow Main Street east four blocks to Rte 51. (0.25 mi.)

➤ Follow Rte 51 south to South Bend, Indiana. (11 mi.)

A trip across Lake Michigan on the SS Badger *is a relaxing shortcut that avoids the Great Lakes region's most congested areas.*

such as the Antique Engine and Tractor Show beginning the Thursday after Labor Day. This four-day event features steam-powered contraptions from around the country displayed on the museum's 80-acre spread.

South Bend, as the home of the Studebaker Automobile Company, was witness to another memorable chapter in American industrial history. Studebaker began as a family carriage business in the mid-1800s and transitioned to horseless carriages at the turn of the 20th century. Studebaker's first car, which debuted in 1902, was electric. With little structure in place to serve gasoline autos, this was an advantage, at first. Within a few years though, the range and power of gas-powered autos spelled the decline of the electric and Studebaker began producing

Ferry Options

Two Lake Michigan ferry options avoid most of the industrial midwest. From Manistee, Michigan, take US 31 to Ludington, Michigan, for a shortcut to Manitowoc, Wisconsin. Ride farther on US 31 south to Muskegon, Michigan, for the Lake Express, a high speed ferry to Milwaukee, Wisconsin.

contemporary autos. The company's best years followed the end of World War II, but an escalating industry price war eventually led to the company's demise. The Studebaker museum preserves the legacy of Studebaker's carriages and cars.

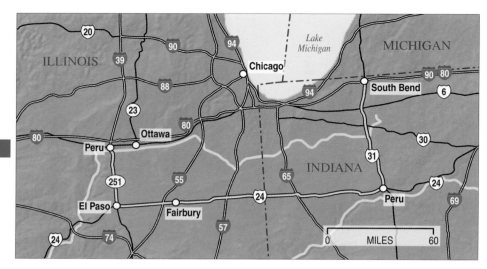

Segment Six
South Bend, Indiana, to Peru, Illinois

This segment swings well south of the Chicago area and into the Illinois heartland. On your way out of South Bend, you might notice that there are a lot of trailers and RVs around. That's because northern Indiana, Elkhart in particular, is known as the trailer capital of the world. What began in the mid-1930s as a small enterprise by a few local folks grew until the war effort diverted materials into essential industries. The post-war

Roads around the Great Lakes are largely empty, tree-lined, and inviting to motorcyclists.

Lake Michigan water temperatures reach the upper sixties by mid-summer. That's brisk.

boom was as good to the trailer industry as it was to automobiles. Folks began hitting the road in record numbers, trailers in tow. Today, the more than 100 manufacturers in the region produce half of all the RVs made.

Northern Indiana is also home to many members of the Amish order (www. amishcountry.org). The Amish, of course, prefer traditional ways of doing things that stress simplicity and the avoidance of modern technology. When you think about what the Amish lifestyle represents and compare it to what the RV lifestyle represents, it's odd to think that the two co-exist in the same place.

Route 24 transports you into the middle of America's Corn Belt, a region that produces much of the country's output, which represents 40 percent of the world's supply.

Route Details – 272 miles

- ➤ From South Bend, Indiana, take US 31 south to Peru, Indiana. (67 mi.)
- ➤ Follow US 24 west to El Paso, Illinois. (157 mi.)
- ➤ Ride Rte 251 north to Peru, Illinois. (48 mi.)

As you ride past mile after mile of corn, sometimes your eyes play tricks on you. Unless, that is, you're passing through Fairbury, Illinois. Here, in a cornfield, a row of frisky horses appeared one night. Over time, the herd has grown to its present size of more than two dozen (www.roadsideamerica. com/tip/17229). Who put them there, and who adds to them remains unknown.

Segment Seven
Peru, Illinois, to Milwaukee, Wisconsin

This segment of the Great Lakes tour takes you to the Milwaukee area, home to American brewing icons, such as Pabst and Schlitz, as well as that other icon I hardly need to name, Harley-Davidson.

Today's route is short and easy, allowing you most of the day to tour Milwaukee. Head due east on US 6 to Route 23 at Ottawa. Route 23 eventually joins US 14 just south of Harvard, Illinois. The left turn you make onto US 14 is a westerly route, but the short portion you'll be on runs due north. Depart US 14 in Walworth, Wisconsin, and follow Route 67 in a northeasterly direction. In Eagle, leave Route 67 in favor of Route 59. Riding east you'll reach Waukesha, Wisconsin, at the

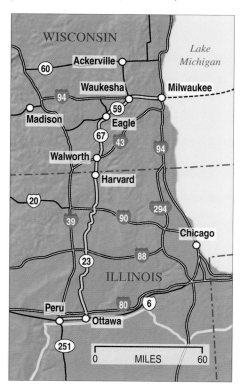

western edge of the metro area, a good spot for setting up camp. Lodging is a little less expensive here than the downtown area.

Though originally settled by French-Canadian traders and trappers, Milwaukee received waves of German and Polish immigrants in the mid-1800s, who brought the traditions of brewing and manufacturing that defined the city's contemporary history. Brewing came first.

At its height, Milwaukee was home to the world's four largest breweries—Miller, Pabst, Schlitz, and Blatz. Miller remains the second largest brewer in the world and continues to operate a massive facility in Miller Valley that packages up to 200,000 cases of beer a day and a distribution center that covers five acres. That is a lot of brew.

The dawn of the 20th century marked a frenzied point in the evolution of American industry and commerce. Inventions and innovations were announced at an astounding pace, transforming American life and laying the foundation for today's world. Automobile and motorcycle manufacturers were at the very hub of innovation, with self-powered contraptions being built in hundreds of garages and machine shops around the country.

Milwaukee had its share of tinkerers, including a pair of boyhood friends, William Harley and his pal Arthur Davidson. Twenty-one-year-old Harley was perfecting the design of his first gas-powered motor in 1901 and, with the help of his friend, built the motor over the next two years in a friend's machine shop. Harley's first motor couldn't generate enough power to move a bicycle up Milwaukee's modest hills without the

Just one of many patriotic riders celebrating the hometown bike maker, Harley-Davidson. You have to wonder how it handles at speed.

4

help of pedals, so the pair began again. By 1904, the two boys, with help from other Davidson family members, completed a prototype that placed fourth in a local race. The Harley legend had begun.

The Harley-Davidson factory continues to occupy its original site on Juneau Avenue (then Chestnut Street) where it produced 50 motorcycles in its first years. Harley-Davidson was one of the only makers to survive not only the industry shakeout in the 1910s when automobiles began to dominate, but also the Great Depression two decades later. (More recently, the company was lucky to survive its ill-fated ownership by AMF.) Harley-Davidson's complete history is meticulously documented and richly presented in

its museum, a must-see not only for Hog fanatics, but for anyone who enjoys the story of motorcycling.

Route Details – 174 miles

➤ From Peru, Illinois, follow US 6 east to Rte 23 in Ottawa, Illinois. (17 mi.)

➤ Ride Rte 23 north to US 14 at Harvard, Illinois. (83 mi.)

➤ Follow US 14 north to Walworth, Wisconsin. (8 mi.)

➤ Continue north on Rte 67 to Eagle. (31 mi.)

➤ Ride Rte 59 into Milwaukee. (35 mi.)

Segment Eight
Milwaukee to Washington Island, Wisconsin

This portion of the tour finally shakes the vestiges of industrial America and returns to the shoreline of the Lakes for the remainder of the tour. Stair-stepping around greater Milwaukee, our route returns to a pastoral cruise through Wisconsin farm country on its way up the Door Peninsula that borders Green Bay. The route out of Waukesha follows a series of state and county routes. You'll see more than one route labled "County Route A," so check your map carefully as you navigate north and east. Route 164 leads north out of Waukesha to Route

60. North on County Road I just outside Grafton leads to a short run on County Road A to Fredonia. From here, you'll pick up Route 57 north.

Milwaukee may feature brats and sausages, but out here the staple food is fresh cheese. You'll find Wisconsin cheese products just about everywhere you stop, but some of the best can be found at shops located at small family-owned farms and dairies along the route. Pick up a map of Wisconsin Cheese Country online and you'll find dozens to choose from on your trip

Milwaukee is famous for more than suds and cycles. It's home to the world-class Milwaukee Art Museum.

Route Details – 208 miles

► From Waukesha, Wisconsin, follow Rte 164 north to Ackerville. (20 mi.)

► Ride Rte 60 east to County Road I (eye). (14 mi.)

► Follow County Road I north to County Road A. (11 mi.)

► Take County Road A east to Rte 57. (2 mi.)

► Follow Rte 57 north to County Road A (near Elkhart Lake). (25 mi.)

► Take County Road A east to Rte 42. (6 mi.)

► Ride Rte 42 north to Northport. (130 mi.)

► Take the ferry to Washington Island, Wisconsin.

(www.eatwisconsincheese.com/assets/pdfs/WisconsinCheeseMap.pdf).

Turn right onto County Route A and head east to Route 42. In Manitowoc, Route 42 runs into US 151 east and US 10 north. You'll pick up Route 42 again on the other side of town and follow it the rest of the way to the ferry at Northport.

When you board the Washington Island Ferry in Northport (www.wisferry.com), you can feel time slow down as you head for one of the earliest Icelandic and Scandinavian settlements in Wisconsin. The calm passage between the mainland and the peninsula belies the area's nickname, "Death's Door," a vivid reference to shifting winds and currents that have contributed to the hundreds of wooden shipwrecks that lie on the bottom of these waters.

Washington Island is everything you'd hope for in a Lakes Island vacation (www.washingtonisland.com). Quiet country lanes pass by small farmsteads, ending at scenic lake shores and harbors. You could probably ride every road on the island in a couple of hours, but it's worth considering spending a day's layover here to explore on foot, or visit nearby Rock Island State Park. Although there are several lodges and inns on the island, it's a good idea to book your lodging a few days ahead while you're on the road, just to make sure you have a room waiting for you.

A visitor enjoys the view from the top of Sand Point Lighthouse in Escanaba, Michigan.

Segment Nine
Washington Island, Wisconsin, to Escanaba, Michigan

This segment returns down the Door Peninsula via a different route, running through Green Bay and turning north along the re-

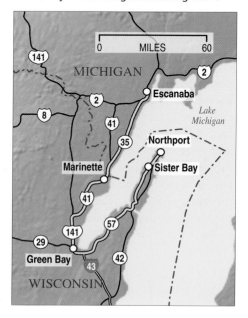

mote upper reaches of Lake Michigan. North of Marinette, you'll enter the "U.P." or Michigan's Upper Peninsula. While this portion of Michigan contains more than a quarter of the state's land area, it holds just three percent of its population. Folks up here, largely of Finn-

Route Details – 197 miles

➤ From Washington Island, return to mainland via ferry

➤ Take Rte 42 south to Sister Bay, Wisconsin. (12 mi.)

➤ Follow Rte 57 west to Green Bay. (75 mi.)

➤ In Green Bay, follow US 141 north to US 41. (20 mi.)

➤ Take US 41 north to Marinette, Wisconsin. (34 mi.)

➤ Ride Rte 35 north to Escanaba, Michigan. (56 mi.)

Stavkirke ("Church of Staves") was modeled after drawings of a similar structure built in Norway in 1150. It was built to honor and reflect the influence of Scandanavian culture on the region.

ish origin, retain a strong regional identity and are frequently referred to as "Yoopers."

Turn down the peninsula on Route 42. For a different way out, follow Route 57 as it meets Route 42 at Sister Bay. Stay with Route 57 into Green Bay, turning onto US 141 north out of town. US 41 joins then splits from US 141 and when it does, follow it. On the north side of Menominee, pick up Route 35 which will carry you into Yooper territory.

For the most part, the road belongs to you alone as you venture north along Route 35. Escanaba, located at the mouth of Little Bay de Noc will provide you with another quiet respite from the road (www.superiorsights. com). The lighthouse makes a fun diversion or a good spot for an evening picnic, or try a sightseeing tour with one of Uncle Ducky's charters for an entertaining afternoon (www.uncleducky.com)

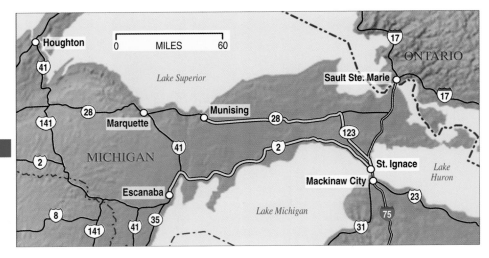

Segment Ten
Escanaba to Munising, Michigan

This segment turns east on US 2 with a stop-over in St. Ignace, the northern anchor for the Mackinac Bridge. This is also a good point to venture over to Mackinac Island.

If you've ever wondered what life was like before motorized vehicles, Mackinac Island is the place to visit. For more than 100 years, most forms of mechanized travel have been prohibited with preference given to the original horse power. Since settlement, this 3.8 square mile island has been used largely as a summer resort and getaway for wealthy industrialists. Homes and inns throughout are swathed in lavishly preserved Victorian trimmings. Whether you explore by foot, bicycle, or horse-drawn carriage, the trip to Mackinac Island really is time travel.

The second half of the route in this segment passes through the Mackinac Wilderness, a region that gained protected status in 1987. The area was severely logged at the turn of the 20th century, but second-growth forests now cover the landscape with some sections now more than 80 years of age.

Travelling through such a remote area might lead you to wonder where you could possibly bed down for the night. After traveling the Mackinac Trail and Route 123 for miles, the options appear to be plentiful for campers. And only campers. Turn west on Route 28 and another 90 minutes will put you in Munising, a good spot to stop for the night. Scenic sandstone cliffs and waterfalls make Munising a popular vacation destination, meaning plenty of travel services are available here (www.munising.org).

Route Details – 266 miles

► From Escanaba, Michigan, take US 2 east to St. Ignace. (142 mi.)

► Follow the Mackinac Trail north to Rte 123. (8 mi.)

► Follow Rte 123 north to Rte 28. (34 mi.)

► Ride Rte 28 west to Munising. (82 mi.)

Michigan's Upper Peninsula, or "U.P.," is a sparsely populated region popular with area riders. Residents here describe themselves as "Yoopers."

Segment Eleven

Munising to Copper Harbor, Michigan

Since you've been in the Upper Peninsula a day or two, you might have noticed that you've been wearing that fleece a little longer during the day than before. Lake Superior strongly influences weather patterns and conditions across the U.P. throughout the year. Air temperatures often vary at different altitudes, creating breezes that keep inland temperatures cooler than areas a little farther away.

While cities like Marquette, Michigan, sprang up around the lake to serve the shipping and mining industries, they also became, and remain, popular summer retreats. You'll pass through Marquette as Route 28

Route Details – 188 miles

➤ Depart Munising, Michigan, on Rte 28 west to US 41 north. (38 mi.)

➤ Follow US 41 north to Copper Harbor. (150 mi.)

Roads leading in and out of the Copper Harbor peninsula are quiet, tree-lined avenues that are perfect for touring by motorcycle.

A trans-Canada trip could bring you near Pukaskwa Provincial Park, renowned for its boreal forests and vistas of Lake Superior.

joins US 41 just south of town. Both routes remain co-signed for fifty miles. Route 41 then makes an abrupt turn to the north heading directly for Copper Harbor.

The road from Munising to Copper Harbor skirts the southern shores of Lake Superior, the largest of the Great Lakes. The turn north on US 41 rides through a canopy of trees for a large portion of the ride. Copper Harbor is Route 41's northernmost point. The other end of US 41 is the junction with US 1 in Miami, 2,000 miles to the south.

Copper Harbor was built as a supply port to support mining activity. Fort Wilkins, a state park today, was built in the 1840s to provide for the orderly development of mining activity and trade, due to the fear that an area with no oversight would become lawless and disorderly. About the only disorderly act you'll find here today is jaywalking.

Who says you have to ride 4,000 miles to get to Alaska? You just have to visit Wisconsin.

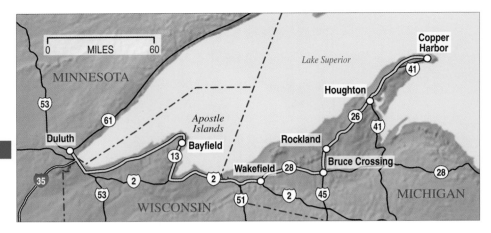

Segment Twelve
Copper Harbor, Michigan, to Duluth, Minnesota

This segment puts in a full day's run, covering more than 300 miles from Copper Harbor to Duluth by way of the Apostle Islands. Route 26 out of Copper Harbor provides something you won't find on most roads around here—curves! The road hugs the Lake Superior shoreline for a few miles before joining US 41 south, then splits for good at Houghton. In Rockland take Route 45 to Bruce Crossing. You're going to find that these are easy miles to cover.

The town at Bruce Crossing marks the point where you'll turn west on Route 28. It looks like most other crossroads towns you'll pass through in this remote region but the large cooperative market you pass on the way through has a special place in the region's history and development.

The economy of Calumet was founded on copper mining, an activity that's been pursued here for the past 7,000 years.

Grand Portal looks like it could be harboring pirates in its large cave structures.

4

Scandinavian cultures have a long history of cooperative self-government and commerce; cooperation borne of necessity. When you live in harsh climates, you have to stick together to survive. The Swedes, Finns, and others who settled the upper Midwest brought those ideals with them, establishing cooperative banks, dairy processing plants, stores, and more.

These community-owned and -governed cooperatives not only provided services in remote areas, they also created markets for farmers to sell their crops and dairy products. Settler's Co-op in Bruce Crossing is a thriving example of a Finnish co-op that remains owned and managed by the people of the community.

At Wakefield, turn west on US 2, reentering Wisconsin at Ironwood. In Ashland, Wisconsin, turn north on Route 13. The visitor center for the Apostle Islands is one block off Route 13 in Bayfield.

The Apostles are a collection of twenty-two islands off the Bayfield Peninsula in northern Wisconsin, known for their dramatic red cliffs and sea caves. Stockton Island is home to one of the largest concentrations of black bears in North America. Some of the islands are populated and can be reached by ferry. The Apostles are a popular summer recreation destination on the cold, clear waters of Lake Superior. To plan a visit to the islands, check out the National Park Service site for complete details including ferry routes and schedules and lodging info (www.nps.gov/apis).

Complete this portion of the journey by continuing on Route 13 to Superior, Wisconsin, where Route 13 ends on US 2/53. Turn north on US 53 to reach Duluth, the stopover point for this tour segment.

Route Details – 326 miles

➤ Depart Copper Harbor, Michigan, on Rte 26 south to Rockland, Michigan. (97 mi.)

➤ Follow US 45 south to Bruce Crossing. (14 mi.)

➤ Take Rte 28 west to Wakefield, Michigan. (40 mi.)

➤ Pick up US 2 and follow it west to Rte 13. (53 mi.)

➤ Ride Rte 13 to Bayfield, Wisconsin. (22 mi.)

➤ Continue on Rte 13 to US 53. (78 mi.)

➤ Follow US 53 to Duluth, Minnesota. (22 mi.)

Grand Portage preserves the ancient footpath that bypasses the waterfalls and rapids over the last twenty miles of the Pigeon River before it flows into Lake Superior. This path was essential to early trade and exploration.

Segment Thirteen

Duluth, Minnesota, to Thunder Bay, Ontario

You don't realize how far north Minnesota stretches until you ride this portion of Route 61 from Duluth to Thunder Bay, Ontario. For most of the ride, you remain firmly on U.S. soil, and you keep going and going and going. It's like riding through Texas. If your bike requires attention for any little thing, fix it before you leave Duluth. You do not want to find yourself needing a tow truck out here. Do you have your passport? You'll need that on this segment of the journey for entry into Canada.

Route 61 has many fans in the riding community as it is easy to settle in and kick back along this road, pointed north and headed for the border. Along the way, folks like to stop at Palisade Head, a large lava flow that juts out into Superior's waters. Looking to the south, you can see where you were yesterday, the Apostle Islands mark the other side of the lake. Another popular spot is Gooseberry Falls, a state park featuring dramatic waterfalls, hiking trails and camp sites. Stone buildings here were erected by the Civilian Conservation Corps between 1934 and 1941.

Route Details – 190 miles

➤ In Duluth, Minnesota, find Rte 61 and follow it to Thunder Bay, Ontario.* (190 mi.)

* Border crossing: be sure to have a current passport for your return to the U.S.

Split Rock Lighthouse was built in 1910 after a gale a few years earlier wrecked dozens of ships.

4

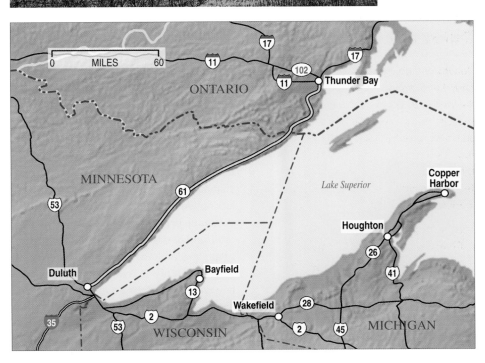

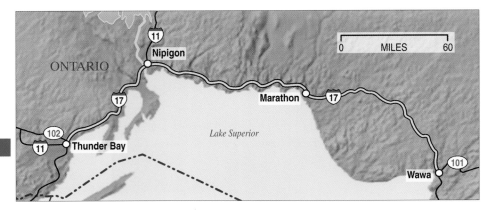

Segment Fourteen
Thunder Bay, Ontario, to Wawa, Ontario

While you're in Thunder Bay, check out the Fort Williams Historical Park, a reconstruction of the North West Company's fur trade post. The Marine Park in Port Arthur draws visitors for views of the Sleeping Giant, a formation of mesas and sills on the Sibley Peninsula.

This segment represents the northernmost portion of the Great Lakes Loop, covering nearly 300 miles between Thunder Bay and Wawa, Ontario. Route 17 to Nipigon is slowly undergoing a transformation to a divided, limited access highway, a reflection of

> ### Route Details – 297 miles
> ➤ From Thunder Bay, follow Rte 17 east to Wawa, Ontario. (297 mi.)

the growing tourist traffic to Thunder Bay. However, once you turn east on Route 17, populations and services vanish. Don't play it too close; gas up when you have the chance.

Route 17 here runs along the northern shore of Lake Superior, often for miles at a stretch. At this point, you're farther north than about 99% of the population of Canada and the Lower 48. During the mid-summer months, twilight gets a late start and it doesn't truly turn dark until 10 or 10:30. That makes for long, fun evenings spent kicking tires and reliving the day's ride.

Hole up in Wawa, a center of mining, forestry, and fur trade. Try out a different type of ride and explore the interior on an ATV. The Bristol Motel in Wawa offers ATV tours, or you can rent one from Jones Powersports here in Wawa (www.jonespowersports.com/rentals.htm). You'll find plenty of accommodations and dining options here.

An observation stand at the Soo Locks in Sault Ste. Marie allows visitors to watch ships navigate between Lake Superior and Lake Huron.

Segment Fifteen
Wawa, Ontario, to Manitoulin Island, Ontario

The route begins to wind down now with a turn around the last portion of Lake Superior through lands dotted with tall, forested hills and thousands of ponds. The mouth of the lake begins to narrow as you approach Sault Saint Marie, a region known as Whitefish Bay. It was here in 1975 that the *Edmund Fitzgerald* foundered in a strong November storm and sank without a distress call.

Gordon Lightfoot's ballad "The Wreck of the Edmund Fitzgerald" topped charts almost exactly a year after the wreck. In his lyrics, Lightfoot suggested that crew error might have been to blame for the wreck. However, when the wreck was found lying broken in half on the lake bottom at a depth of 530 feet, it was speculated that unexpected severe weather encountered by the ship caused it to break apart on the surface. Learning this,

Lightfoot changed his lyrics to remove any idea the crew may have been at fault.

The water flows from Lake Superior to Lake Huron in the Saint Mary's River, which loses elevation quickly in a series of treacherous rapids and falls near Sault Saint Marie. Fur traders and explorers traveling between the two lakes regularly passed through the area because of the need to portage around the falls, which resulted in the creation of a settlement, followed shortly by a 7-Eleven and a Starbucks.

Route Details – 355 Miles

➤ From Wawa, Ontario, continue on Rte 17 to McKerrow. (284 mi.)

➤ Follow Rte 6 to South Baymouth, Manitoulin Island, Ontario. (71 mi.)

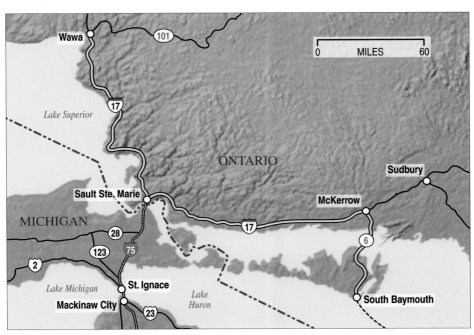

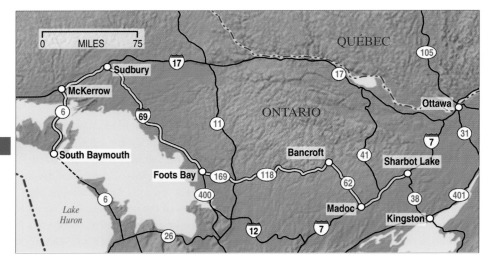

Segment Sixteen
Manitoulin Island, Ontario, to Sharbot Lake, Ontario

Manitoulin is the largest island in the Great Lakes, in fact, it's the largest island in a freshwater lake to be found anywhere. More than a thousand square miles in size, Manitoulin is large enough to have its own freshwater lakes. Route 6 leads you over the island's one-lane swinging bridge. No, this is not like the swinging bridge you used to jump up and down on to scare your sisters. This bridge pivots in the middle, turning to align with the river channel when boats need to pass. It then swings back into place for traffic to cross.

Take a day, or two, or three to enjoy Manitoulin's laid-back atmosphere. Think of it as a chance to return to summer camp. Hiking trails lead to dramatic cliffs and perfect picnic spots. Or rent a bicycle and explore quiet lanes that end at the shore. Or maybe you're an old salt yourself. Canadian Yacht Charters can set you up with a sloop or a catamaran to explore the island's hundreds of inlets and gunk holes for yourself (www.cycnorth.com).

Though the day's ride from Manitoulin to Sharbot Lake is the longest on the tour, it's an easy run if you get an early start. Return

Route Details – 449 miles

➤ From Manitoulin Island, return to McKerrow, Ontario, via Rte 6. (71 mi.)

➤ Follow Rte 17 to Sudbury. (43 mi.)

➤ Take Rte 69 south to Foots Bay. (124 mi.)

➤ Follow Rte 169 east to Rte 118. (6 mi.)

➤ Take Rte 118 to Bancroft. (111 mi.)

➤ Follow Rte 62 south to Madoc. (44 mi.)

➤ Take Rte 7 east to Sharbot Lake, Ontario. (50 mi.)

Manitoulin Island is the largest in the Great Lakes. It features many quiet country lanes that are perfect for exploring on two wheels.

to the mainland on Route 6, east on Route 17, and south on Route 69. A couple of turns will keep you off the busier divided highway and cruising through the bogs of northern Ontario all the way to Sharbot Lake, the last stop on the tour before returning to Buffalo.

Road Tip – Beating Fatigue

Do you suffer from road fatigue on long rides? Find it hard to keep your eyes open after just a few hours on the road? Simple changes in your diet will help you stay alert and focused. Road fatigue is often the result of dehydration and sugar crashes. Keep water handy (no sodas or coffee) and sip it continuously. Avoid big meals during riding hours. Eat small meals and snack on the road. This will keep your blood sugar at a more consistent level and help you avoid that hateful drowsiness that comes an hour or so after a meal.

Sharbot Lake, Ontario, to Buffalo, New York

By now, you should have checked off just about everything on your To Do list for a northern lake vacation. But, just in case you have one or two things left, Sharbot Lake is just the right place to finish them off. Maybe you have yet to undertake some canoeing, or you've carried those golf clubs in your trailer now for a couple thousand miles (a couple thouuusand miles, wow) and haven't yet pulled them out for a round.

Sharbot Lake and surrounding villages offer dozens of out-of-the-way vacation and fishing camps. Even if you don't complete the entire circle tour, the area from Sharbot Lake to Manitoulin is worth a ride up from the Lower 48 on its own.

Route 38 leads to Route 2 in Kingston

where you can pick up the Wolfe Island Ferry to cross the Saint Lawrence River, reentering the U.S. at Cape Vincent by way of a second ferry. Wolfe Island is the largest of the Thousand Islands, an archipelago of islands that straddle the Canada-U.S. border in the Saint Lawrence River. The islands, numbering 1,793 in all, stretch about 50 miles downstream from this point. In order to qualify as an island, a candidate spit of land must be larger than one square foot, stay above water all year, and support at least one tree. And yes, this is the Thousand Islands that gave its name to the popular salad dressing, which later played a starring role as Big Mac's "secret sauce."

Once into the United States you'll slip out

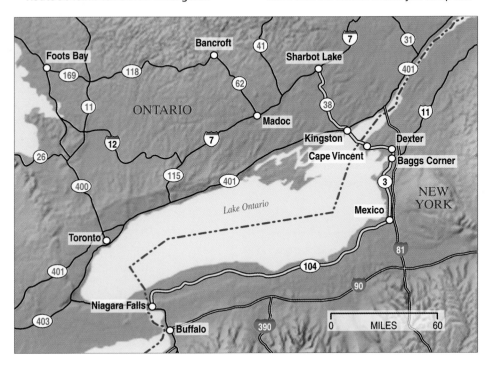

The archipelago of islands in the Saint Lawrence River between Ontario and New York is called the "Thousand Islands" because the "One Thousand Seven Hundred Ninety-Three Islands," the actual number, is too long to fit on touristy tchotchke.

of the tourist traffic that defines the border crossing, returning to quiet lanes that keep company with Lake Ontario. Reaching the Rochester area means that you're just an hour and a half from completing the last leg of your journey.

Think about it. You've covered a distance nearly equal to two cross-country runs in one of the most beautiful, unhurried, and underappreciated sections of the country. You've undertaken a ride that few have considered and even fewer will ever attempt. You've ridden well, probably made a few new friends, tried some new things, and I'm sure you've eaten well.

The only question that remains is, "Where to next?"

Route Details – 287 miles

➤ Depart Sharbot Lake heading south on Rte 38 to Kingston, Ontario. (45 mi.)

➤ Take Rte 2 south to the ferry crossing to Wolfe Island. (3 mi.)

➤ On Wolfe Island, cross on Rte 95 and take the ferry to Cape Vincent, New York. (8 mi.)

➤ From Cape Vincent, follow Rte 12E south to Dexter. (19 mi.)

➤ Take Rte 180 south to Baggs Corner. (4 mi.)

➤ Follow Rte 3 south to Mexico, New York. (41 mi.)

➤ Ride Rte 104 into Niagara Falls, New York. (167 mi.)

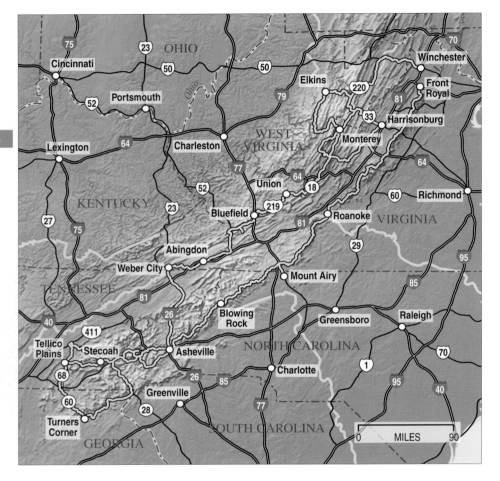

5 APPALACHIAN ADVENTURES

This tour ranges from 8 to 14 days and covers about 2,000 miles. The route includes the length of both Skyline Drive and the Blue Ridge Parkway, and features layovers in North Carolina, Virginia, and West Virginia where you can enjoy hundreds of miles of pastoral and mountainous byways, including the famous "Dragon."

Raise your hand if the Blue Ridge Parkway is on your bucket list. You're not alone. Riding Skyline Drive and the Blue Ridge Parkway is a thoroughly satisfying motorcycling experi- ence, drawing riders each season from around the world. Few roads in the U.S. fea- ture the Parkway's combination of long sce- nic vistas, unending curves, and a ban on

One of the most famous motorcycling roads in the United States may be this portion of US 129 that crosses the southern boundary of the Great Smoky Mountains. Known far and wide as The Dragon, it's a better ride during the week than on a weekend.

This may be the South, but you'll still encounter icy spots at the beginning and end of the riding season, as was found here on the Richard B. Russell Scenic Byway near Helen, Georgia.

Ghost towns aren't exclusive to western states. Eastern towns with an economy based on natural resources like timber or coal experienced rapid growth and decline. A few, such as Thurmond, West Virginia, have been preserved.

commercial traffic for more than 550 miles. What's more, riding off the Parkway is just as rewarding. Thousands of miles of central Appalachian roads are smooth and lightly-traveled, accommodating a wide range of riding styles, from those who prefer a gentle cruise to those who like to get after it.

But the Appalachian region offers more than roads. Mountain traditions of music, art, and craftsmanship have influenced the world. Much of the nation's early history was shaped by these ancient hills and the folks who scratched out a hardscrabble existence here. The fertile lowlands feature vast tracts of cultivated, rolling fields that color the foreground of panoramic vistas. This is also a region of stark contrasts between haves and have-nots, but in spite of the apparent disparity, the high-dollar weekend retreats and the cabins that cling tenuously to rocky hillsides have something in common: a view that's priceless.

The most pleasurable time to travel in the region runs from April through October. In the spring, flowering mountain laurel and rhododendron grace most roadways in the upper elevations. July and August feature hot weather and a good chance for afternoon thunderstorms. If you want to travel the region during the height of fall color, the peak usually comes to the mountains in mid-October. Best months: May, June, September, and October. Excepting the occasional winter storm, most roads remain passable throughout the year, but the winter months are chilly.

Connections

This tour runs in close proximity to the American South loop and, via US 50, can connect with Crossing the Heartland.

If you have an idea that the eastern states of the U.S. are crowded and noisy, you just haven't been riding in the right places, like VA 311.

Segment One
Front Royal to Roanoke, Virginia

This tour loop begins at what most riders take for the logical start of a run down the spine of the Blue Ridge: the northern entrance to Skyline Drive in Front Royal, Virginia. Skyline Drive runs the length of Shenandoah National Park for 115 miles, terminating at Afton Mountain, near Waynesboro, Virginia. Skyline offers expansive views of the rolling Virginia Piedmont to the east and the Shenandoah Valley to the west. A good target for the end of Segment One is Roanoke, Virginia, a ride distance of about 235 miles.

At milepost 120, look for the spur road leading to the Mill Mountain Star, an 88-foot neon star that lights the Roanoke skyline each night. Make sure you find time to visit

Route Details – 235 miles

➤ Follow Skyline Drive from Front Royal, Virginia, to Afton Mountain. (115 mi.)

➤ Continue on the Blue Ridge Pkwy south to milepost 120 at Roanoke. (120 mi.)

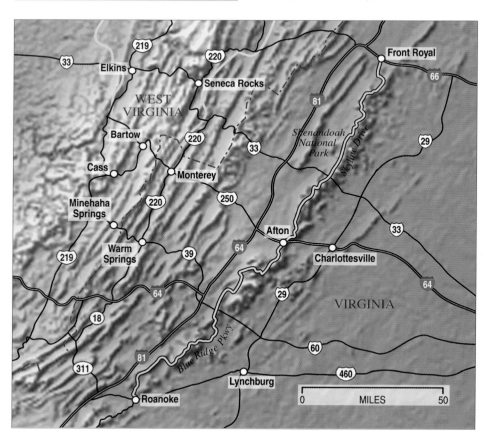

5

On your way through Culpeper, look for the author parked outside Baby Jims.

the O. Winston Link Museum in downtown Roanoke. Link is remembered for developing innovative photographic techniques that al-lowed him to capture striking nighttime im-ages of locomotives in the last days of steam-powered engines.

Segment Two
Roanoke, Virginia, to Blowing Rock, North Carolina

Departing Roanoke, the Parkway begins a long, slow ascent into the highlands of southern Virginia. The mix of rolling farmlands, forests, and hills turn to high mead-ows and mountains as you travel toward the border.

This section includes some of the Blue Ridge Parkway's most famous icons. At milepost 176 is the Mabry Mill, possibly the world's most photographed grist mill. It's so popular, vintage post cards promoting tourism in other states can still be found featuring the Mabry. (www.virginia.org/Listings/HistoricSites/MabryMill). Just a mile down the road, the exit on US 58 at mile marker 177 leads to Willville (willvillebikecamp.com), a motorcycles-only campground at Meadows of Dan, Virginia.

At milepost 199, take a detour off the

Route Details – 201 miles

➤ Blue Ridge Pkwy milepost 120 to milepost 199. (79 mi.)

➤ US 52 south to Mount Airy, North Carolina. (30 mi. round trip)

➤ Blue Ridge Pkwy milepost 199 to 291 at Blowing Rock, North Carolina. (92 mi.)

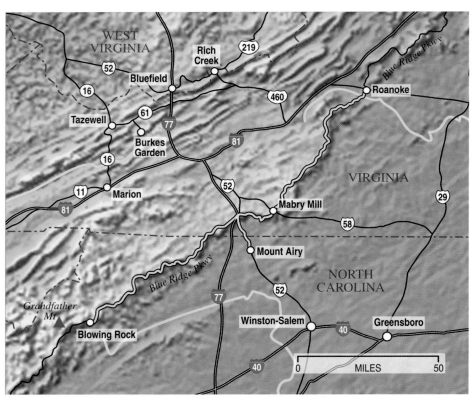

5

Riders enjoy a perfect spring day along the Blue Ridge Parkway. The parkway allows no commercial traffic and is laced with countless twists and turns along its entire 469-mile run.

5

Parkway on US 52 for 15 miles and you'll arrive at Mount Airy, North Carolina, better known as the inspirational setting for the fictional town of Mayberry. Wander through Mount Airy toward the end of September and you'll arrive just in time for Mayberry Days (www.surryarts.org), an annual celebration of the simpler times and slower living epitomized by the popular television show.

A good overnight destination is Blowing Rock, North Carolina, one of the region's early tourist destinations. Its high altitude offered a welcome respite from the summer heat in the lowlands, guaranteeing a visit from the eastern gentry each year. The town takes its name from the unusual rock formation that rises more than 1,500 feet above the Johns River Gorge, which creates updrafts that return small objects thrown over the edge. You'll find plenty of accommodations, restaurants, and a walkable downtown area.

Road Tip – Beware the Dreaded Looky-Lou

When riding Skyline, beware of cars stopped unexpectedly in the middle of the road. There's no accident, just a couple of deer. Maybe a bear. And a few carloads of excited urban dwellers whose previous experience with wildlife are the raccoons rummaging through garbage cans. Plan your Skyline trip for a Monday through Thursday and you'll encounter fewer impromptu roadside safaris.

Segment Three
Blowing Rock to Asheville, North Carolina

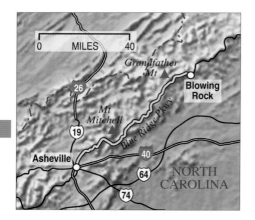

5

Make a stop at the Linn Cove Viaduct at milepost 304. This section of the Parkway was the last to be completed (1987). It was designed to skirt Grandfather Mountain, one of the oldest peaks and most ecologically sensitive portions of the Appalachian range.

The entrance to Grandfather Mountain is just a short distance away and worth the visit (grandfather.com). In 1794, French botanist Andre Michaux scaled the ancient mountain, later recounting that he had "Reached the summit of the highest moun-

There are points on Skyline and the Blue Ridge Parkway where it's tempting to take your eyes off the road. Better to use the turnouts, or you'll end up in the valley!

Hiking trails depart from the roadside at many points. Pack a picnic lunch in your saddlebags and hike to a nearby overlook for a memorable meal with view.

tain in all of North America, and with my companion and guide, sang the "Marseillaise" and shouted 'Long live America and the Republic of France, long live liberty!'" God bless the excitable French.

Michaux should have saved his enthusiasm for Mount Mitchell forty miles down range. At 6,684 feet, Mount Mitchell tops Grandfather (5,946 ft) by more than 700 feet, claiming the highest elevation east of the Mississippi. A short trail from the Mount Mitchell parking lot leads to a stone observation platform with 80-mile views of the surrounding area.

Plan to call it a day in Asheville (www. exploreasheville.com). Downtown Asheville is filled with one-of-a-kind restaurants and plenty of people-watching.

Route Details – 220 miles

- ➤ Follow Blue Ridge Pkwy milepost 291 to 304 (Linn Cove Viaduct). (13 mi.)
- ➤ US 52 south to Mount Airy, North Carolina. (30 mi. round trip)
- ➤ Blue Ridge Pkwy milepost 199 to 291 at Blowing Rock, North Carolina. (92 mi.)
- ➤ From milepost 304 ride to US 221 at milepost 305. (1 mi.)
- ➤ Take US 221 south to Grandfather Mountain and return (1 mi.)
- ➤ From milepost 305 ride to 355 (Mount Mitchell). (50 mi.)
- ➤ From milepost 355 ride to 388 at Asheville, North Carolina. (33 mi.)

Segment Four
Asheville to Stecoah, North Carolina

As you travel between Asheville and Cherokee on this leg of the trip, you'll find some of the most dramatic views along the Parkway. Have your camera ready for milepost 431; it features the highest elevation along the Parkway. As you near the end of the Parkway, milepost 455 holds a special treat. Exit here and follow US 19 east toward Maggie Valley to reach Wheels Through Time (www.wheelsthroughtime.com). Wheels bills itself as "the museum that runs" because every motorcycle housed here is restored to running condition and operated on a regular basis, no matter how rare or unusual the motorcycle.

Return to the Parkway via US 23 for the last 14 miles. If you think Skyline and the

Parkway were a good run, you'll be happy to know the riding in the days to follow is at least the equal to what you've enjoyed so far.

The Parkway terminates in Cherokee, North Carolina, home to the eastern band of the Cherokee Indian Nation. In 1838, many

Make sure your run down the Parkway includes a stop at the Wheels Through Time Museum, just off the Parkway in Maggie Valley, North Carolina.

A good sign of things to come.

of the Cherokee were forced to abandon their ancient homelands and relocate in Oklahoma Territory, a march that became known as the Trail of Tears. Despite this, some managed to hold on to their land, others hid, and a few returned to their homes by foot. Over time, members of the tribe re-purchased portions of their land and gained protection through federal recognition. Stop for a picture with a roadside chief (bit.ly/i62hO5) and learn more about the story of the Cherokee at the Musuem of the Cherokee Indian (www.cherokeemuseum.org).

When you're ready to call it a day, follow US 441 south out of Cherokee to US 74 west. Turn west on North Carolina 28 and follow it to Stecoah, North Carolina, and the Iron Horse Motorcycle Lodge (www.ironhorsenc.com). The Iron Horse was de-signed especially for riders and is located in an area renowned for great riding. Set up basecamp here for at least a couple of days because the rides on Segments 5 and 6 start and finish from this location.

Route Details – 123 miles

- ➤ From milepost 388, ride south on the Blue Ridge Pkwy to milepost 455. (67 mi.)
- ➤ Follow US 19 east to Wheels Through Time in Maggie Valley, North Carolina. (10 mi. round trip)
- ➤ Continue on the Pkwy south to its end. (14 mi.)
- ➤ Take US 441 south to Cherokee, North Carolina. (3 mi.)
- ➤ In Cherokee, follow US 441 south to US 74. (4 mi.)
- ➤ Follow US 74 west to Rte 28. (15 mi.)
- ➤ Follow Rte 28 to Stecoah. (10 mi.)

Segment Five
Dragon's Lair

Route Details – 155 miles

- ➤ From Stecoah, follow Rte 28 north to Rte 143. (1 mi.)
- ➤ Follow Rte 143 south to Robbinsville, North Carolina. (9 mi.)
- ➤ Take US 129 north to Rte 143. (2 mi.)
- ➤ Follow Rte 143 (the Cherohala Skyway) west to Tellico Plains (becomes Tennessee 165). (53 mi.)
- ➤ Follow Rte 360 north to US 411. (22 mi.)
- ➤ Ride US 411 north to Rte 72. (4 mi.)
- ➤ Follow Rte 72 to US 129. (9 mi.)
- ➤ Ride US 129 (The Dragon) south to Deals Gap, North Carolina. (33 mi.)
- ➤ Follow Rte 28 to Stecoah, North Carolina. (22 mi.)

The riding agenda today includes two well-known motorcycling roads, the Cherohala Skyway and The Dragon. Running from Robbinsville, North Carolina, to Tellico Plains, Tennessee, the Cherohala Skyway bisects the Cherokee and Nantahala National Forests. Dedicated in 1996, the Cherohala is a rider favorite, sought after for its sweeping curves, long distance vistas, and virtual absence of traffic.

Just before entering Tellico Plains, pick up Route 360 on your right. Route 360 skirts through fields and lakes, ending on US 411. Follow US 411 north for a short distance to Route 72. The right turn on Route 72 leads you to the perfect starting point for riding Deal's Gap.

The section of US 129 that crosses Deal's Gap between the Foothills Parkway and Route 28 has achieved a certain notoriety

From Robbinsville, North Carolina, to Tellico Plains, Tennessee, the Cherohala Skyway is a beautiful and entertaining ride.

It's hard to take a wrong turn in western North Carolina. Every road is packed with curves and scenic views

both for the curvy eleven-mile section known as The Dragon (www.tailofthedragon.com) as well as the antics of would-be racers on sport bikes. However, you don't have to be a knee dragger to have a good time riding this famous slab of pavement if you keep a few pointers in mind. It's curvy, but US 129 isn't a technical challenge. Just keep your speed to posted limits and don't feel tempted to wick it up beyond your comfort level. Expect faster bikes to come up on you quickly and regularly. Just move to the right and let 'em do their thing.

Approaching the end of the Dragon, the gaggle of bikes parked and buzzing around the Deal's Gap Motorcycle Resort (www.dealsgap.com) will present an irresistible stopping point. No matter how exotic your ride is, you're likely to find a kindred spirit at this popular motorcycle watering hole in the far western North Carolina mountains.

The last segment of your run on the Dragon's Lair is just about as much fun as the Dragon itself. The last portion of Route

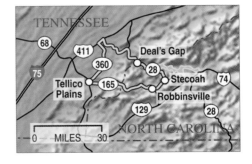

28 is a twisty, turny strip of pavement hugging the shore of Cheoah Lake.

Route 28 passes directly by the Fontana Dam, the largest dam on the east coast and, thanks to its starring role in *The Fugitive,* one of the most recognizable. When completed in the early 1940s the 480-foot structure holding back the Little Tennessee River inundated several small towns and villages including its namesake, Fontana, North Carolina. The resulting lake covers over 10,000 acres. Stop by the visitor center at the dam and take a stroll out on the observatory deck for up-close views.

Segment Six
Northern Georgia Loop

This will be a long day in the saddle, but well worth it. The last few days have featured lower miles and more stopping points. Today, it's all about the ride. While roads like the Skyway and The Dragon get all the attention in these parts, many of the roads throughout western North Carolina and northern Georgia traverse a varied landscape full of mountain-filled vistas and laced with curvaceous strips of pavement.

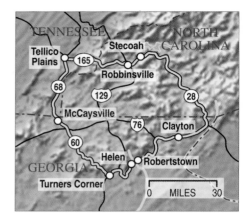

Follow Route 28 south out of Stecoah through the state and into Georgia. This segment of 28 is almost as entertaining as the portion leading up to The Dragon. The right turn onto Warwoman Road leads you through beautiful Georgia hills where folks have cut out a few narrow strips for farming. For the most part though, you'll travel along a mostly empty, smooth road along quiet streams and lakes. Arriving in Clayton, Georgia, stick with the road you're on and as you pass through town, it becomes US 76. Known as the Lookout Mountain Scenic Highway, this portion of the tour will offer you some great shots of the rough and tumble landscape of the southern Appalachians. A left turn on Georgia 197 begins a long,

The Russell Scenic Byway near Helen, Georgia, offers great views of the northern Georgia mountains and valleys.

quiet run along the shores of Lake Burton. The right turn onto Georgia 356 offers more of the same. Turn left on Georgia 75 for the short ride into Helen.

Northern Georgia is known for its pottery and Helen serves as a showcase for the region's handiworks. You can find a sampling of works from artists around the region at the Helen Arts and Heritage Center (www.helenarts.org). Helen is also home to a collection of what may be the world's most in-timidating arachnids: tarantulas. Although the bite of certain tarantula species can make you sick, they won't kill you as popular lore or their fierce appearance would have you believe. When you visit the folks at the Live Tarantula Gallery, they'll even set you up with a specially made cage so you can enjoy one of these furry critters as a pet. Your better half would enjoy that, don't you think?

The return ride begins out of Helen following Georgia 75 ALT south for a short portion to US 129 north and US 19 south. The reason for cutting across the state like this is to get to a special return road, Georgia 60. Prepare to wear down your sidewalls, as Route 60 contains curves from one end to the other, earning its well-deserved reputation as one of the best motorcycling roads in northern Georgia.

Route Details – 280 miles

➤ From Stecoah, North Carolina, take Rte 28 south to Warwoman Road. (64 mi.)

➤ Ride west on Warwoman Road to Clayton, Georgia. (15 mi.)

➤ Continue west on US 76 to Rte 197. (11 mi.)

➤ Go south on Rte 197 to Rte 356. (12 mi.)

➤ Follow Rte 356 south to Roberts-town. (11 mi.)

➤ Take Rte 17/75 into Helen. (1 mi.)

➤ Reverse direction on Rte 75, following Rte 75 ALT south to US 129. (10 mi.)

➤ Follow US 129 to US 19 at Turners Corner. (7 mi.)

➤ Follow US 19 south to Rte 60. (6 mi.)

➤ Ride Rte 60 (becomes Rte 68 in Tennessee) to McCaysville, Georgia. (46 mi.)

➤ Follow Route 68 to Tellico Plains, Tennessee. (37 mi.)

➤ Turn east on Rte 165 (becomes Rte 143 in North Carolina) to Stecoah, North Carolina. (49 mi.)

➤ Take Rte 143 to Stecoah. (11 mi.)

Follow the old alignment of US 19 under the New River Gorge Bridge and you'll find this original crossing near the bottom of the gorge.

Iron Horse Lodge is a rider favorite in western North Carolina, featuring camping areas and cabins along a quiet mountain creek.

Segment Seven

Stecoah, North Carolina, to Abingdon, Virginia

Today the route turns north, following US 74 through Asheville. Take some time on your way through to visit the Biltmore Estate (www.biltmore.com). Originally built by George Vanderbilt, the home opened to visitors in 1895 after six years of construction. It includes 34 bedrooms, 43 bathrooms, and more than four acres of floor space. A proper tour of this vast estate takes a couple of hours and you can easily spend a half day roaming a small portion of the 8,000-acre grounds.

Out of Asheville, follow I-26 across the mountains into Tennessee. Despite the Interstate designation, this wide-open portion of road does not feature heavy traffic and is a pleasure to ride. Crossing into Virginia pick up US 58, known as The Crooked Road. It's

With a view to the Blue Ridge in the distance, Biltmore's Deer Park, built by visionary landscape architect Frederick Law Olmsted, was designed to resemble English countryside.

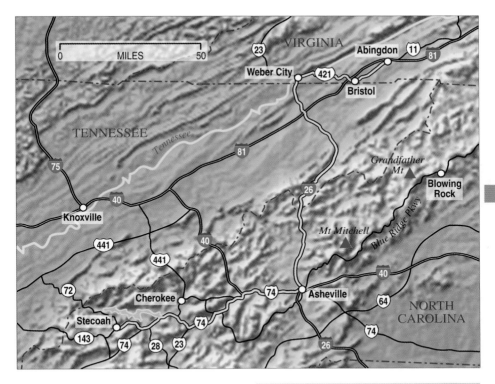

also a music heritage trail, taking you through Hiltons, Virginia, home of the Carter Clan, the first family of country music. Family members still operate the Carter Fold (www.carterfamilyfold.org) where you can enjoy original and contemporary country music acts in a setting perfect for reliving this uniquely American form of music. Route 58 also runs directly through Bristol (www.visitbristoltnva.org), a city that straddles Virginia and Tennessee. Bristol is rightly considered the birthplace of country music and there are dozens of historic sites to visit here to complete your musical education.

Follow US 11 out of Bristol to Abingdon, Virginia, the perfect spot to stop in preparation for the next day's ride.

Route Details – 212 miles

➤ From Stecoah, North Carolina, follow Rte 28 to US 74 east. (10 mi.)

➤ Follow US 74 east to Asheville, North Carolina. (71 mi.)

➤ Ride I-26 (becomes US 23 in Virginia) north to Weber City, Virginia. (88 mi.)

➤ Follow US 421 to State Street in Bristol, Tennessee. (26 mi.)

➤ Follow State Street to Piedmont Ave. (1.5 mi.)

➤ Turn left on Piedmont, following to US 11. (1 mi.)

➤ Follow US 11 north to Abington, Virginia. (15 mi.)

Segment Eight
Abingdon to Monterey, Virginia

The first part of today's route features a section of Virginia 16 that some consider a contemporary of The Dragon. You'll want to pull up any low-hanging highway pegs for the next forty miles. It's gonna be a curvy ride, so hang on!

In Tazewell, head east on Route 61, following the turnoff for Burkes Garden at Virginia 623. Burkes Garden, one of the more unusual geographic features of the Appalachians, is included on today's route. Referred to as God's Thumbprint, the formation of

this valley looks like a sunken volcanic caldera, but actually resulted from the collapse of limestone caverns. The area was first discovered in the 1740s by James Burke on a hunting expedition. Burke planted potato peelings by the campfire of a 1748 surveying party and the next year, a fine crop of potatoes was found, giving rise to the name "Burkes Garden."

The remainder of the ride today follows rural routes across several Appalachian ranges for one of the curviest days through-

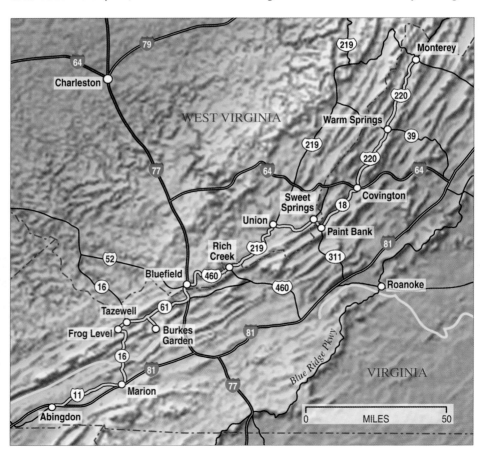

out the entire route. Route 61 east to US 52 is a flat, fast road following the northern edge of the mountains that form Burkes Garden. US 52 north avoids most of the traffic on Interstate 77. Rather than join I-77, opt to continue on Route 598, an old alignment of US 52. This portion of the route skips along the Virginia-West Virginia border atop East River Mountain before connecting to US 460 in Bluefield. Follow US 460 east back into Virginia, turning north on US 219 in Rich Creek.

Had enough curves yet? There are plenty more to come. The right turn onto West Virginia 3 winds through low hills and farmlands, but the turn onto West Virginia 311 ups the ante considerably. The run from here, along Virginia 18 into Covington, and US 220 north to Monterey, is filled with altitude changes, valley runs, tight sweepers through dense forests, and wide open road through broad valleys. Set up camp in Monterey, Virginia. There's more great riding to be had on this unforgettable Appalachian journey, and it all starts here.

An impressive steel arch bridge spans the New River Gorge at Fayetteville, West Virginia. Bridge Day, held annually in mid-October, features BASE jumpers performing thrilling acts of derring-do for the crowds.

Route Details – 283 miles

- ➤ Continue on US 11 from Abingdon, Virginia, to Marion. (29 mi.)
- ➤ Follow Rte 16 north to US 19 Business in Frog Level. (31 mi.)
- ➤ Follow US 19 Business through Tazewell to Rte 61. (5 mi.)
- ➤ Take Rte 61 to Rte 623. (5 mi.)
- ➤ Follow Rte 623 to Burkes Garden and return. (16 mi.)
- ➤ Continue east on Rte 61 to US 52. (20 mi.)
- ➤ Follow US 52 north to Rte 598. (4 mi.)
- ➤ Continue on Route 598 to US 460 in Bluefield, West Virginia. (7 mi.)
- ➤ Follow US 460 to US 219 in Rich Creek, Virginia. (30 mi.)
- ➤ Take US 219 north to Union, West Virginia. (27 mi.)
- ➤ Follow Rte 3 to Rte 311 in Sweet Springs, West Virginia. (20 mi.)
- ➤ Take Route 311 to Route 18 in Paint Bank, Virginia. (7 mi.)
- ➤ Follow Rte 18 north to US 220 in Covington, Virginia. (27 mi.)
- ➤ Follow US 220 north to Monterey, Virginia. (55 mi.)

Segment Nine
Greenbrier Valley Loop

Monterey, the county seat of Highland County, is central to some of the most spectacular riding in the Appalachians. With the highest average elevation east of the Mississippi, Highland is aptly named. You just can't build a straight road here, and that's a good thing.

Head west on US 250 over Monterey Mountain through the bucolic Blue Grass Valley and into West Virginia. A short ride will bring you to the Green Bank Observatory (www.gb.nrao.edu), home to some of the most powerful radio astronomy telescopes in the world. The entire facility is free of

The Glade Creek Grist Mill, in Babcock State Park in West Virginia, was built from the pieces of several historic mills in the area. Fully operational today, the mill sells freshly ground corn meal and buckwheat flour to visitors.

charge and features a tour of the grounds and an up-close view of the big 'scopes including the 300-meter GBT, the world's largest fully-steerable telescope.

Nearby you'll find Cass Scenic Railroad (www.cassrailroad.com). The coal-fired Shay locomotives that once performed logging duties in these rugged hills now dutifully pull passenger cars along the same steep tracks. Cass also offers accommodations in state-owned and restored company houses.

The run west on West Virginia 66 passes through Snowshoe, an all-year resort that's home to Freedom Fest (www.snowshoemtn. com/freedom-fest/index.htm), a popular all-marque motorcycle rally.

A right turn on US 219 leads you on a narrow path through the mountains. Most of US 219's route through West Virginia follows the Seneca Trail, a major Indian footpath that followed the contours of the mountains from north to south.

Turn east on US Route 33 to begin the return portion of the loop, joining US 220 in Franklin, West Virginia. The run south to Monterey will be a fitting end to a pleasant day's ride.

Route Details – 179 miles

➤ From Monterey Virginia, ride west on US 250 to Bartow, West Virginia. (24 mi.)

➤ Turn south on Rte 92 to Route 66. (12 mi.)

➤ Follow Rte 66 to US 219. (16 mi.)

➤ Take US 219 north to Elkins. (44 mi.)

➤ Follow US 33 east to Franklin, West Virginia. (60 mi.)

➤ Ride south on US 220 to Monterey, Virginia. (23 mi.)

5

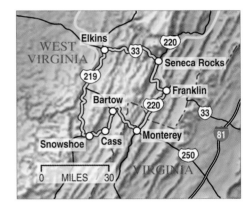

US Route 250 rolls across an unending array of mountains and lush farm valleys in western Virginia.

Segment Ten
Staunton Loop

This loop ride out of Monterey heads in the opposite direction, turning down US 220 south. A short ride brings you to the first turn onto Virginia 84, a backdoor entrance into West Virginia that seems virtually untraveled. As Route 84 ends, turn south on West Virginia 92, a tight, flat little road that hugs the western edge of the narrow valley floor. Minehaha Springs is the next junction. Turn left here onto West Virginia 39 and fol-

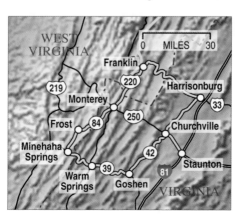

low it over the tall mountains and ridges into Warm Springs, Virginia. Warm Springs (www.discoverbath.com) represents one of the earliest forms of tourism, drawing wealthy farmers and merchants from the lowlands to "take the healing waters." Warm Springs' most notable pools are marked by the round buildings at Jefferson Pools, named for Thomas Jefferson who took to the soothing spring waters in his later years. Separate facilities for men and women highlight the fact that bathing suits are optional—the better to permit that natural spring water to penetrate your crevices. Leave your camera on the bike. There will be no photo opportunities here today, I guarantee.

After a refreshing dip, continue east on Virginia 39, turning north on Virginia 42 at Goshen. Arriving at Churchville on Virginia 42, turn east on US 250 to visit Staunton, Virginia, one of the Shenandah Valley's old-

These riders are exploring Virginia 42, a popular north-south highway in western Virginia

est cities. Although agriculture still dominates the local economy, Staunton's downtown has undergone a significant revival in the last decade, transitioning from its heritage as a center of trade and industry to an arts center (www.visitstaunton.com) . Downtown you'll find the Blackfriars Playhouse, the world's only re-creation of Shakespeare's indoor theater featuring plays from the Bard every evening. The eastern side of town includes the Frontier Culture Museum, a living history display of English, Irish, and German cultures that settled throughout the region.

Retrace your path on US 250 west and turn north once again on Virginia 42, passing through Bridgewater and the southern edge of Harrisonburg. The portion of US 33 west between Harrisonburg, Virginia, and Franklin, West Virginia, is a regional favorite. Expect to see many fellow riders enjoying the twists over Shenandoah Mountain. After completing the challenge of Route 33, US 220 south to Monterey seems tame by comparison. It's the perfect stretch of road for cooling down after a hard day's run.

Route Details – 214 miles

- ➤ From Monterey, Virginia, ride south on US 220 to Rte 84. (4 mi.)
- ➤ Follow Rte 84 into West Virginia to Frost. (20 mi.)
- ➤ Take Rte 92 south to Minehaha Springs, West Virginia. (11 mi.)
- ➤ Ride east on Rte 39 to Goshen, Virginia. (43 mi.)
- ➤ Follow Rte 42 north to Churchville. (27 mi.)
- ➤ Follow US 250 into Staunton, then return to Rte 42. (20 mi.)
- ➤ Continue north on Rte 42 to US 33 in Harrisonburg, Virginia. (25 mi.)
- ➤ Follow US 33 west to Franklin, West Virginia. (41 mi.)
- ➤ Ride south on US 220 to Monterey, Virginia. (23 mi.)

Segment Eleven
Monterey to Winchester, Virginia

This leg through the Appalachians traverses a scenic and easy-to-ride route between Monterey and Winchester, Virginia. Follow US 220 north out of Monterey and into West Virginia, turning west on US 33 at Franklin. Follow Route 33 west to Seneca Rocks. Rock climbers from all over flock to Seneca to scamper up the sheer cliffs and ledges of this unique formation. You might be just as happy to watch them from the porch of the general store. I would.

Here at Seneca Rocks, turn north on West Virginia 55 and follow the road into Petersburg. US 220 joins the route here. After spending so much time on utterly empty roads, the little bit of traffic you encounter through Petersburg and Moorefield will seem like a lot, but after riding just a few miles north of Moorefield, you'll return to the road less traveled. US 220 intersects with US 50 at Junction. Turn east on US 50 for the run into Winchester.

Winchester, Virginia, was a center of trade from the early days of American history (www.visitwinchesterva.com) . During the American Civil War, it was a position desired by both sides. Control of Winchester meant control of the Shenandoah Valley, regarded as the breadbasket of the Confederacy. No wonder it changed hands more than 70 times during the four-year conflict. Stonewall Jackson's Valley headquarters are preserved here along with dozens of other sites related to major campaigns of the war.

Winchester is more than a crossroads for folks from the Valley. It also marks the end of this tour through the central and southern Appalachian mountains and a decision point for you. Where will your journeys take you next? You're sitting right on US 50, one of the few remaining signed US highways that runs the entire span of the U.S. A run to the west coast could be in order. Better yet, close your eyes, flip through the rest of the book, and let fate decide. Spontaneity is a hallmark of an unforgettable journey.

West Virginia features some of the finest riding to be found on the East Coast. Just off the Blue Ridge Parkway, you'll enjoy a riding paradise that is truly underrated.

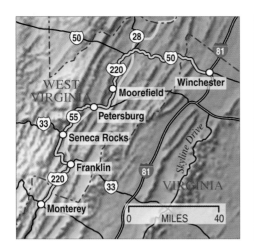

Route Details – 152 miles

➤ Ride north out of Monterey, Virginia, on US 220 to Franklin, West Virginia. (23 mi.)

➤ Follow US 33 west to Seneca Rocks. (25 mi.)

➤ Ride north on Rte 55 to Petersburg. (23 mi.)

➤ Follow US 220 north to US 50 at Junction, West Virginia. (32 mi.)

➤ Follow US 50 east to Winchester, Virginia. (49 mi.)

5

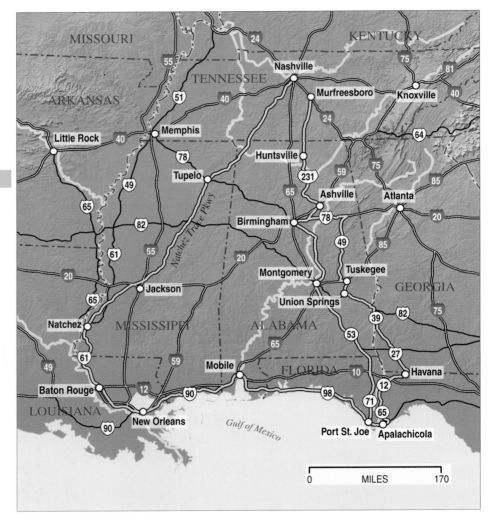

MILES

0   170

6 AMERICAN SOUTH

This tour loops through an area of the United States known as the American South, ambling through Tennessee, Mississippi, Louisiana, Florida, Georgia, and Alabama, a region that has inspired poets, musicians, and writers for centuries. The roads aren't so bad either. We'll follow the length of the Natchez Trace from Nashville, Tennessee, to the Mississippi River and then to New Orleans, Louisiana. We'll ride along the warm, clear waters of the Gulf Coast through Apalachicola before turning north through Huntsville, Alabama, and back to Nashville. At an average of 250 miles per day, completing this loop would require about two weeks, depending on weather and the length of stopovers.

If you're interested in developing a well-rounded picture of American ideals, values, and attitudes, the South is an important part of your education. It's more than a motorcycle ride; it's a voyage that informs you about social, political, and religious forces which, sometimes for the better, sometimes for the worse, influenced the course of a nation and continue to shape it today.

Some would say it's no longer possible to tour the American South as it has classically been defined and written about over the years. Folks who live here will say that the South they knew has vanished, that it's been crowded out, overtaken by folks moving in from every which way. That's not entirely true. Southern culture may no longer pre-dominate, but a long ride through this part of the country reveals a multitude of cus-

Southern states don't have as many hills as others, but they do have curves.

Palm trees, warm, open water, and a limitless stretch of sand mark the southern shores of the United States. I can almost taste the margaritas and grilled grouper.

Longwood Mansion is an excellent example of a southern antebellum mansion, at least from the outside. At the outbreak of the Civil War, workers put down their tools and returned to the North, leaving the mansion unfinished on the inside. >

toms, literature, music, and cuisines that remain unique to this region and continue to thrive. There is still plenty of "southern" in The South.

From the outset, let me encourage you to use these routes as a starting point for exploring, and not necessarily as your exclusive route. The travels documented in this section will highlight some of the better roads and points of interest, but "off the beaten path" takes a special meaning when you're exploring a region and a culture. Holing up in a place like Tupelo and following the back roads of the Mississippi Delta will help you find those features of the South that aren't lost, just overlooked.

The southerly location means an early start to the riding season. It might be chilly initially, but as you head south on the Natchez Trace in mid-April, you'd be in warmer climes by the time you reach New Orleans. Hang out on the Gulf Coast for a week, then make a slow return to the north. By then, completing the loop through the Appalachians will be comfortable as well.

The Natchez Trace is a beautiful ride during the spring. The fall isn't too shabby either.

Connections

Ready for some more touring through this fine country of ours? This tour through the American South runs close to the Appala-chian Adventures as well as Crossing the Heartland tours. But don't rush off now. Sit a spell. Enjoy some fresh sweet tea.

The Pharr Mounds are burial mounds made by local Indians between AD 1 and AD 200.

Segment One

Nashville, Tennessee, to Tupelo, Mississippi

Like the Blue Ridge Parkway, the Natchez Trace is a route that every rider should plan to visit at least once. This 444-mile roadway is a commercial-free two-lane route between Nashville, Tennessee, and Natchez, Mississippi, that links the Cumberland, Tennessee, and Mississippi Rivers. It is an easy and pleasurable way to explore the interior of the Mississippi Delta.

Unlike the Parkway, the Natchez Trace started out as a working road, not one built for motoring pleasure. Its original path was developed well before motorcycles or European settlers or even American Indians.

When you're out west sometime, give a tip of the hat to the American bison. It was their ancestors that originally blazed this trail, following a geological ridgeline to migrate between the delta grasslands and the salt licks around present-day Nashville. The first people here used the trace to establish trade between villages along its path. The path saw continuing development for trade until routes along the Mississippi River became more efficient and travel along the trace fell into decline. The construction of the Natchez Trace Parkway was a work of the 1930s Civilian Conservation Corps, preserving the trace and constructing a roadway that followed its general path. Many portions of the original trace can be enjoyed today as short hikes.

The Natchez Trace doesn't hit many population centers, but it does run directly through Tupelo, Mississippi, the birthplace of The King. If you don't know who I'm talking about, just ask anyone in Tupelo. After

Route Details – 225 miles

➤ Follow Natchez Trace south to Tupelo, Mississippi (225 mi.)

they recover from a near stroke, they'll point you to the shotgun house where Elvis Presley was born. This neatly preserved home now includes a museum that commemorates and interprets his early years and influences. (www.tupelo.net/things/elvis_in_tupelo). Tupelo also sports a well-known automobile museum, featuring a rare Tucker, a Lincoln previously owned by Elvis, other movie and celebrity vehicles, Hispano Suizas, a Duesenberg, and many more rare brands and American favorites.

This point in the tour offers you an opportunity to branch off and further explore the region's musical heritage. You're just a hundred miles from Memphis, Tennessee, a city that played a central role in the evolution of many styles of music, and was home to Elvis Presley's Graceland. Even if you're not an Elvis fan, you can still enjoy a visit to his home. If you don't see Graceland, it's a little like saying you went to Orlando and didn't visit Disney World, or you went to Colorado Springs but didn't ride up Pikes Peak. Just down the road is Clarksdale, Mississippi, generally acknowledged as the birthplace of Mississippi Delta blues, a musical form that influenced musicians from Elvis to contemporary artists such as Eric Clapton.

The King may have made his name in Memphis, but he was born in a modest shotgun house in Tupelo, Mississippi.

6

Did you ever hear the story about the fellow who sold his soul to the devil to become the best blues player who ever lived? According to the legend, Robert Johnson found himself hitchhiking on the road to Clarksdale, unable to pick up a ride. As he reached a lonely crossroad near town, he met a figure who asked for his guitar. The figure "tuned" the guitar and played a few songs with it. Returning it to Johnson gave him mastery of the instrument in exchange for his soul. Following US 61 south out of Memphis will lead you to the spot at the intersection of US 61 and US 49.

When you tire of riding, set yourself on the front porch of the Springfield Plantation for a respite. Mint juleps advised, but not included.

Tupelo, Mississippi, to New Orleans, Louisiana

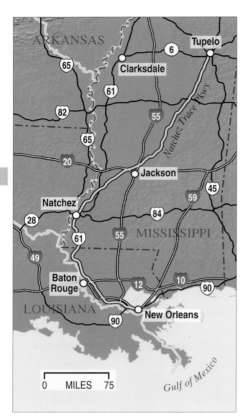

The Trace continues to wind its way through small towns and villages throughout Mississippi. If you'd lived along the road during its heyday, you'd have seen a continuing parade of colorful characters pass by from the south to the north. Those were the "Kaintucks," boatmen who pushed flatboats filled with goods down the Ohio and Mississippi to points south. Arriving in New Orleans, they'd sell their goods as well as the logs in their boats, then return home to Tennessee, Kentucky, and Pennsylvania by foot. Had the trail continued to grow and expand, it might have supported the development of large population centers. But as railroad and steamboat traffic increased, the Trace became obsolete and failed to support growth along its path. Sometimes, those failures work out just fine.

The Trace ends in Natchez, Mississippi, on the banks of the Mississippi River. Natchez is an old city, blending the influences of Native American, European, Southern, and African cultures—all of which have given the city an

Built in the late-1700s, King's Tavern is the oldest building in Natchez, and possibly the most notorious. Work performed on the building in the 1930s revealed three skeletons bricked up in the chimney wall, along with a jeweled dagger.

Inside, the Lorman Store is a clean, comfortable restaurant serving classic southern cuisine.

Route Details – 432 miles

➤ From Tupelo, Mississippi, continue on the Natchez Trace south to Natchez, Mississippi (262 mi.)

➤ In Natchez, pick up US 61 south to New Orleans, Louisiana. (170 mi.)

endless supply of charm, grace, and romance. The rich soil around Natchez supported the development of massive plantations, whose owners grew rich by using slave labor. Frequently those fortunes were used to build the massive antebellum and Greek Revival homes you'll see there today.

Stories about US Route 61 are as colorful as the people who live here. Some call it the Blues Highway for the musical communities it connects along its way. The portion between Baton Rouge and New Orleans is called the Airline Highway because it provides a direct route between the two cities in contrast to other routes that meander through the state. Some credit Governor Huey Long with the development of this part of the route because it provided the fastest access between Baton Rouge, the capital, and the bars and dives in New Orleans. This might be a stretch where you choose to im-provise, following any of the numerous roads that make up the river route. I guess it all depends on how quickly you want to get to the party on Bourbon Street.

In New Orleans, it's probably best to find a spot to park your bike for a couple of days and explore the city by foot. Staying somewhere in the downtown area or along a streetcar line will put you within reach of anything you'd want to see, without dealing with the hassles of pedestrians and traffic. If you've been to New Orleans before, you probably have a list of must-do's that you didn't get to last time. But if this is your first visit, here are a few ideas that will give you a good feeling for what the Crescent City is all about:

- A guided walking tour of French Quarter architecture
- Riding a streetcar to the Garden District
- The special "Friday lunch" at Galatoire's
- Traditional jazz at Preservation Hall
- A cemetery tour hosted by the Voodoo Museum
- Beignets for breakfast (or anytime) at the Café du Monde
- An evening on Bourbon Street
- A visit to the Audubon Zoo and Gardens
- Shopping or looking on Magazine Street

US 89 traces the edge of the Gulf of Mexico almost turn for turn from Mobile, Alabama, to St. Marks, Florida.

Segment Three

New Orleans, Louisiana, to Apalachicola, Florida

When it's time to decamp from New Orleans, turn east on US 90 for the run along the Gulf Coast. To some folks, the southern coast of the United States is a beach bum's paradise, a string of towns along the sparkling waters of the Gulf of Mexico that offer hundreds of miles of sugar-white sand, sunsets over the water, fresh seafood, and margaritas-by-the-sea. Others see this stretch of US 90 and 98 as a sweltering, commercialized, hurricane-prone, concrete jungle.

A successful visit here depends on your at-titude toward the beach and the time of year you travel here. Come in the summer and it's hot. And humid. Visit here between Christmas and Easter and the place is swamped with snowbirds who've flocked here to escape the cold winters of the upper Midwest. Spring break is filled with college kids, wet T-shirt contests and . . . wait a minute, maybe spring is okay. But let's say your focus is on riding and enjoying the seashore. In that case, I'd recommend coming down in May or June, then September through November. Just remember, autumn is hurricane season,

Motorcycle Journeys Through North America

New Orleans' French Quarter looks quiet in this photo near the House of Voodoo. It's probably best not to make a big racket around here, lest a voodoo priestess starts "working" you.

so keep one eye on the road and one eye on the water. Tricky? Not really. There's a voodoo powder for that. Luckily, you know just where to get some.

The route out of New Orleans on US 90 is largely smooth thanks to its rebuilding after Hurricane Katrina. The first portion of highway looks as though it has been swept clean of buildings; that's because it has. Hurricane Katrina made landfall here with a storm surge that pushed houses and boats six to twelve miles inland.

The next insult to hit the area was that little oil spill you may have heard about from the Deepwater Horizon well. While we won't know the full environmental impact of that spill for decades, the present reality shouldn't stop you from visiting here. The beaches are clean, the water is clear, and the seafood is safe to eat.

Given that this segment is a 400-mile run, you may want to split it in two. Navarre Beach is a good option (www.navarrebeach.com) for a mid-point stopover. The beach is a barrier island just off the coast, made of the pure white sand the Gulf is famous for. Navarre has rentals of all types and with so much competition, prices are affordable year round. Off season, the deals are smokin'. You can find a beachfront condo for around a hundred bucks a day.

Route Details – 383 miles

➤ Depart New Orleans on US 90 east to Mobile, Alabama. (147 mi.)

➤ From Mobile, follow US 98 east to Navarre, Florida. (98 mi.)

➤ From Navarre, follow US 98 east to Apalachicola, Florida. (138 mi.)

Segment Four
Apalachicola, Florida, to Birmingham, Alabama

There are two alternate routes planned for this segment. The first route follows a series of US and state routes that feature more two-lane highways and pass through small towns and rural countryside. If you find there are too many roads to follow, you can opt for the simpler route that sticks to US highways.

You hear a lot about Old Florida down here in the same way you hear about the Old South; the forest you pass through on the way north is a real example of it. Apalachicola National Forest is the largest in Florida and preserves one of the last portions of longleaf pine and wiregrass in the area. The savannahs within the forest contain the greatest diversity of wildflowers in the pan-handle, including pitcher plants, sundews, wild orchids, asters, black-eyed susans, blazing star, Harper's Beauty, sneeze weed, and meadow beauty, among others. You'll also catch glimpses of cypress swamps, magnolia bays, creeks, sloughs, and groves of oak hammocks.

European settlers weren't the first to clear the forests here for agriculture. Native Americans cleared tracts to plant maize, beans, and other staples. Soil conditions here have enabled a diversity of uses, making this region the most agriculturally diverse in western Georgia and Alabama, producing cotton, peanuts, poultry, cattle, some vegetables, and forestry products. Roadside stands offer produce right out of the fields and an opportunity to chat with folks whose families have likely lived here for generations. Try a bag of boiled peanuts sometime, you'll find them everywhere. It must be an acquired taste.

Road Tip – GPS Freelancing

Routes through the south are well-suited to freelancing with the GPS using the "pushpin method." Pick a spot on the map a couple hours ahead and enter that into the GPS, but don't depend on it for directions. Follow whatever roads you care to that are headed in the general direction and refer to the GPS just to remain aware of your arrival time. When you get to that point, pick another spot an hour or two ahead and repeat. That gives you the freedom to explore an area you don't know with the comfort that you'll eventually end up where you planned to be.

The 1957 Aermacchi Chimera 175 featured here is just one of hundreds of rare motorcycles you'll find in the Barber Motorsports collection.

Thousands of acres of woodland and open field also makes for world-class hunting. Union Springs, Alabama, at the intersection of US 82 and 29, is known for quail hunting and bird dog trials. Union Springs is also a classic example of the southern small town with a downtown anchored by the county courthouse and the surrounding streets lined with Queen Anne, Victorian, Greek, and classic revival style homes .

North of Union Springs you'll enter Tuskegee, Alabama, home to one of many important chapters in the evolution of the civil rights movement in the South. In the 1940s Tuskegee, Alabama was home to a "military experiment" to train America's first African-American military pilots. In time, that experiment produced a highly accomplished and decorated air corps that became known as the Tuskegee Airmen. It's said that the men who served in the ranks of the Airmen fought two wars, the one in Europe and the one at home. Over time, the accomplishments of these men on both fronts has been recognized more fully and today is immortalized at the Tuskegee Airmen National Historic Site (www.nps.gov/tuai).

Route Details – 470 miles

➤ Depart Apalachicola, Florida, on US 98 east to Rte 65. (10 mi.)

➤ Ride Rte 65 north to Rte 12. (72 mi.)

➤ Take Rte 12 east into Havana, Florida. (17 mi.)

➤ Follow US 27 north to Blakely, Georgia. (66 mi.)

➤ In Blakely, take Rte 39 north to US 82. (39 mi.)

➤ Follow US 82 west to Union Springs, Alabama. (46 mi.)

➤ Ride US 29 north to Tuskegee. (23 mi.)

➤ Follow US 80 west to Cty Rte 49 (becomes State Rte 49 at I-85). (8 mi.)

➤ Continue on Rte 49 north to Rte 281. (88 mi.)

➤ Follow Rte 281 to US 78. (16 mi.)

➤ Take US 78 west into Birmingham. (85 mi.)

Alternate Route – 333 miles

➤ From Apalachicola, ride west on US 98 to Rte 71 at Port St. Joe, Florida. (23 mi.)

➤ Ride north on Rte 71 (becomes Rte 53 in Alabama) to Sylacauga, Alabama. (270 mi.)

➤ From Sylacauga, follow US 280 west into Birmingham, Alabama. (40 mi.)

Route 49 north is a great ride through the heart of the state, culminating in a run through the Talladega National Forest. Race fans will recognize the name Talladega, home to the world's largest superspeedway. Automobile racing grew up here on dusty

The interaction of light between water and clouds puts on a dramatic show nearly every evening, as the sun sets along the Gulf.

red clay tracks as an organized outlet for guys who began as moonshine runners. Although the sport has gone nationwide through the NASCAR series, dirt track racing remains an important southern pastime. I'll bet on your ride up Route 49 you'll see at least a half-dozen hand-lettered signs reading RACE TRACK that point down some narrow lane into what looks like the middle of nowhere. Around here, "Friday Night Lights" means something more than football, it means action at the local racetrack.

Birmingham is a logical stopover for the halfway point on this leg and there's a special place nearby that is a must-visit on any rider's agenda. Birmingham native and successful racer George Barber has amassed one of the largest and most important collections of vintage motorcycles to be found anywhere; they're kept at the Barber Motorsports Park on the east side of the city (www.barbermuseum.org). There are approximately 600 of the collection's 1,200 motorcycles on display at any given time, all in running condition. Barber's collection ranges from 1902 to current-year production including bikes from 20 countries and 200 different manufacturers. Common street bikes are included in the collection, as are rare, one-off Gran Prix race machinery.

If someone says they're "walking in high cotton" it means they're wealthy. Riding in high cotton isn't so bad either.

The alternate route between Apalachicola and Birmingham follows a more direct route, still sticking to back roads, but with fewer stops. The route out of Apalachicola turns west on US 98, then due north on Route 71 through the largely agricultural western Florida panhandle. At the state line, the road remains the same but changes numbers from Florida 71 to Alabama 53. Follow Route 53 north to Sylacauga, a small town just outside Birmingham whose most famous son is probably Jim Nabors. You may know him better as "Gomer Pyle." Nabors began acting when he attended the University of Alabama. He moved west for relief from asthma and was discovered by Andy Griffith in a small Santa Monica, California, tavern.

Sylacauga is also the first known site to record an object from space falling to strike a person. On November 30, 1954, a 4 kg meteorite crashed through the roof of a house, bounced off a radio, and struck Ann Hodges, who was taking an afternoon nap. Mrs. Hodges was badly bruised but not seriously injured. It's still a subject of conversation in town.

In town, pick up US 280 heading west all the way into town. A short jaunt out I-20 will take you to the Barber Motorsports Museum. And while you're at it, keep an eye on the sky.

Segment Five
Birmingham, Alabama, to Nashville, Tennessee

The last segment of the American South route follows the Heart of Dixie Highway from Birmingham to Nashville. That seems like an appropriate way to wrap up this loop. Not only is the road well-named, it's also a sweet ride. US 231 north is mostly two-lane, open, and easy to ride with plenty of passing lanes to get around any gents you run up on who are driving Miss Daisy around.

As you head north, Route 231 passes through just one large population center: Huntsville, Alabama, the original home of the National Aeronautics and Space Administration (NASA) at the Marshall Space Flight Center (www.nasa.gov/centers/marshall). Marshall was the home of NASA's rocket building program and it was here that German rocket builder Wernher von Braun led a team to design and build vehicles that would launch the space age.

The U.S. Space and Rocket Center (www.ussrc.com) here in Huntsville houses a large collection of space gear and exhibits. Like viewing the Great Wall of China and the Hoover Dam, standing near the *Saturn V* is a humbling experience and leads one to marvel at the things mankind can accomplish.

The *Saturn V* was by far the largest vehicle ever flung into space. At launch, the 363-foot rocket weighed 6.7 million pounds. More than 5.5 million pounds of that weight was the fuel in the first two stages required to launch the vehicle into orbit. The five engines of the first stage generated over 7 million pounds of thrust to boost the rocket the

The U.S. Space and Rocket Center in Huntsville, Alabama, includes a Saturn V *rocket, the type used in the Apollo missions. If you've never seen a Saturn, you'll be floored by its size.*

Route Details – 202 miles

➤ From Birmingham, follow I-20 east to US 411 at Leeds, Alabama. (16 mi.)

➤ Follow US 411 north to US 231 south of Ashville, Alabama. (23 mi.)

➤ Take US 231 north to Murfreesboro, Tennessee. (163 mi.)

first 36 miles. It might not have been as quick off the line as your bike is, but once it built up a head of steam, it put up some pretty good numbers—a mile and a half per second for a top speed of around 5,300 mph. Not too shabby.

From high tech to high country, you'll notice that the terrain north of Huntsville begins a gradual transition to the foothills that dominate the Tennessee countryside. Coastal plains give way to rolling meadows and pastures. As you near Murfreesboro, the pace of traffic begins to pick up and you're less than 30 miles from the junction with I-40. Continue on US 231 to US 70 in Lebanon, turn west and you'll run into the country music capital of the world. Turn east and a very long stretch of US 70 begins just a few miles down the road, leading to Sparta, Tennessee, then Knoxville, Tennessee, and the

Appalachians. The sound of the Grand Ole Opry or the sound of the highway. Either way you turn will be music to your ears.

Y'all come back now. Ya hear?

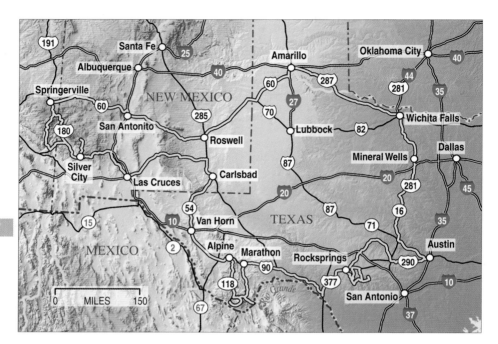

7 LONE STAR LOOP

Covering almost 3,000 miles in the central southwest, this loop includes a relaxing blend of open highways and country lanes through high desert and Texas hill country. It also includes a route extension that lets you explore the unique geological features and ancient cultures of New Mexico. Budget about ten days for this run. Extend your itinerary if you plan to take a break from riding along the way. Many of the roads in this section encourage long riding days, but there are a surprising number of attractions and distractions.

Spend some time touring here in the Lone Star State and you'll come to appreciate the true meaning of the phrase "Everything's bigger in Texas." This typically happens around day two or three. You've bagged yet another three-hundred miler, you haven't left the state, and then you realize—you could ride for another two weeks and still not complete a loop. Friends, Texas is a big state.

From many different perspectives—economically, geographically, culturally—Texas is diverse. But for many folks, Texas means The West. Throughout history and in popular culture, Texas is depicted as the home of the cowboy, long cattle drives, and nights spent

A variety of microclimates within Big Bend means that some areas receive more precipitation and support different types of plants and wildlife.

Vast, dramatic views are found throughout Big Bend National Park in southern Texas.

round the campfire sipping coffee and singing "Tumbling Tumbleweeds." It's an image and a lifestyle that residents here wholly embrace and celebrate, even if most of them have never broken an ornery bronco or encouraged a little dogie to get along.

Unlike other areas of the country, where the primary focus is on the roads, touring in Texas offers you an opportunity to discover your own "inner cowboy." Just like those cowpokes of old, you can chase distant horizons on long, empty trails, then spend the evening at a local watering hole recounting your tales with other riders of the purple sage.

On entering Hill Country, you'll experience a completely different Texas. This is a region filled with meandering byways that offer all the thrills you would expect on twisty mountain roads, but which pass over and through soft-shouldered canyons filled with yucca, prickly pear, mesquite, and Texas live oak. Standing on a hilltop overlook, you can almost picture a column of dust in the distance, kicked up by a stagecoach nearing a group of bandits who lie in wait.

The most dramatic landscapes are found as you journey through Big Bend National Park. Although it appears nearly lifeless, this protected portion of the Chihuahuan Desert includes more than 1,200 species of plants and hundreds of species of birds, reptiles, and mammals. Every turn has the potential to star as a backdrop for a classic John Ford western.

A lot of folks ride this region throughout

Ever thought you'd want to see a performance featuring bats? At Carlsbad Caverns, hundreds of thousands of bats rise from the caverns at dusk, putting on quite a show. The swirling mass looks like a black tornado.

the spring, then park the bike for July and August. The sun is relentless here at the height of summer. July and August are also the wettest months. Come September, folks start rolling again into the late fall. Portions of the tour run into the high desert, where it can cool down considerably after the sun sets, any time of the year. If you do find yourself touring in mid-summer, a highly-ventilated mesh jacket with removable liner will help you face the wide range of temperatures you can expect to encounter. Hydration here is important, too. Pack plenty of water and keep it handy.

Connections

The Lone Star Loop connects with the Desert Tracks tour. It's not much of a stretch to connect this loop to the Crossing the Heartland and Rocky Mountain Way tours as well.

The White Sands of New Mexico are formed by the continuous action of erosion and crystallization of gypsum from nearby mountains. Even in the hottest weather, you can walk across the sands barefoot.

Segment One
Austin to Mineral Wells, Texas

Every city gives off a distinct vibe you can feel as you tour the downtown and walk the streets. Some have a funky, artistic feeling while others seem to ooze urban sophistication and a certain modern chic. Others have a laid-back, anything goes attitude. Austin is all three rolled into one. If you like live music, this is your city. Nearly two hundred venues throughout the city offer live music day and night. And in true "everything is bigger" form, the Texas state capital, located here, is styled after the U.S. Capital in Washington. Except taller. Thirteen feet, to be exact.

The initial run of this Lone Star Loop begins on Texas 71 heading west out of town. It doesn't take long to run out of city and

into the eastern limits of Texas hill country, an area we'll visit in much greater detail as we complete the loop. In Llano, turn north on Route 16 to Comanche where you take Route 67 to Dublin.

If you happen to be a diehard fan of Dr. Pepper, this may be as far as you care to ride. That's because Dublin is home to the oldest Dr. Pepper bottling plant, cranking out a refreshing tonic for mind, body, and spirit since 1891 (www.dublindrpepper.com). Pop the cap on a frosty cold one and you'll notice something different about this Pepper right away. It tastes like soda used to taste. That's because the Dublin bottler still uses the original formula which includes cane sweetener. When you pay a visit to the plant you'll see original bottling equipment, some still in use, along with an old-fashioned soda fountain and a museum.

Continue on US 67 to Stephenville, then turn north on US 281 to Mineral Wells, where this segment concludes. Mineral Wells is a small town about 80 miles west of the Dallas-Fort Worth metro region. A lot of little towns that form around natural springs claim their waters possess special healing

Route Details – 235 miles

➤ From Austin, Texas, travel west on Rte 71 to Llano. (70 mi.)

➤ Turn north on Rte 16 and ride to Comanche. (88 mi.)

➤ In Comanche, pick up US 67 heading north to Stephenville. (34 mi.)

➤ In Stephenville, turn north on US 281 to Mineral Wells. (43 mi.)

The Dr. Pepper bottling plant in Dublin, Texas, has been churning out this refreshing beverage using the original, unchanged formula, since 1891.

powers. Skeptics would say it's the fresh air and relaxation that provides the most benefit. But Mineral Wells is different—take the case of the Crazy Water Well.

According to local lore, the water provided by the well here was taken by folks all over town, including a woman with a mental disorder who was known as the "crazy woman" (affectionately, I'm sure). After taking water from the well regularly over a period of time, she was cured. Later, an analysis of the water showed higher than normal levels of lithium which today is the basis for a number of treatments for mental health issues. When the folks hold up a glass of water around here and toast "to your health," they really mean it!

Mineral Wells is a convenient launching point for daytrips into the Dallas-Fort Worth (DFW) area while maintaining a lower hotel rate than facilities closer to town. Here are a few ideas for fun things to see and do that are unique to the DFW region:

- *U.S. Bureau of Engraving* (www. moneyfactory.gov). This western branch of the U.S. Mint is the only location outside Washington, D.C. that prints paper money.

- *Southfork Ranch* (www.southforkranch. com). This iconic ranch will be forever remembered as the setting for *Dallas* and the home of the infamous Ewing clan.

- *Dallas Cowboys Stadium Tour* (stadium. dallascowboys.com). Stops include the players' and cheerleaders' locker rooms. (Note: If they find you hiding in a cheerleader's locker, you are removed by a team member. It could be worth it.)

- *Fort Worth Stockyards* (www. fortworthstockyards.org). Fort Worth has long been associated with the livestock trade and the stockyards tell the tale.

- *Dallas Segway Tours* (www. dallassegwaytours.com). Have you tried the other two-wheel experience? Even if you're a crusty old rider, you'll find a Segway a blast to ride. After an orientation, you'll find yourself scooting around with ease. The Dallas Segway Tour also includes an experienced tour guide who will point out famous landmarks, historic sites, and favorite local hangouts.

You can spend an entire day visiting museums, the stockyards, a rodeo, a vintage railroad, the cowboy hall of fame, and much more.

Segment Two
Mineral Wells to Amarillo, Texas

It looks deceptively simple on a map, but the run from Mineral Wells to Amarillo is a long haul and in this segment, it's more about the destination than the journey—the destination being Amarillo, the city known as the Yellow Rose of Texas. That's not to say the ride won't be fun—it will be. On a bright, sunny spring or fall day, sometimes the best ride is an easy one. Not every ride has to be about the curves. Let this one just be about the ride. The long straights on US 281 and 287 will allow you to settle into a comfortable riding rhythm and the miles will melt away.

Plan to arrive hungry in Amarillo. Located along a stretch of historic U.S. Route 66, Amarillo offers a wealth of dining options that appeal to folks with big appetites. First, there is the Big Texan (www.bigtexan.com), home of the world-famous 72-ounce steak. That's four and a half pounds of meat. It's free if you finish the meal in an hour, but you'll pay in advance. Competitive eater Joey Chestnut finished one in just under nine minutes, but the true record holder downed one of these slabs in just ninety seconds. Well, okay, that diner was a 500-pound Siberian tiger. It is not noted whether the tiger paid in advance or got a refund for finishing the meal.

Roads throughout Texas Hill Country look like this: swoopy, sweet, and empty.

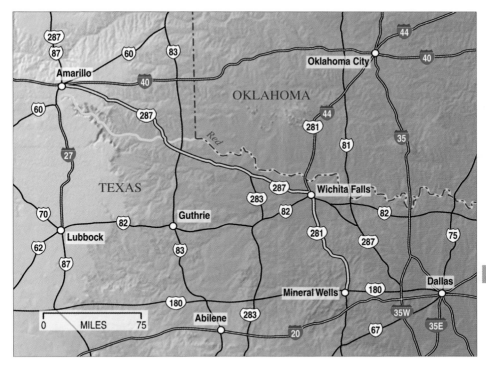

So you can go for volume, or you can go for local color. That would mean a trip to Smokey Joe's Café on 6th Avenue , the original Route 66 corridor through town. Smokey Joe's offers the usual steak fare you'll find elsewhere, but the mix of locals and visitors, live music, and large outdoor pavilion give the place a carnival atmosphere. The beer's icy cold, too. That's a plus.

The chances are pretty high that as you explore Amarillo, you're going to encounter some strange road signs. "If you have a world famous figure, why be selfish with it?" or "Tarzan had four navels." What the? Those signs, and others, are the work of

Route Details – 315 miles

➤ Leave Mineral Wells, Texas, on US 281 heading north to Witchita Falls. (90 mi.)

➤ In Witchita Falls, turn west on US 287 to Amarillo. (225 mi.)

Stanley Marsh III, son of a successful local oilman and a patron of the arts with, shall we say, eclectic tastes. His most famous work, the Cadillac Ranch, resides on the west side of town and draws a steady stream of visitors from around the world (www. roadsideamerica.com/story/2220).

This looks like an interesting road. Better make sure your tire repair kit and air pump are on board, and your gas tank is full.

Segment Three
Amarillo, Texas, to Roswell, New Mexico

Segment Three is an easy ride from Amarillo to Roswell, so if you haven't had the chance, you can stop by the Cadillac Ranch for a couple of photo ops on your way out of town. US 60 and US 70 continue the straight, open highway mode. Easy riding.

When you think of the history of modern American rock-and-roll music, you tend to think of Cleveland, Ohio, and Memphis, Tennessee, but Clovis, New Mexico, also claims a spot on that list. Clovis is the home of Norman Petty Studios, where Buddy Holley and the Crickets, Roy Orbison, and Waylon Jennings all recorded. Today the studio is open by appointment only, but the Clovis Music Festival (www.clovismusicfestival.net) held each September typically features groups that once recorded at the studio.

Segment Three ends in Roswell, New Mexico. Like famous celebrities, most folks know whereof you speak when you just say "Roswell." Something strange happened here in the summer of 1947. It was a time when sightings of unidentified flying objects were reported all over the country. But in early July, something fell from the sky and crashed on a ranch just outside of town. Known now as the Roswell Incident the crash launched a storm of speculation about visitors from outer space which reverberates through the community today.

Initially, folks in these parts were slow to

Route Details – 217 miles

➤ From Amarillo, Texas, head west on US 60 to Clovis, New Mexico. (106 mi.)

➤ From Clovis, take US 70 west to Roswell, New Mexico. (111 mi.)

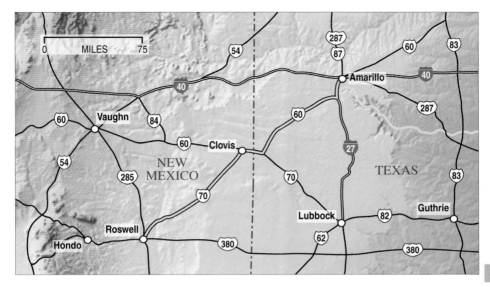

embrace their status as an alien landing site. Today, having discovered its commercial value, Roswell happily trades on its international reputation with attractions like the UFO Musuem. The Chamber of Commerce logo features a flying saucer and the words "Visitors Welcome." Especially those paying by cash or credit.

So what did really happen here? Did a fly-ing craft made of metal with strange, otherworldly properties really crash here as locals claim, or was it just a weather balloon as the government would have you believe? Pay a visit and make up your own mind. In defense of the folks here, I'll say this: I've never heard of another weather balloon crash that generated such a rapid and thorough response from Uncle Sam.

The UFO Research Center and Museum in Roswell, New Mexico, "provides information to those seeking the truth about the 1947 Roswell Incident." Does "information" equal "facts?" You'll have to decide.

Segment Four

7 | Roswell, New Mexico, to Springerville, Arizona

Your route choice here depends on the time you have available. If you prefer to stick to a smaller loop and complete your tour sooner, follow US 285 to Carlsbad and pick up the loop again at Segment Seven. But if you have the time, this portion of the tour explores New Mexico and eastern Arizona in greater detail.

Following US 70 out of Roswell, you'll begin a long slow climb from 3,600 feet to more than 7,000 feet as you enter high desert country. After a run of more than 300 miles, you'll likely want to hole up in Springerville for the evening to reset for the next day's run. Located at the gateway to the White Mountains, Springerville has a good selection of lodging and restaurants.

This battered sign in Roswell marks the path to where the alleged UFO crashed in 1947.

Route Details – 323 miles

➤ Depart Roswell, New Mexico, west on US 70 to Hondo. (48 mi.)

➤ Ride west on US 380 to San Antonito. (109 mi.)

➤ Take Rte 1 north to Socorro, New Mexico. (13 mi.)

➤ Pick up US 60 west and follow to Springerville, Arizona. (153 mi.)

Segment Five
Springerville, Arizona, to Silver City, New Mexico

Segment Five follows a portion of the Coronado Trail out of Springerville. This route roughly parallels the Native American footpath through this region that was followed by Spanish conquistadors, prospectors, and later by settlers. It's a varied and scenic route quite unlike the open and flat highway of the past few days. The roadway curves playfully through the mountains, encouraging you to lean forward in the saddle a little and dial up a little more throttle.

In Alpine, turn onto US 180 and head south toward Silver City. While US 180 doesn't have the same high curve-per-mile ratio as southern portions of US 191 (we'll get to those in the Arizona tour), it still delivers high smiles per mile through the forested hills of western New Mexico. It's a beautiful ride through the Gila National Forest and the roadway is almost always yours alone.

The run to Silver City isn't long—just a little over 100 miles—but this segment doesn't end here. In town, turn north on Route 15 and head for the Gila Cliff Dwellings (www.

> ### Route Details – 235 miles
>
> ➤ From Springerville, turn south on US 180 to Alpine, Arizona. (27 mi.)
>
> ➤ Continue on US 180 south to Silver City, New Mexico. (118 mi.)
>
> ➤ North on Rte 15 to Gila Cliff Dwellings. (45 mi.)
>
> ➤ Return via Rte 15 to Silver City. (45 mi.)
>
> ### Alternate Route – 300 miles
>
> ➤ From Springerville, turn south on US 180 to Alpine, Arizona. (27 mi.)
>
> ➤ At Alpine, continue on US 191 south to Three Way, Arizona. (103 mi.)
>
> ➤ Follow Rte 78 east to US 180. (35 mi.)
>
> ➤ Continue on US 180 south to Silver City, New Mexico. (45 mi.)
>
> ➤ North on Rte 15 to Gila Cliff Dwellings. (45 mi.)
>
> ➤ Return via Rte 15 to Silver City. (45 mi.)

7

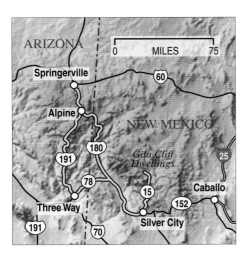

nps.gov/gicl). Studies show that the dwellings there were occupied for just a few decades between the late 1200s and early 1300s before they were abandoned. Steep, rugged canyon walls are hidden by heavy stands of forest including ponderosa pine, Douglas fir, juniper and pinion pine. If you're willing to walk a mile or so, a well-worn path will lead you close to the ruins for an up-close look

Segment Six
Silver City, New Mexico, to Carlsbad, New Mexico

The route out of Silver City continues on a string of lightly-traveled mountain roads with photo opportunities around every bend. The first stop on this segment is White Sands National Monument. The dunes here are formed in a unique natural process that draws on deposits of gypsum from the mountains you just descended. Unlike regular sand, gypsum doesn't absorb heat as readily, so you can walk on the sands at any time, even in bare feet.

The national monument is at the southern

The lake bed here is filled with minerals, including large amounts of gypsum. When it rains, minerals are leeched from the alkali flat and dissolved. When the lake dries, the gypsum crystals are carried by the winds and collect in the dunes, thus forming the white sands.

The scale of the interior of Carlsbad Caverns defies appreciation until you see it firsthand.

end of the White Sands Missile Range and is just a few miles from the Trinity site, the location of the first atomic bomb test, conducted on July 16, 1945. Detonation of the test bomb here signaled the arrival of the nuclear age and only weeks later the nuclear bombs were dropped on Hiroshima and Nagasaki. The Trinity site, which is on restricted range property, is open just twice a year on the first Saturday in April and October. (www.atomictourist.com/trinity.htm)

Enjoy the ride along US Route 82. This is the last oasis of high mountain road and forest before returning to long, lonely stretches of highway.

Route Details – 356 miles

- ➤ From Silver City, ride east on Scenic Rte 152 to Caballo, New Mexico. (76 mi.)
- ➤ Ride south on Rte 187 to Hatch. (27 mi.)
- ➤ Continue south on Rte 185 to Las Cruces. (38 mi.)
- ➤ Turn east on US 70 to Alamagordo. (68 mi.)
- ➤ Continue east on US 82 to Artesia. (110 mi.)
- ➤ Follow US 285 south to Carlsbad. (37 mi.)

The Guadalupe Mountains feature habitats ranging from low desert brush to lush mountain evergreens.

Segment Seven
Carlsbad, New Mexico, to Terlingua, Texas

7

Carlsbad Caverns National Park is located about eighteen miles south of town and should be included on your must-see list. Chambers in the caverns are some of the largest known to exist and extend for miles into underground limestone, once the floor of a vast and deep lake. Over three hundred caves are part of the system but only Carlsbad and Slaughter Canyon Cave are open to the public. An easy-to-hike trail will lead you on a tour of the most famous Carlsbad features, including rooms with mammoth displays of stalactites and stalagmites on a scale that's hard to comprehend.

It's said that local resident Jim White dis-

Route Details – 301 miles

➤ From Carlsbad, New Mexico, ride south on US 62 to Rte 54. (64 mi.)

➤ Follow Rte 54 south to Van Horn, Texas. (55 mi.)

➤ Ride US 90 south to Alpine. (100 mi.)

➤ Follow Rte 118 south to Rte 170 (the access road to Terlingua). (78 mi.)

➤ Ride Rte 170 to Terlingua. (4 mi.)

An eclectic art group created this mock Prada store on the north end of Marfa, Texas, as either some type of statement, or joke, or . . . I don't know. It's weird. Funny, but weird.

covered the cave when he observed whirlwinds of smoke that would appear each evening around sunset. Curious about the origin of the smoke, White hiked to the area to find that it wasn't smoke coming from the caverns, but endless waves of Mexican free-tail bats. Today, visitors can observe this strange and beautiful phenomenon at the park from April through October in an amphitheater located just outside the large cave entrance. As the sun drops, you'll begin to see that black cloud rising from the depths of the cave as hundreds of thousands of bats circle in a vortex, eventually rising above the entrance and off to the east, where they will feed on insects near the Pecos River.

Lonely. Barren. Dry. Desolate. A place that makes Nowheresville feel crowded. Welcome to US 62 through southeastern New Mexico and West Texas. If you're looking for a stretch of road for contemplating life's meaning, for releasing everyday cares and concerns, for getting your priorities in order, this would be it.

Route 62 is empty, but the landscape isn't featureless. To the far south and west, the Guadalupe Mountains keep watch over your ride along the entire length of US 62. Folks who traveled this route by stagecoach in centuries past used these mountains (now part of Guadalupe Mountains National Park) as a guide. Inside the park, Guadalupe Peak marks the highest point in Texas at 8,749 feet.

Make your departure from Guadalupe on the Texas Mountain Trail, starting with Route 54. Entering a vast salt plain, the road feels dead-level flat, squeezing through a gap between the Beach and Baylor Mountains be-

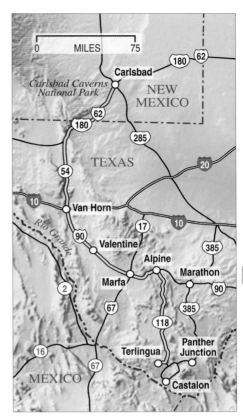

7

The Starlight Theater was built in the 1930s and abandoned when the mines in Terlingua went bust in the 1940s. It has since been reinvented as a popular watering hole.

A pair of riders prepare to enter Big Bend National Park, often considered "three parks in one" because of its widely varied terrain and its huge size.

fore entering Van Horn. Top off here if you have less than half a tank. On second thought, just top it off, regardless.

Continue south on US 90 south of Van Horn. It's the same song, different verse. US 90 runs straight and level, passing through Valentine, a town established by a Southern Pacific Railroad construction crew on February 14, 1882. Entering town from the north, what's that on the right? A Prada store? Here? Actually, it's a permanent sculpture entitled *Prada Marfa* that is designed to mimic a real Prada store. You could call it "a work of pop architectural land art" as its European creators Michael Elmgreen and Ingar Dragset call it. Or funny. Or inspiring. Or you could just call it weird. Whatever meaning it takes for you, it's most definitely one of the most memorable photo stops you'll encounter along today's route.

Natural architecture will regain your attention as you follow US 90 through Marfa, turning south on Route 118 at Alpine. From here, it's a straight shot due south through the Chihuahuan Desert. Time to tie up your horse and put on the feed bag.

The Terlingua of today (www.historic-terlingua.com) is a happening place with plenty of lodging, restaurant, and entertainment options. Consistently rated as one of the nation's top bars for its food, and its unusual setting, La Kiva is one of the best known spots in Terlingua, but you'll have to look for it. La Kiva is a cave bar, cut into the side of a hill and on any given night, more folks arrive by horseback than by car. To be unique your visit to Terlingua should include an overnight stay at the Mansion on the Hill. It looks like a ruins, and it is. But two rooms in this former grand palace have been fully renovated and are available for your stay. After you stay here at the Mansion, you can tell folks that you not only visited a ghost town, you slept there, too.

Texas is known for its barbeque, especially brisket, but I would be hog tied and strung up if I failed to call out that other famous dish—Texas chili. And if you're a chili lover, early November is the perfect time to be in Terlingua. That's when the Chili Appreciation Society hosts its annual celebration. Since it's in Texas, you would suspect that it's the largest and grandest chili celebration to be found anywhere, and you'd be right (chili. org/terlingua.html). The four-day event draws more than 10,000 chiliheads, featuring a jam-packed entertainment schedule and the famous chili cook-off on Saturday.

Big Bend offers roads with sweeping 360-degree views. You won't know where to look next.

Lone Star Loop

Segment Eight
Terlingua to Marathon, Texas

No trip through Texas would be complete without a ride through Big Bend National Park. Its austere landscape belies a world filled with life. Thanks to its various elevations and expansive scope, Big Bend is home to hundreds of species of plants and animals, many unique to the region.

The Apollo astronauts visited Big Bend in the mid-60s to train because NASA felt conditions in Big Bend would resemble what would be encountered on the moon. Your entrance into the park by way of Route 118 does resemble pictures of the lunar landscape. But at the right time of year, the stark colors of this desolate terrain are transformed by the appearance of hundreds of varieties of wildflowers.

Many of the cactus found in Big Bend produce large, showy flowers in shades of red, yellow, pink, and purple. Yuccas, especially the impressive giant dagger, put on a grand display usually in February thru April. Shrubs such as the fragrant yellow huisache in the southeast part of the park, and the fruity-

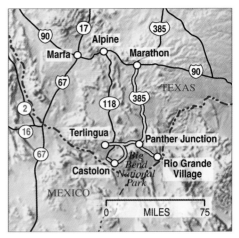

smelling Texas mountain laurel bloom in March and April. Ocotillo produce bright red bunches of flowers at the ends of the spiny whip-like branches, also in March and April, providing nectar and pollen for hummingbirds, bees, and butterflies. Spring flowering season is followed by another flowering period in mid- to late summer, fueled by the monsoon rains that drench the area.

There are two scenic drives off the main

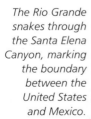

The Rio Grande snakes through the Santa Elena Canyon, marking the boundary between the United States and Mexico.

Big Bend National Park is a spectacular place to visit on a bike, especially during the spring wildflower season. The unobstructed view from the seat of a bike is preferable to that of a cage.

route through the park. You'll encounter the first, Ross Maxwell Scenic Drive, about fifteen miles from Terlingua. This route to the southern border passes the Sotol Vista Overlook, which features panoramic views of the Chisos Mountains and the Santa Elena Canyon, some 20 miles in the distance. As you ride toward the end of the drive, you'll pass through Castolon where the Park Service continues to operate the trading post. Following the road to the very end brings you to the Santa Elena Canyon. Here the Rio Grande flows through steep canyon walls, one of the most impressive and majestic sites in all of the National Park System.

Retrace your steps to the main park road and turn right to reach Panther Junction. At the junction, stay to the left to exit the park or ride to the right to head to the eastern end of the park and Rio Grande Village. A short run will take you to the Boquillas Canyon Overlook, similar to the Santa Elena, but not quite as tall. Still, seeing the Rio Grande flow through either is a grand view.

At the visitor center, you'll find gas if you

Route Details – 198 miles

➤ From Terlingua, Texas, take Rte 118 to Big Bend National Park. (4 mi.)

➤ Follow Old Maverick Road (the main park road) left to Ross Maxwell Scenic Drive. (9 mi.)

➤ Take the round trip on Ross Maxwell to Santa Elena Canyon Overlook and back. (62 mi.)

➤ Follow Old Maverick Road from Ross Maxwell Scenic Drive to Panther Junction. (13 mi.)

➤ Round trip on Park Rte 12 to Rio Grande Village and back. (42 mi.)

➤ From Panther Junction, follow US 385 north to Marathon. (68 mi.)

need it. It's not a bad idea to top off before you head out of the park, especially out here. Marathon, Texas is the end point for this segment, about 70 miles north of Panther Junction. That means you'll have plenty of time on your ride from Terligua to explore Big Bend from one end to the other.

Be careful when you pop over a rise in Hill Country. A rain elsewhere can send a wall of water down a creek for dozens of miles, resulting in an instant wash.

Segment Nine
Marathon to Rocksprings, Texas

This segment positions you for a ride that encompasses some of the best the state has to offer. The route out of Marathon, like many roads in the state, is straight, flat, and fast. But that'll change soon. Hill country appears on the horizon like a battlement as you ride east on US 90 and the 240 miles to Rocksprings can be covered surprisingly quickly.

As you enter the hills, highway cuts reveal the underlying geological formation of the region. About the same time the Appalachians were being formed, the hills in this region were also being made. As they were lifted, a fault caused them to fold, resulting in nearly vertical layers of rock.

Settlements in the west often appeared where water was discovered; such is the case with Rocksprings. Folks moving west discovered a steady stream of water pouring from a cut in the earth here, and a town was

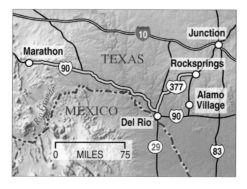

Route Details – 242 miles

➤ From Marathon, Texas, follow US 90 east to Del Rio. (170 mi.)

➤ Follow US 377 north to Rocksprings. (72 mi.)

born. Situated in the highest area of the Edwards Plateau, Rocksprings enjoys a milder climate than many parts of the state, both in summer and winter. The big business here is mohair, reflected in the name of the newspaper, the *Rocksprings Record and Texas Mohair Weekly*. Mohair is a fine, silk-like fabric made from the hair of Angora goats.

While you're here, stop at the interesting and popular Historic Rocksprings Hotel (www.historicrockspringshotel.com) and ask them for access to the Rocksprings Gallery, a collection of original works by Texas artists that features landscapes and animals. They'll also let you into the Texas Miniature Museum, a collection of dollhouses, furnishings, and dolls from the 1900s to present.

If you've arrived in town early and are itching for a ride, try running down Ranch Road 674 to Alamo Village. This was the setting built for John Wayne's 1960s flick *The Alamo*. Alamo Village (www.alamovillage.

Road Tip – Hydration
Staying hydrated is an aspect of motorcycle travel that is like tire pressure—many riders just don't give it the attention it deserves. Keeping your fluids topped off isn't just for riders crossing deserts. Proper hydration will help you stay alert and keep you cooler in warm weather. Keep a bottle of water or sports drink handy and stay away from drinks with high levels of sugar or caffeine.

com) is both an active set and an attraction, so expect to pay an admission fee. Mock gunfights and other events are staged throughout the year, so check their website or give them a ring for details. The ride down RR 674 and back is an entertaining run, too, and a preview of the next day's ride.

7

Texas Hill Country features some of the best riding in the Lone Star State. Low, green hills and twisty roads invite riders to explore at length.

Routes 335, 336, and 337 around Leakey, Texas, are known as the Three Sisters, and they comprise the best of the best riding in Texas Hill Country.

Segment Ten
The Three Sisters

Are you the type who's always wondered if you could handle triplets? Here's your chance to find out. I'm talking about roads, of course. Three Farm-to-Market roads here in central hill country that consistently rate among the best motorcycling roads in the region and the country are on today's agenda.

Do a web search on "Three Sisters" and

"Texas" and you'll find write-up after write-up detailing nearly every turn through this section of Hill Country. The three roads we're visiting today aren't the only good roads through the region, but collectively, they give you a good day's run. Consider them Hill Country's Greatest Hits.

The difference between the Three Sisters and other routes through the region probably has to do with the intimacy of the setting and the relation of the road to the landscape. For example, US 90 is an attractive road as you come into Del Rio, but the hills seem remote, as though you are viewing them in a picture. On back roads like Route 335, the road feels as though it originated from the land and was shaped by an artisan. The hills here are bunched together and frequently cut by streams. The area is carpeted with wild grasses, flowers, and shrubs.

Head east out of Rocksprings on Route 55

and in Barksdale, turn north on the first sister, Route 335. Portions of this road feature fast ups and downs and include sharp turns. Some turns are not very well marked, so take your time. Run up to Route 41, hang a right, and look for the next route, Route 336, in about fourteen miles. Take Route 336 south to Leakey (that's pronounced LAY-key, by the way).

Once in Leakey, turn left on Ranch Road 337 and head out to the Lone Star Motorcycle Museum located in Vanderpool (lonestarmotorcyclemuseum.com). When RR 337 intersects FM 187, turn left and head north about three miles to the museum on the left. The museum features motorcycles from around the world dating back to 1910. The onsite Ace Café is a good spot to pick up a bite for lunch before you turn back toward Rocksprings.

The final leg of the run returns down FM 187 to RR 337, passing through Leakey and back to Camp Wood. The section of RR 337 between Vanderpool and Camp Wood offers some of the best vistas running in the east-to-west direction. In Camp Wood, turn right

Route Details – 185 miles

➤ From Rocksprings, Texas, go south on Rte 55 to Barksdale. (26 mi.)

➤ Ride north on Ranch Road 335 to Rte 41. (30 mi.)

➤ Turn east on Rte 41 to Ranch Road 336. (14 mi.)

➤ Turn south on Ranch Road 336 to Leakey. (27 mi.)

➤ From Leakey, turn east on Ranch Road 337 to Vanderpool. (16 mi.)

➤ Go north on Farm-to-Market Road 187 to Lone Star Motorcycle Museum. (3 mi.)

➤ Return to Vanderpool on FM 187. (3 mi.)

➤ Ride west on Ranch Road 337 to Camp Wood. (36 mi.)

➤ Return to Rocksprings on Rte 55 north. (30 mi.)

on 55 for the return back to Rocksprings. Or, for that matter, head back to RR 335 and run the Three Sisters again. No one would think twice about it if you did.

Be on the lookout for wild beasts. These ain't your run-of-the-mill whitetail deer.

A pair of hombres belly up to the bar in Luckenbach, Texas.

Segment Eleven
Rocksprings, Texas, to Austin, Texas

It's the last day on the road for this unforgettable journey, so it seems only fitting to
pay parting respects to the Lone Star State
by visiting a couple of towns and venues
that are uniquely Texan.

Fredericksburg is a large, vibrant Texas
town furnished with ornate buildings representing every manner of architectural flour-
ish and embellishment you can imagine. The

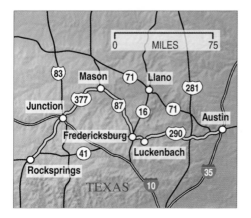

town was originally settled by German immigrants in the mid-1800s pursuing religious
freedom, a heritage you'll see today in the
town's lavishly appointed downtown
churches.

If you time your visit just right, you can include a visit to the Fredericksburg Trade Days
(www.fredericksburgtradedays.com). More
than 350 vendors gather at this giant flea
market on the Sunday Farms on the third
weekend of every month. What they offer
ranges from antiques, tools, and furniture,
to crafts, jewelry, and more, spread over
acres of ground under six big-as-Texas barns.

Before heading back to Austin, stop off
and see Waylon, Willie, and the boys in
Luckenbach. Follow Ranch Road 1376 for a
couple of miles where signs will point you to
the Luckenbach Dance Hall. The dusty little
outpost here was first established in 1849
and the post office, store and beer joint were
built decades later. The town was saved

Route Details – 212 miles

➤ From Rocksprings, Texas, ride north on US 377 to Mason. (91 mi.)

➤ Follow US 87 south to Fredericksburg. (42 mi.)

➤ Ride US 290 east to Ranch Road 1376. (5 mi.)

➤ Follow Ranch Road 1376 to Luckenbach. (5 mi.)

➤ Continue on Luckenbach Road to US 290. (4 mi.)

➤ Follow US 290 east to Austin. (65 mi.)

from disappearance in the early 1970s when it was purchased by a group of locals who began a revival of sorts. Fortunes took a full turn for the town when a song, written by Bobby Emmons and Chip Moman and sung by Waylon Jennings and Willie Nelson, put Luckenbach on the map for good. "Luckenbach Texas (Back to the Basics)" became a worldwide smash hit, and before long, busloads of folks began stopping by on their travels between Fredericksburg and Austin.

Today, Luckenbach is in little danger of disappearing. The event calendar at the hall

Rider Trip Hilliard enjoys a break at the Luckenbach Post Office and General Store. The Luckenbach Dance Hall features a full slate of regional and nationally-known country music performers.

is packed with an uninterrupted string of live performances by local and national country artists. Willie Nelson and friends visit town every Fourth of July for a special concert. Whether you're in town for an event large or small, the time you'll spend here in a place where "Everybody's Somebody" is a fitting way to end your epic Texas adventure.

Austin, Texas, is an attractive, vibrant city with a wealth of entertainment options and a vibrant night life for those seeking things to do after a long day in the saddle.

8 CROSSING THE HEARTLAND

Crossing the Heartland covers nearly 1,500 miles through the central plains and rolling hills of the American Midwest and Mississippi River Valley to connect the front range of the Colorado Rockies with the Allegheny Mountains of the central Appalachians. You'll find the long, open stretches of highway that you expect, along with plenty of high-speed sweepers and hills that will surprise you. Quaint mom-and-pop hotels, roadside cafés featuring hearty fare, and friendly folks who'll take a genuine interest in your travels will usher you back to a time when travel was for the adventurous and the privileged. This tour is designed to be ridden comfortably in five days.

For all the accolades garnered, all the breathless articles written, and pictures taken that feature the Rockies and the Appalachians, the Ozarks, and the Alleghenies, a scrapbook kept for articles written about the flatlands that lie between might be a little, well, sparse. If the Great Plains were a middle child, surrounded by such glamorous and successful siblings as these, it might require counseling. Fortunately, the prairie isn't so sensitive.

When you look carefully at the map, there are a lot of legitimate reasons to take it down a notch and enjoy a leisurely tour

through the American Heartland. Despite what you've heard, there are interesting roads here. You'll find a surprising number of things to see and do when you aren't whizzing by on the slab. Landmarks of American history are found here, as is the culture that shaped our identity and continues to influence us today. And there's no doubt that some of your most memorable meals will be found along this route. Monuments, markers, and museums document the movement of a young, expanding country. And when someone felt their part of the middle needed a little more scenic grandeur,

When you arrive in Kinsley, Kansas, you're halfway to San Francisco, California, or halfway to Ocean City, Maryland, depending on which direction you're headed.

they just might make something up, whether it's the world's largest ball of twine or an American icon like the Liberty Bell made out of whatever's handy.

For as many interesting things as you find, there's no question that the region's greatest asset is its people. Folks in the Plains States go about their business quietly, but that doesn't mean they're standoffish. In fact, get a word or two beyond "Howdy"

and they can become downright chatty. Tell them you're taking your time to explore the Midwest. That's a real compliment. Don't be surprised if you find yourself whisked off on a personally guided tour of the town or an invitation to dinner.

A tour across the middle rewards the rider with a keen eye. Subtle changes can be seen in each segment of this tour, marking a transition from arid western terrain to the rich

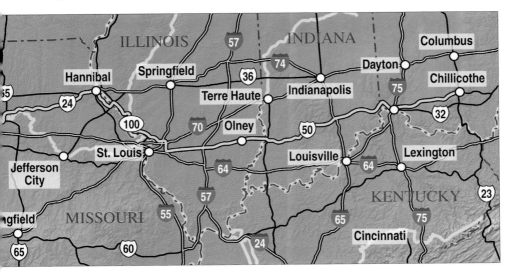

A cross-country run through the central U.S. will go right through the heart of the Rockies. Both US 40 (pictured) and US 50 are good options through Colorado.

highlands and pastures of the East. High grasslands, cultivated fields, and prairie morph ever so slowly into fertile fields of the river delta. Over distance, undulating swells of rolling farmland become foothills, the GPS marking a steady climb as the elevation grows. Toward the end of your crossing, the ancient mountains of the Appalachians ascend into view, rising slowly above the eastern horizon.

Considering the track of this tour, it's hard to say what's "average" for weather. The prairie is a semi-arid area with wettest months coming in May and June while the Mississippi River Delta experiences rainfall more evenly throughout the year. In either region, spring brings the greatest chance of severe weather, as competing weather systems collide over the central U.S. With little to break the wind, you'll experience strong head and side winds any time a weather front is moving through. And there's no escaping the sun here. Keep some sunblock handy and apply it frequently.

One of the unique benefits of traveling is seeing and experiencing other cultures, especially those that resist modern society's pressure to conform.

They don't shoot-em-out on the streets of Dodge City like they used to, but it still retains a distinct flavor of the Old West.

So take your bike out of hyperdrive, turn away from the slab, and settle in for a journey across America's breadbasket. Discover what lies in the middle. There's more to it than you think.

Connections

You can connect to a lot of great riding from this central location. A day's ride from Chillicothe will bring you to the starting point for the Appalachian Adventures tour. You're also within easy reach of The Nor'easter tour and Great Lakes Loop to the north or a ride along the Natchez Trace in the American South tour, starting near Nashville, Tennessee.

8

Often, the most enjoyable part of the journey is when you make those unplanned discoveries, like Carhenge in Nebraska.

Segment One
Pueblo, Colorado, to Great Bend, Kansas

Depart Pueblo, Colorado, on US 50 heading east. A last glimpse of the Rockies sets in your mirrors as you ride into the sprawling landscape of eastern Colorado. Brightly colored crops in irrigated fields stand in stark contrast to faint green and brown brush that subsists here on scant precipitation that isn't scrubbed out of the air by the tall mountains to the west.

In La Junta, take a break from Route 50 and turn north on Route 109 in town. Just a mile ahead, turn east again, this time on Route 194. This route parallels US 50 and passes the entrance to Bent's Old Fort, a national historic site (www.nps.gov/beol).

Trading posts like Bent's dotted the plains in the mid-1800s. These isolated commerce centers were a place where trappers, traders, travelers, and plains Indians could reliably gather for trading on peaceful terms. Passers-by found shelter, food, supplies, and repairs at these outposts. Even in these early days, goods from around the world could be had on the frontier. Glass beads from Italy, cloth from England, and silver jewelry from Germany. Even dyes from China could be found on the shelves here.

Bent's was located along the Mountain Branch of the Santa Fe Trail, a path you are largely following on your trek to the east. Pioneered in 1822, the Santa Fe Trail connected Missouri with New Mexico, opening the southwest to exploration and settlement. It remained a vital throughway until the completion of the Santa Fe Railway in 1880.

As you near Dodge City on US 50, a sign points out a two-mile stretch of the original Santa Fe Trail that remains clearly visible. It's a remarkably moving sight. This set of worn dirt tracks is a strong link binding the past with the present, reminding us of those who blazed the trails we continue to enjoy today. You can't help but feel a little chill up the spine looking at these tracks, following them with your eyes as they disappear in the distance. The mind's eye draws a vivid picture

The second floor of Bent's Fort served as the "gentlemen's club" where gambling, drinking, and other vices were enjoyed.

of mule-drawn wagons, laden with family and possessions. You have to marvel at their motivation, pulling up stakes to travel into the vast unknown, and you wonder what happened to the people who passed this way.

Some of them never made it past Dodge City, Kansas, your next stop. Towns like Dodge City exploded in population as transportation infrastructure stretched west, intersecting with cattle trails. In the 1870s and '80s, Dodge City became Queen of the Cow Towns. You've heard of it, no doubt. In 1952, a serial radio program set in Dodge City debuted, telling epic tales of the American West. Its memorable cast of characters, U.S. Marshal Matt Dillon, deputy Chester Proudfoot, Doc, and Miss Kitty created a vivid portrait of the west that gave our generation a picture of life-as-it-was in the same way that Buffalo Bill's Wild West Show entertained throngs of easterners in the late 1800s and early 1900s.

Rapid economic growth brought both opportunity and trouble. The population of gamblers, gunfighters, and general trouble-seekers grew seemingly overnight. During the town's busiest days, a string of marshals and appointed lawmen helped keep order including William "Bat" Masterson, Wyatt Earp, and Bill Tilghman. Boomtimes faded quickly and by 1886, the cattle trade shifted farther west. Dodge City returned to its sleepy ways but its place in history was assured. Much of the town's history is retold at the Boot Hill Museum which features regularly scheduled reenactments of some of the town's greatest gun battles.

Follow US 50 east out of Dodge to Kinsley, which claims to be the halfway point along US 50 between east and west coasts, with a sign marking the spot. (In truth, the actual spot is two miles to the west but out here, what's a couple of miles anyway?) Turn northeast on Route 56 to reach Great Bend, Kansas.

Route Details – 360 miles

➤ From Pueblo, Colorado, ride east on US 50 to La Junta. (67 mi.)

➤ Turn north on Rte 109. (1 mi.)

➤ Ride east on Rte 194 to Bent's Old Fort National Historic Site. (6 mi.)

➤ Continue on Rte 194 east to US 50. (14 mi.)

➤ Follow US 50 east to Dodge City, Kansas. (188 mi.)

➤ Continue on US 50 east through Kinsley. (36 mi.)

➤ In Kinsley, turn northeast on US 56 and continue to Great Bend. (48 mi.)

A few examples of the original tallgrass prairie still exist. The Konza Prairie near Topeka preserves about 8,000 acres.

Segment Two
Great Bend to Topeka, Kansas

Rather than take a direct route to Topeka (what would be the fun in that?), the route out of Great Bend heads north on US 281. Riding north, you'll pass through rolling fields, shimmering with amber waves of grain in the growing season.

In some parts of the country, towns are built around a village square, a church, or a notable natural feature like a spring. Out here, communities are marked by grain elevators. Any speck that appears ahead on the horizon is likely to resolve into a slim concrete tower standing watching over a handful of businesses and a few dozen houses arranged on a grid of dirt streets.

On occasion, you'll pass something different, like an oil derrick. Russell, Kansas, hometown of U.S. Senator Bob Dole, is also known for petroleum production. The displays at the Oil Patch Museum depict how oil was formed, and subsequently discovered, and it includes a tour through an oil storage tank. That's not something you'll see every day. And neither is the next stop.

Some areas are lucky enough to have a claim to fame that is built upon a natural feature or a site of historical significance. When you think of Estes Park, Colorado, or Jackson, Wyoming, mountains come to mind. Say "Golden Gate" and you instantly think of San Francisco. When you're a tiny town in a remote part of a rural state, you have to try harder. That's why you have to admire places like Cawker City—home of the world's largest ball of twine.

You can't miss it. Really. Weighing in at nearly 9 tons, and containing nearly 8 million feet of twine, Cawker City's homemade landmark rests comfortably in a shelter in the center of town. Unwound, it would stretch from Cawker to Boston, the Bahamas, Cuba, Mexico City, Vancouver, Hudson Bay, or Canada's Northwest Territories.

The competition for claiming the largest ball of twine is more active than you might think. The original "largest twine ball" was started in Darwin, Minnesota. When local resident Frank Stoeber got wind of this in 1953, he began his own ball and within a few years his efforts yielded a ball eight feet high weighing five thousand pounds. In 1961, Stoeber donated the ball to the town of Cawker and the quest to create the world's largest ball became a community effort. Folks continue to add to the ball, and even visitors are encouraged to participate. Stop in, grab a length of twine, and do your part to help the folks in Cawker maintain their monument to self promotion, Kansas-style.

Flush from your excitement, the next 115 miles are apt to pass quickly. Route 24 cuts across the Sunflower State taking a turn to the southwest into Manhattan, home to Kansas State University. As a college town, things are always buzzing in Manhattan.

When we talk about the Midwest, we often refer to the "prairie," but with the vast majority of the plains under cultivation, what did the wild fields actually look like? Ride just a few miles south of Manhattan on Route 177 and see for yourself. The Konza Prairie Natural Area preserves 13.5 square miles of native tallgrass prairie as it would have looked to Laura Ingalls Wilder, the well-known author of the "Little House" series of books recounting her family's life on the frontier. The semi-arid climate of the central plains would not support large forests but

Route Details – 272 miles

➤ From Great Bend, Kansas, ride north on US 281 to Osborne. (87 mi.)

➤ Follow US 24 east to Cawker City. (19 mi.)

➤ Ride US 24 east to Manhattan. (115 mi.)

➤ Continue east on US 24 to Topeka. (51 mi.)

enough moisture falls to foster the growth of tall grasses and wildflowers. Three hiking trails allow you to get off the bike for an up-close look at a landscape that has almost vanished. June and September are peak months for wildflowers and are the most popular and photogenic months to visit.

Continue on US 24 to reach Topeka, the state capital of Kansas. You'll find a wealth of travel services and restaurants here, including Bobo's Drive-In. Named one of the "Eight Wonders of Kansas Cuisine," this 1940s era hotspot was featured on the Food Network's *Diners, Drive-ins, and Dives* for its juicy cheeseburgers and homemade onion rings and apple pie.

8

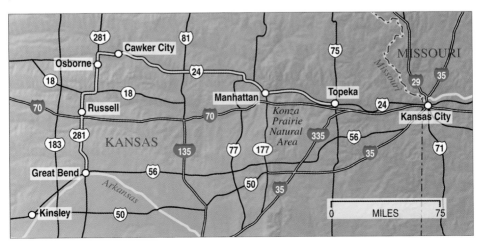

Segment Three
Topeka, Kansas, to Hannibal, Missouri

If you thought there was nothing to see or do on a ride across the heartland, this segment should dispel that notion for good. That's because this portion of the ride is marked by historic and cultural landmarks at the beginning, middle, and end of the ride. Oh, and there's some great riding, too.

In 1951, thirteen parents filed a lawsuit in Topeka, Kansas, on behalf of their children to end racially segregated schools. The case, originally decided in favor of the school system, was overturned by the Supreme Court in 1954, laying the foundation for the beginning of the equal rights movement and the end of racial segregation. Monroe Elementary School was at the heart of the case and today serves as home for the Brown vs. the Board of Education National Historic Site (www.nps.gov/brvb). Ranger-led tours, movies, and displays depict the events that led to a historic decision that has helped ensure that everyone has equal access to the opportunities a free and open society provides.

Spend a couple of hours at the national park site, then hop on the bike for a short ride on US 24 to Kansas City. Time it to arrive for lunch. Hungry. Kansas City has a reputation for good food, and an even greater reputation for barbeque. How many other cities do you know with a Barbeque Society or a barbeque competition circuit? Well they do here in Kansas City and the resulting rivalries have created some of the most flavorful cooking in the country.

Savor this award-winning example and you'll see what I mean. On your GPS, punch in the address for Oklahoma Joe's BBQ (3002

8

Route Details – 273 miles

➤ From Topeka, Kansas, follow US Rte 24 east to Kansas City. (71 mi.)

➤ Continue on US 24 east to Monroe City, Missouri. (180 mi.)

➤ Follow US 36 east to Hannibal. (22 mi.)

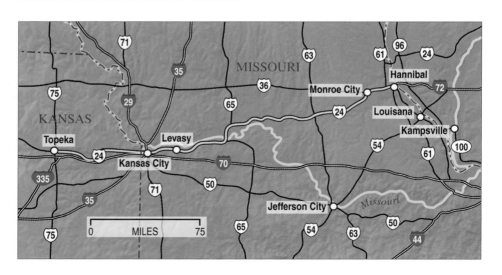

A simple landscape can be a very pretty one.

West 47th Avenue, Kansas City, Kansas 66103) and prepare to strap on the feedbag. Whether you go with the it'll-please-anyone barbeque chicken, the delicate taste of smoked pork laced with tangy Carolina sauce, or the slap-your-momma-they're-so-good ribs, there's little chance you'll walk (or waddle) away disappointed with this feast.

Recognized as a regional specialty, "burnt ends" are cut from the tip of brisket, requiring extra long cooking and smoking. Burnt ends are featured on many menus around town, but there is no restaurant better qualified to prepare this smoky delicacy than Arthur Bryant's BBQ (www.arthurbryantsbbq.com/). Established in the 1920s, Bryant's is the granddaddy of them all, famous for serving up massive piles of wood-smoked meats.

There's nothing better to follow a good lunch than a good ride and that's just what's on tap for the balance of this segment. US 24 heading east out of downtown Kansas City belies the notion that roads through the midwest lack character or riding appeal. Once you motor past Levasy, Missouri, the road returns to its rural roots, once again following old portions of the Santa Fe Trail.

If you're from the East Coast, the ride into Missouri begins to feel familiar. The terrain begins to roll and pitch ever so slightly more here in Missouri than its western neighbor. Roads are lined with tall, thick, green grasses. Fields are a bit greener here with corn and soybean being the primary crops.

Route US 24 still manages to convey that special feeling that many people associate with its more famous Midwestern cousin, Route 66. Small towns that could be the inspiration for model train sets come and go in the blink of an eye, as you work your way across the Show Me State. In most, a café on the corner and a mom-and-pop motel on the edge of town offer homegrown hospitality to weary travelers.

Perhaps it's fitting then that this segment ends in the place that bills itself as "America's Hometown," Hannibal, Missouri. If that name sounds familiar, it should, as it's the boyhood home of Samuel Clemens, known better as Mark Twain.

Segment Four
Hannibal, Missouri, to Olney, Illinois

Hannibal, Missouri, had a powerful influence over Mark Twain. That much is clear from his writing. Whether it's the epic list of memorable characters Twain recalled from his childhood or his affectionate and detailed description of places and events, it's clear that Hannibal was a place much loved by its famous son.

Before you mount up today, take a little time to check out Twain's legacy in and around town. Twain's boyhood home is as good a place to start as any. In addition to Twain's home, you can visit the Thatcher house, Huck Finn's place, the Justice of the Peace, and other places from Twain's works.

Next, take a cruise aboard a paddlewheel riverboat to enjoy a perspective that Twain cherished: life on the Mississippi (marktwainriverboat.com). Or check out the cave that figured so prominently in Twain's *Tom Sawyer*. Guides will point out all the places in the cave that were recounted in the book. To this day you'll get the feeling that Injun Joe or Ol' Pap could be lurking around any corner. (marktwaincave.com)

Route Details – 248 miles

- ➤ From Hannibal, Missouri, ride south on Rte 79. (32 mi.)
- ➤ Follow US 54 east to Rte 96. (7 mi.)
- ➤ Ride Rte 96 south to Kampsville, Illinois. (28 mi.)
- ➤ Take Rte 100 south to Alton. (47 mi.)
- ➤ Follow Rte 143 east to Rte 4. (23 mi.)
- ➤ Ride Rte 4 south to Lebanon. (13 mi.)
- ➤ Take US 50 east to Olney. (98 mi.)

8

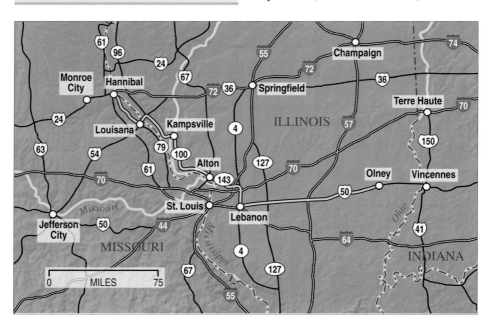

Departing Hannibal, head south on Route 79 toward St. Louis. If you have plans to visit the city, this route will bring you to the northwestern edge. If you stick to the route that's outlined, you'll pass to the north and east of the city with an easy run to the Gateway Arch.

The eastern bypass crosses the Mississippi on US 54 at Louisiana, Missouri. Ride over to Atlas, Illinois, on Route 96 south. This is a quiet rural two-laner that runs south, then abruptly turns east, connecting to Kampsville, Illinois. The next 47 miles on Illinois Route 100 is part of a federally-designated scenic byway that follows the Illinois River on its way south. Route 100 makes a turn to the east, marking the confluence of the Illinois and Mississippi Rivers. State and federal parkland is found throughout this part of the run and what land remains is agricultural. It's a quiet, pleasant country ride.

Route 100 ends in Alton, Illinois. Riding south on US 67 will bring you into St. Louis directly, if you choose. To continue the de-

Sometimes you just see a setting that strikes you as funny. Do you think he's helping her pick out the dress?

tour, ride east on Route 143 through Alton and take Route 4 south to Lebanon, Illinois. Here you'll reconnect with our old friend US 50, the road that will carry you the rest of the way to the Appalachians.

Here's a little bit of good news: Mom and Pop eateries are alive and well in the center of many small towns. And worth seeking out.

Segment Five
Olney, Illinois, to Chillicothe, Ohio

Be careful on your way out of town, will you? Olney, Illinois, is the white squirrel capital of the U.S. and, well, probably the world. Unlike their grey brethren who almost blend in with the pavement (sometimes, literally), white squirrels stand out in nature. Generally, that's a bad thing. Easily seen equals easily eaten. Unless you're a white squirrel living in Olney. Folks go out of their way to tend to their native population, and squirrels (the white ones, anyway), have the right of way. Hit one with your bike and it'll set you back $500. The best place to catch a glimpse is at the city park where the

rattle of a potato chip bag rings like a dinner bell to these little critters.

Notice how the hills have been growing on your ride east? You're about to put the flatlands behind you for good as you begin to climb the foothills of the Appalachians. By the end of this segment, you'll arrive in one of the country's best kept riding secrets: southeastern Ohio.

Route 50 crosses the Wabash River at Vincennes, entering the Hoosier State. Past Loogootee, the road begins to wind and weave as you ride through southern Indiana's Hoosier National Forest and Big Oaks National Wildlife Refuge. Compared to the time it took to cross Kansas, riding through Indiana goes by quickly. Just a couple of hours will put you on the Indiana-Ohio border and you're on the doorstep of Cincinnati.

8

Route Details – 318 miles

From Olney, Illinois, follow US 50 east to Chillicothe, Ohio. (318 mi.)

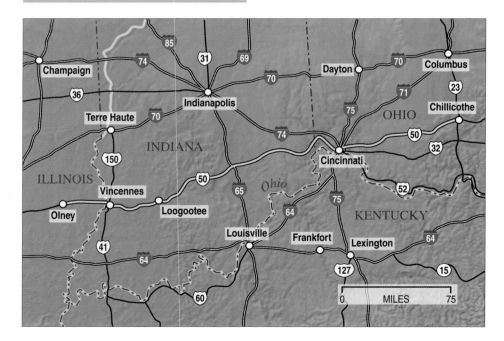

A few of the old ways of life are still preserved, like these hand-operated locks on the Muskingum River in Ohio.

Chili is to Cincinnati as barbeque or steak is to Kansas City. Immigrants arriving here from Macedonia in the early 1920s are credited with developing this popular regional style of chili, first as a topping and later as a stand-alone dish. Unlike Texas chili, Cincinnati chili is thinner with a tomato base sauce and is flavored with cinnamon, cloves, and allspice. Parlors like Skyline Chili (skylinechili.com) have managed to create a sizeable regional following with multiple locations while specialists like Camp Washington Chili (campwashingtonchili.com) have kept things small. You can't go wrong with either one.

The last third of the route, between Cincinnati and Chillicothe, rolls through scenic southern Ohio. Chillicothe is recognized as the center of Indian Hopewell tradition ("tradition" is a label given to practices that are shared among distinct Indian cultures). Indian cultures that were part of the Hopewell tradition established trade routes that extended west to the Rocky Mountains and south to the Gulf of Mexico (en.wikipedia.org/wiki/Hopewell_tradition).

In this region, tribes observed the practice of mound building for ceremonial and burial purposes. Examples of Hopewell mounds are found all over southern Ohio. More study has revealed that some of the shapes and locations of the mounds correspond to celestial events, adding credence to theories that the mounds served a wider range of purposes than we might have first believed.

Roads here don't plow through the hills, they are draped over them. Pick any state side road, especially those heading east, farther into the hills, and see for yourself. Having ridden from portions of the country that can't buy a bend in the road to those that have curves to spare, the transition is complete.

Crossing the Heartland

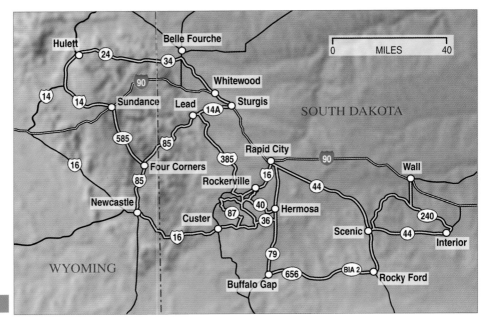

Motorcycle Journeys Through North America

9 THE BADLANDS

The loops in this journey include some of the most famous roads and sights in the Black Hills region of South Dakota. The thousand miles of riding covered by this journey could easily fill a week and are sure to satisfy the mind, body, and spirit.

The inextricable link of the history of motorcycling with the Black Hills and Badlands of South Dakota can be summed up in just one word: Sturgis. In 1936, with a world economy still mired in the Great Depression, Clarence "Pappy" Hoel opened an Indian dealership in his hometown of Sturgis, South Dakota, and played a leading role in forming the Jackpine Gypsies, a group organized to promote motorcycle races and touring.

Sturgis had a long history of support for local racing, so it wasn't surprising when two years later the city of Sturgis joined with the Gypsies to promote a racing rally to be held in early August.

The rest, as they say, is history. The Sturgis rally has grown from a couple of days of rac-

ing to a weeklong biker bacchanalia attended by a half-million or so riders from around the world, where you are likely to find any form of diversion, ranging from family-friendly entertainment to decidedly adult indulgences. Some folks enjoy big rallies like Sturgis; others avoid them. But one thing everyone can agree on is this—the region can't be defined by the Sturgis rally alone: the Black Hills are beautiful and the riding is spectacular.

The area covered by these loops includes the southwestern corner of South Dakota and eastern Wyoming. The topography and the ride change dramatically, according to which direction you depart from your base camp in Rapid City. A ride toward the east

Mount Rushmore plays peek-a-boo along US 16A.

features open plains and grasslands. A ride to the west means a twisty run through hills, mountains, and canyons.

The Black Hills are home to some of the nation's classic vacation hotspots and tourist traps. Any visit to the area should include a stop at icons like the Mount Rushmore and Crazy Horse Monuments, and a cold cup of water (and more!) at Wall Drug. Visiting the Badlands is a given. While you're there, you're within striking distance of Wind Cave, Sundance, Deadwood, and Devils Tower.

There are two seasons in the Black Hills: hot and cold. After a short, cool spring in May, temperatures climb quickly through June. July and August are hot and dry. With the area's high elevation, lack of shade, and dry climate, you need to keep hydrated and protect yourself from the sun. By the end of

What're you lookin' at, pal? You want a piece of me?

summer, the weather turns surprisingly fast. The first freeze arrives in the Black Hills by late August or early September, and snow is common in October. Suffice it to say, this is

The Badlands are a product of relentless winds and periodic monsoon-like rains that simultaneously pounded and swept away the soft rock of southern South Dakota.

Remarkable roads like the Needles Highway help make the Black Hills Motorcycle Classic (at Sturgis) one of the most popular motorcycle rallies in the world. If you come for the riding, that is.

a classic summer riding destination. You won't find a fall color ride here.

The scope of riding in the Black Hills is a bit different than other journeys in this book. With so much riding available in the region, it's hard to plan one big loop that would cover it well. So, this chapter consists of four day-ride loops in the vicinity of Rapid City, Sturgis, and Custer. A fifth loop takes in a couple of sections of US 14 and 16 of particular interest to canyon carvers.

Connections

The Badlands Loops don't directly connect to other tours in the region. That's the bad news. The good news is, the roads that do connect you to other tours are awesome. US 14 and 14A west connect to the Northwest Passage tour through the Bighorn Mountains. Sweet pavement and scenery, curves, and—thanks to I-90—nearly zero traffic. Reaching the Rocky Mountain Way tour is easy via US 85 south.

Segment One
Badlands Loop

This run through the scenic barrens of South Dakota begins at the higher elevation of Rapid City and explores the lowlands via Route 44. The grassy plains toward the east were once populated with millions of bison that roamed the continent from season to season. Imagine how awesome the sight must have been to those who saw herds numbering in the tens and hundreds of thousands come rumbling over the hills. Portions of the ride today run through areas where a limited number of bison still exist, so it's possible you'll see a few on the ride, especially through Indian lands.

The turn toward Badlands National Park begins at Scenic, South Dakota, on Sage Creek Road, a dirt road. It's hard packed and easy to navigate. This approach allows you to view the Badlands from the higher elevations first, then ride down through the canyons.

Just before entering the park, you can turn north for a ten-mile ride up to Wall, South Dakota, home to the famous (or infamous)

Wall Drug (www.walldrug.com). It's fair to say that the town should just rename itself Wall Drug, because the one-time drugstore is now the town. Purchased by Ted Hustead in 1931, business was slow for the first few years, but when Mount Rushmore opened in 1939, Ted's wife Dorothy got the idea to offer free ice water to thirsty travelers. Wall Drug became famous for its self-promotion on billboards and signs. Today, businesses line the streets of Wall, most of them a part of the Wall Drug empire.

At one time or another, anyone who has traveled through this region has given it the same name: Badlands. The Lakota, likely the first people to inhabit the area, called this desolate expanse *Makhóśièa*, meaning, literally "bad land." French trappers named it *les mauvaises terres à traverser* (the bad lands to cross). The Spanish referred to it as *tierra baldía* (waste land). A lack of ground cover paired with infrequent, intense rain and ceaseless winds have whipped this terrain of soft rock, loose dry soil, and deep sand into steep slopes, canyons, hoodoos, ravines, and gullies.

As you stand on the rim and look over the area, you can easily see what they were talking about. On first approaching the rim of the Badlands, your instinctive reaction will be to grab for your water bottle. It's a beautiful sight, but your mouth will feel parched just looking across this colorful but very dry wasteland.

This ride loops around the foot of the area, where you can see up close just how soft and fragile the land is. Fossil beds are frequently found in areas like this, as exposed layers and soft rock make surveying and fossil hunting easy. The Badlands are home to some of the most productive fossil beds anywhere, the finds of which include the remains of camels, three-toed horses, and even rhinoceroses. Imagine what it would be like to hear a thundering herd approach from a distance and discover it's rhinos!

Route Details – 249 miles

➤ From Rapid City, South Dakota, ride east on Rte 44 to Scenic. (39 mi.)

➤ Follow Sage Creek Road (unpaved) to Rte 240. (26 mi.)

➤ Ride north on Rte 240 to Wall, and return. (16 mi. round trip)

➤ Turn east on Rte 240 Badlands Loop Road to Ben Reifel Visitor Center. (22 mi.)

➤ Ride south on Rte 377 to Interior. (3 mi.)

➤ Take Rte 44 west to Scenic. (31 mi.)

➤ Ride south on Bombing Range Road to Rockyford. (20 mi.)

➤ Turn west on BIA 2 (becomes County Rte 656) and follow to Buffalo Gap. (47 mi.)

➤ Follow Rte 79 north to Rapid City. (45 mi.)

9

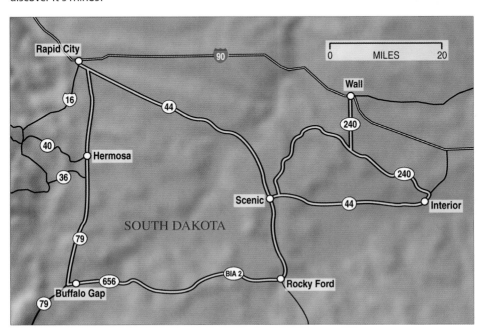

Tall grass shimmers on the prairie like ocean waves, helping explain why covered wagons were referred to as "prairie schooners."

Segment Two
Devils Loop

This loop begins in Sturgis, South Dakota, making a run into eastern Wyoming to Devils Tower, returning by way of Sundance and entertaining roads like Route 585 and US 85 through Lead and Deadwood.

There are two Sturgis, South Dakotas. The first is that dusty little town by the Interstate, just west of Rapid City. Just another

jumping-off spot like you see every twenty miles or so on a road so changeless you could steer with your knees (though not recommended). Churches on the street corners, rows of neatly-kept houses, and a few blocks of commerce in a downtown business district that has its share of successes and failures. It could be any small town on the high

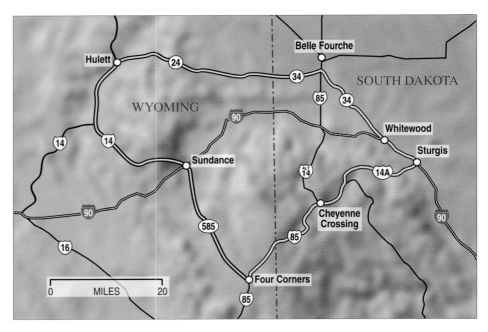

western plains. As you drive through, you might think it's kind of unusual to see a couple of tattoo parlors on a main street. And there seem to be plenty of bars here, too. It is dry around here. Folks must be thirsty. If you left it at that and got back on the Interstate, you'd forget about the place in an instant.

Then there's the other Sturgis, one that begins to stir in late July and for a couple of weeks in early to mid-August swells to full-scale Mardi Gras proportions. Half a million folks leave their day-to-day persona at home to pursue the "biker lifestyle," however they define it. Want to walk on the wild side? You can find that here if it's what you seek. There's plenty of live entertainment, games,

Route Details – 181 miles

> ➤ Depart Sturgis following Rte 34 to Whitewood, South Dakota. (8 mi.)

> ➤ At Whitewood, continue north on Rte 34 (becomes Rte 24 in Wyoming) to Hulett, Wyoming. (58 mi.)

> ➤ Continue on Rte 24 to US 14. (15 mi.)

> ➤ Follow US 14 east to Sundance, Wyoming. (21 mi.)

> ➤ Take Rte 585 south to Four Corners, Wyoming. (28 mi.)

> ➤ Ride US 85 north to Cheyenne Crossing, South Dakota. (25 mi.)

> ➤ Take US 14A east to Sturgis. (26 mi.)

9

Deadwood, South Dakota, is where Wild Bill Hickok met his fate in a poker game. Hickok was reportedly holding aces and eights which later became known as the "Dead Man's Hand."

and racing, too—stuff that won't later require penicillin shots or a DNA test.

From Sturgis take Whitewood Road, which runs parallel to the Interstate, and splits off onto Route 34 at Whitewood. As you pass from South Dakota to Wyoming, Route 34 becomes Route 24. This route is uncluttered, unpopulated, and untrafficked, a seductive ribbon of highway which, in part, captures the essence of the open road. The road begins a southward turn at Hulett when, around a bend in the road, a strange figure appears on the horizon ten miles distant. That's your introduction to Devils Tower (www.nps.gov/deto).

The tower is a column of magma that, eons ago, penetrated a soft area of rock, once part of a vast seabed. The seabed was raised by the same action that created the Black Hills and the Rockies. Over time, the much softer sedimentary rock eroded away, leaving the tower. Standing more than 1,200 feet above the surrounding terrain, Devils Tower does give off a mystical vibe. Long before Europeans showed up, American Indians considered this sacred ground. Those

Devils Tower in northeastern Wyoming gives off an otherworldly vibe that has drawn tinfoil-hatted visitors and movie producers for decades. It is considered sacred ground by area tribes.

who think *Close Encounters of the Third Kind* was a documentary still poke around for evidence of an alien landing. Let 'em look, I say. It'll keep them occupied.

Run Route 24 south to US 14 and turn east toward Sundance (www.sundancewyoming.com). Although this is not the location of the popular film festival,

Turns are so tight on roads in the Black Hills, it was necessary to engineer pigtail or spiral turns that provided the necessary turning radius in a small amount of space.

Once, the prairies were so full of these beasts the land would look black to the horizon. Get these fellas on a stampede and that would be some real rolling thunder.

it is the spot where Harry Longabaugh adopted his nickname "Sundance Kid" after his release from the local jail. The town took its name from the Sun Dance ceremony performed by the native cultures.

In town, turn down South 6th Street, cross under I-90, and continue on Route 585 then north on US 85. As you reenter the Black Hills, the road begins to gain elevation, winding through thickening stands of trees as you go. At Cheyenne Crossing, turn west on US 14A for what is typically a fast, fun run up the Spearfish Canyon Highway.

At Spearfish, turn east once again on US 14A for the return run to Sturgis via Deadwood. As icons of the Old West go, Deadwood, South Dakota, would rank on anyone's Top 10 list. Born as the result of a gold rush, a haven for gamblers and outlaws, and the final resting place of one of the West's most colorful characters, Deadwood has the authentic look and feel of the Wild West that the best Disney imagineers couldn't replicate. Even the name sounds western. The folks here know they've got a good thing going and they've worked hard

to preserve it. Today the streets look and feel much as they did at the turn of the 19th century and when you ride your iron horse into town here and climb out of the saddle, you can practically feel the eyes of the townsfolk sizing you up. Is that the gambler from Missouri everyone's been talking about? Or that posse from Dodge City, come to grab an outlaw in hiding? Oh, it's just a couple on a Beemer. That'll be two sparkling waters, neat.

Amble in to the Lucky Nugget where you'll find some card action and a little history. Wild Bill Hickok was already a legend when he sat at a table here in 1876. Having made a name as a gunfighter, lawman, and gambler, Hickok followed the gold west to the Dakota Territory, landing in Deadwood. Hickok played poorly that day, having had a premonition that this trip to the West might be his last. With his back uncustomarily turned to the door, Hickok was bushwhacked by the brother of man killed some years earlier by Wild Bill. The cards Hickok was holding, aces and eights, became known as the "Dead Man's Hand," a reference to Hickok's untimely demise.

Segment Three
Lead Loop

Originating in Custer, generally acknowledged as the oldest established town in the Black Hills, site of the first gold discovery and home to George Armstrong Custer's 7th Cavalry in 1874, this loop follows a series of well-known winding roads through the Black Hills, ending at the Crazy Horse Monument.

The jumble of mountain passes plays havoc with the route numbering system here in the Black Hills. Within a couple hours time, it's not unusual to be on different stretches of the same highway multiple times headed in opposite directions. It just works out that way. But if you get turned around, the worst that can happen is that you have gone a few miles out of your way. In these parts, that's not a bad thing.

Head east on US 16A. This road was purposely designed as a highway for touring, with portions of single-lane divided highway, pigtail bridges that loop around on themselves, switchbacks, and scenic one-lane tunnels designed to frame the faces on Mount Rushmore. It's a wild ride. As you approach Route 244, you have the option to turn left to visit Mount Rushmore which is discussed in more detail in the next loop.

Route 16A rejoins US 16 north of Keystone. Turn west heading toward Hill City. You won't reach the town before you hit the

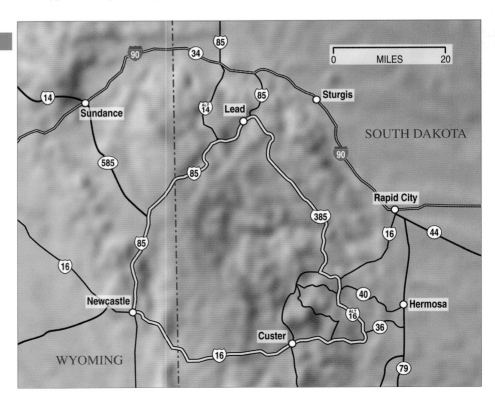

Route Details – 164 miles

➤ From Custer, South Dakota, ride east, then north on US 16/16A to US 385. (39 mi.)

➤ Ride north on US 385 to Lead, South Dakota. (38 mi.)

➤ Follow US 85 south to Newcastle, Wyoming. (51 mi.)

➤ Take US 16 east back to Custer, South Dakota. (36 mi.)

➤ Optional: Take Rte 16/385 north to Crazy Horse Memorial. (10 mi. round trip)

The Crazy Horse Memorial is the world's largest mountain carving and located not far from Mount Rushmore. No completion date has been estimated but it's probably safe to assume you and I won't see it finished.

junction with US 385. At this point, turn north toward Lead. US 385 is an interesting route. It's an extension of Route 85 and runs from here 1,206 miles to Big Bend Park in Texas. Visit that area in the Lone Star Loop and you'll have the opportunity to ride the very end of the road.

Lead (pronounced "leed") is another mining town, home to the Homestake Mine, the world's deepest and most productive gold mine (www.leadmethere.org). Over its lifetime the mine produced 40 million ounces of gold and reached a mile and a half below the surface of the town. The mine closed in 2002 but today is being redeveloped as an underground laboratory where sensitive physics experiments can take place without being affected by cosmic radiation.

US Route 85 south follows the Cheyenne-Deadwood stagecoach route leading to the rider-friendly town of Newcastle, Wyoming, one of many towns that sprang up in anticipation of the route the railroad would take through the area. Real estate speculation ran rampant. Nearby communities like Tubb Town and Whoop-Up were built and promoted as the next stop along the line, often based on little more than faint hope. When the railroad came through Newcastle, residents from the towns that lost the competition packed up and left and the towns disappeared altogether. Frequently you'll find riders gathered in Newcastle around the Antlers Hotel along Main Street enjoying some victuals before returning to the trail.

Our old friend US 16 returns to lead us back to Custer. But before calling it a day, head north on US 16/385 to the Crazy Horse Memorial (www.crazyhorsememorial.org). Sculptor Korczak Ziolkowski and Lakota Chief Henry Standing Bear officially started Crazy Horse Memorial in June 1948 to honor the culture, tradition, and living heritage of North American Indians. It is the world's largest mountain carving and is being built entirely by private funding. Due to the complexity of the carving and the availability of funds, it has no projected completion date. However, the work that's been done over the last 60 years gives you a clear impression of where the project is headed. The museum contains a large collection of artifacts related to the history of the sculpture and the subject of its study, Crazy Horse.

9

Segment Four
Rushmore Loop

This route explores sideroads through the Black Hills leading to a visit to Mount Rushmore. At just 80 miles, it's designed to give you plenty of time to explore the Rushmore exhibits and take part in activities like a guided program or a hike.

It's a 13-mile run from the eastern terminus of US Route 16 in Rapid City to Rockerville. Take the left-hand exit for Rockerville, follow that to Main Street, and then turn left onto South Rockerville Road.

After some easy riding with wide views of the hills and grasslands, things quickly get interesting as you turn north on Route 87. The road narrows to one lane, steepens, and enters a series of slow-speed switchbacks that pass through an occasional single-lane

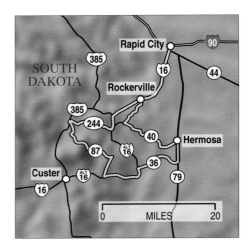

tunnel. It's an intimate ride through the Black Hills and one that will stand out as a highlight of your travels through the region.

Route 87 and 244 are separated by a short stretch on US 16 heading east toward Rapid City. Route 244 leads directly to Mount Rushmore, the primary stop on this loop.

The original plan for the carvings on Mount Rushmore (www.nps.gov/moru) is a reminder that our interest in popular culture isn't a new phenomenon. It began as a plot to lure tourists to the area with likenesses of

Local promoters originally planned to carve Manny, Moe, and Jack into the side of Mount Rushmore, but decided presidents would make a better draw.

9

Route Details – 103 miles

➤ From Rapid City, South Dakota, take US 16 south to Rockerville. (13 mi.)

➤ Take South Rockerville Road south to Rte 40. (6 mi.)

➤ Follow Rte 40 east to Hermosa. (13 mi.)

➤ Take Rte 79 south to Rte 36. (1 mi.)

➤ Follow Rte 36 west to US 16/16A. (9 mi.)

➤ Take US 16/16A west to Rte 87. (9 mi.)

➤ Follow Rte 87 north to US 385. (20 mi.)

➤ Take US 385 to Rte 244. (0.2 mi.)

➤ Follow Rte 244 east to US 16A. (11 mi.)

➤ Follow Rte 16A then US 16 north to Rapid City. (21 mi.)

The Needles Highway passes through fourteen miles of unique granite structures, tunnels, and pine forests.

famous personalities carved into the granite. Sculptor Gutzon Borglum, who was commissioned to develop the site, decided to create a more national theme by devoting the memorial to four U.S. presidents. Construction of the site began in 1927; in 1933 the National Park Service took control of the monument. It was completed in 1939 and became an instant American icon, drawing now up to 2 million visitors annually. You have to wonder who would have been featured if Borglum hadn't challenged the original design. I don't think that 60-foot carvings of Chico, Harpo, Zeppo, and Groucho Marx would have had the same appeal.

Road Tip – Quick Cooldown

If you find yourself in hot riding conditions and need to cool down, here's an idea that brings rapid relief. Soak a hand towel, bandana, or other piece of cloth that's long enough to wrap around your neck and wet down your hair. Cooling your neck will lower the temperature of blood flowing through the carotid arteries while wetting your head will speed the transfer of heat out of your body. As you ride, the evaporating moisture will take the heat with it.

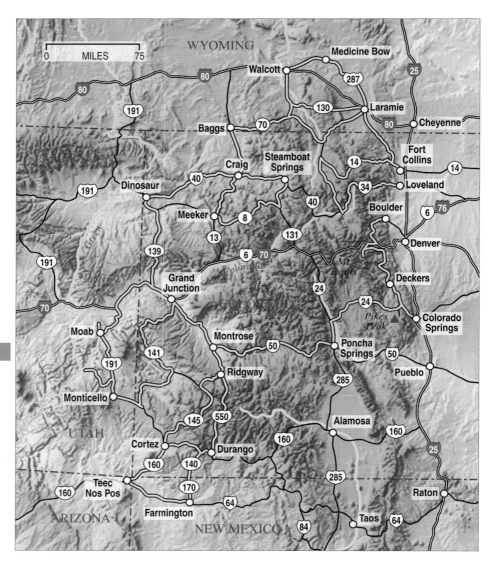

10

10 ROCKY MOUNTAIN WAY

This chapter describes a 2,600-mile ride through the Colorado Rocky Mountains over the course of ten days. The main loop circles the state with five separate day-ride loops covering the most prominent riding locales, including excursions into central Wyoming and eastern Utah. You'll enjoy well-known roads like the Million Dollar Highway and Trail Ridge Road, plus hundreds of miles of lesser known but equally entertaining byways.

This tour around the Rocky Mountains is like a highlight reel of the western U.S. It has everything. Cow towns and cattle drives. Fly fishing in snow-fed waters against the backdrop of monolithic mountains. Ghost towns. High desert and lush mountain forest. Plateaus and canyons. And the region's best roads that lead you through it all.

Colorado might think about changing its nickname to "The Outdoor State," because that's where you'll find most of its residents. More than in many other states, folks in Colorado engage in many outside activities—hiking, bicycling, mountain climbing, and rafting—the list goes on and on. Spend enough time here and you'll find yourself drawn into the outdoor lifestyle, too.

This loop focuses on the western two-thirds of the state and features some rides in very remote places. Some include unpaved sections with hard-packed gravel surfaces; however, they aren't quite like that steep, rutted gravel road leading into the campground where you dropped your bike that cold, rainy night. The few dirt sections included in this route are generally flat and dry and can be ridden comfortably at near-touring speeds.

One big loop encircles the western portion of the state, and six sub-loops cover areas both inside and outside the main loop. Each sub-loop returns to one of the stopover points on the main loop. This gives you a plan for experiencing a variety of landscapes

Built today, the Million Dollar Highway would probably be the Billion Dollar Highway. Come to think of it, it probably wouldn't exist at all. So ride, and enjoy!

There are more than 2,000 cataloged arches in Arches National Park. An opening must span at least three feet to be considered an arch formation.

Balanced Rock is one of many strange formations in Arches National Park.

and lifestyles while reducing the lodging arrangements you need to make.

Many of the passes here exceed 10,000 feet altitude. Sustained riding at higher elevations demands a few extra considerations.

For starters, plan your ride here for June through August. Many roads at higher elevations are open seasonally and some aren't fully cleared of snow until the end of May.

Rental bikes are easy to find in the Denver-Boulder area. If you're going to fly and ride, consider the dual-sport option. In addition to the streetbike-friendly roads in this chapter, there are thousands of miles of dirt trails through the canyons and passes that are best suited to bikes with knobby tires and higher ground clearance.

Colorado's robust tourist economy means travel services are abundant in towns throughout the state . . . .when you can find a town. The western portion of the state has remote areas where you might find nothing for seventy or eighty miles at a stretch. I'd recommend that any time your gas falls below half a tank, top it off at the next station.

Your fuel-injected bike should have no problem adapting its air-fuel mixture to adjust for the lower oxygen at higher elevations, but your body may not comply as quickly. Sunscreen is essential to counteract

A group of youngsters (who are still flexible enough to do handstands), offer a variation on the old four-states-at-one-time photo at Four Corners Monument.

the higher UV exposure you'll experience. Also, altitude sickness can affect some folks, especially above 8,000 feet. Staying hydrated will help, as will avoiding alcohol. Prescription remedies are available to alleviate the flu-like symptoms of altitude sickness, so you might take preemptive action and talk with your doctor before your trip (www.ncbi.nlm.nih.gov/pubmedhealth/ PMH0000766). Dress in layers. It'll be chilly at the top.

Connections

This tour intersects the Desert Tracks loops and comes close to Crossing the Heartland. By a short stretch ("short" as defined out west), you can connect to the Badlands loops and the Northwest Passage tour.

10

The high country of Rocky Mountain National Park is home to herds of elk.

Segment One
Fort Collins Loop

When you get to a place like Colorado, you want to jump right into the good stuff, especially if you've ridden overland to get here. So, let's start big. This tour begins with a loop out of Fort Collins, encompassing classic Rocky Mountain roads, passes, and

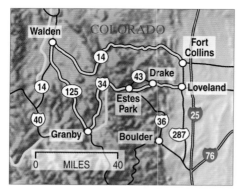

canyons that will give you chills—and not just from the high elevations.

Start your run on US 34 out of Loveland, headed for Estes Park. Route 34 is also known as the Trail Ridge Road, portions of which top 12,000 feet, making it the highest continuously paved road in the states. A popular option with riders is to dip off of 34 at Drake and follow Route 43 to Estes Park. If you do this, beware of a couple of technical switchbacks with a 10 percent grade that require some skill to ascend safely. However, this is a spectacular and lightly traveled alternative for the first portion of this ride.

Estes Park is the eastern gateway to Rocky Mountain National Park. Continue from here west on US 34 to reach the first park visitor center at Fall River. Route 34 scales the

Imagine riding through an area as pretty as this and having only one or two exposures left on a roll of film!

At 12,000 feet, Trail Ridge Road is the highest continuously paved road in the U.S.

mountains as you continue on. It's tempting to try to enjoy the views and ride at the same time, but that's hard to do on this road; there's just too much to see. Use the overlooks for gawking and stay focused on the road when you're moving! US 34 tops out at 12,183 feet before beginning a slow descent toward Granby.

In Granby, you have a couple of options. The Laramie Loop describes a ride originating out of Steamboat Springs. Riding west on US 40, you could make the loop through Steamboat Springs, then return to Fort Collins on the second half of this loop.

To complete this segment, head west on US 40 for a short distance, then turn north on Route 125. This lightly-traveled two-lane road transports you to a landscape of high plains that looks utterly different from the rugged mountain terrain of the Trail Ridge Road. By the time you reach Walden, the mountains have all but disappeared. That speck approaching you on the horizon could be the High Plains Drifter, the outlaw Josey

Wales, The Preacher, or any of a half dozen other Clint Eastwood characters. Or, it could just be another rider.

Heading east from Wanden, Route 14 gains elevation through the area known as North Park. As you approach from the west, the Rockies gradually reappear on the eastern horizon where you'll cross Cameron Pass at 10,400 feet. As you descend, you'll run through Poudre Canyon on the way back to Fort Collins. It may start out straight and flat but the last two-thirds of this loop will give you all you want for excitement. A good start to your journey through the Rockies.

Route Details – 236 miles

➤ US 34 west out of Loveland, Colorado, to Granby. (92 mi.)

➤ US 40 west to Rte 125. (2 mi.)

➤ North on Rte 125 to Walden. (52 mi.)

➤ East on Rte 14 to Fort Collins. (90 mi.)

Segment Two
Fort Collins, Colorado, to Laramie, Wyoming

The ride from Fort Collins to Laramie is a short run of only 65 miles, so you can combine this segment with either the Fort Collins Loop or the Laramie Loop for a complete day of riding.

The road north on US 287 roughly parallels portions of the Overland Stage Route. Had you been traveling through here 160 years ago, you would likely have made a stop at Virginia Dale. The county road that runs off to the right just behind the now-closed café and post office leads to the Virginia Dale Stage Station, a remarkably well

Route Details – 65 miles

➤ Take US 287 north out of Fort Collins, Colorado, to Laramie, Wyoming. (65 mi.)

preserved log cabin stagecoach stop just a mile or two off the main road.

This part of the Overland Trail followed a southerly path in an attempt to avoid "Indian problems" that had developed over the heavily traveled Oregon Trail. The station that stands at Virginia Dale was built in 1862 by Jack Slade, a rough character who developed a reputation for hard drinkin' and hard livin'.

Slade was experienced with stage routes, since just a few years prior he'd supervised the construction of some 200 relay stations for the Pony Express. The station he built here, and named after his wife, became one of the most prominent stops on the Overland route. Slade oversaw personnel on the route, hiring drivers including a young fifteen-year-old named William Cody.

The Centennial Highway peeks from the foreground as early spring clouds gather above Horsetooth Reservoir near Fort Collins.

Today Slade would probably be called a "logistics manager." It was his job to see that nothing prevented the stage from running, whether the threat was weather, Indians, or competitors who set up along the way. One local trader, Jules Beni, pumped the contents of a six-shooter into Slade and finished him off with a couple loads of buckshot. Or so he thought. Like a scene out of a classic western movie, Slade vowed revenge on Beni, promising that one day he'd wear Beni's ears on his watch chain. It's a promise he kept. Slade surrendered himself at Fort Laramie and was promptly dismissed by officers at the fort who were well familiar with the story of the original attack.

If you have an extra day in your itinerary, why not get a real feel for the country by spending the day on a local ranch? The 2 Bars 7 is a working family ranch near Virginia Dale that caters to city slickers (a broad definition including anyone not from here) who

seeks an authentic western experience (www.2bars7.com). The ranch hosts a range of activities including horseback riding along trails, or on the open range with a wrangler. Just remember to keep an eye out for a bullet-ridden old coot wearing an ear on his watch chain. Jack Slade was such an ornery old cuss, he still may not be dead.

Segment Three
Laramie Lasso Loop

This loop is based from Laramie, exploring the Medicine Bow Forest and passing through the Snowy Mountain Range.

Any mountains here that contain the word "snowy" should alert you to expect the white stuff throughout the year. Usually, the roads through this area are open by Memorial Day, but snow can still be found roadside for an impromptu snowball fight into July.

You won't find snow on the first part of the ride though. Route 230 traverses flat

high country on a southwesterly course into Colorado. The scenery grows, literally, as you ride farther south. First, stands of pines begin to appear, signalling that you've entered the Medicine Bow Forest area. Then the hills begin to grow.

Over the Colorado line, Route 230 becomes Route 127. At the intersection with Route 125, turn north to run back into Wyoming. Route 125 becomes Route 230, again. The return via 130 is a treat, especially the middle portion. Cutting through the heart of the Snowy Mountain Range, Route 130 offers you the first serious set of curves on your Colorado journey, a preview of coming attractions. Landscape and road compete equally for your attention. Open range riding is framed by distant mountains. Wide sweepers are offset by snow-capped cliffs. In the end, the road wins the competition with the occasional high-speed 180 switchback that invites you to forget what you're look-

A pair of Road Kings stop for a photo op with Medicine Bow Peak in the background along Route 130, the Snowy Range Scenic Byway.

Near Fort Laramie, Wyoming, you can still see ruts carved by the iron rims of heavily laden wagons heading west on the Oregon Trail.

ing at, lean into a sweet curve, and turn up the wick.

On the eastern side of the mountain, you'll pass through Centennial. When the post office was established here in 1876, the town was named for the year's big event—the country's centennial celebration. You'll find plenty of provisions here for yourself and your iron pony including one popular hangout, the Old Corral Hotel and Steakhouse.

Road Tip – Weather Permitting

As you make your way around the region, it's not a bad idea to have access to local road condition reports. Frequently, road conditions can be obtained by dialing 511 on your cell phone. Most transportation departments maintain information online as well. Just search the name of the state and "highway conditions" or "department of transportation." (www.wyoroad.info/highway/conditions/dist1.html)

Route Details – 165 miles

➤ From Laramie, Wyoming, follow Rte 230 south (becomes Rte 127 in Colorado) to Kings Canyon, Colorado. (45 mi.)

➤ Follow Rte 127 to Rte 125. (4 mi.)

➤ Turn north on Rte 125 (becomes Rte 230 in Wyoming) to Encampment, Wyoming. (36 mi.)

➤ Continue on Rte 230 to Rte 130. (10 mi.)

➤ Ride east on Rte 130 to Laramie. (70 mi.)

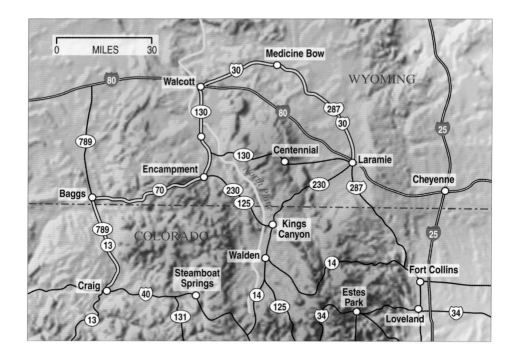

Segment Four
Laramie, Wyoming, to Craig, Colorado

If things sounded rough in Virginia Dale, it wasn't any better in the early days of

---

Route Details – 232 miles

➤ From Laramie, Wyoming, follow US 30 to Medicine Bow. (57 mi.)

➤ From Medicine Bow, continue on US 30 to Walcott. (36 mi.)

➤ Turn south on Rte 130 to Saratoga. (22 mi.)

➤ Continue straight on Rte 230 to Encampment. (19 mi.)

➤ Turn west on Rte 70 to Baggs, Wyoming. (57 mi.)

➤ Follow Rte 789 (becomes Rte 13 in Colorado) south to Craig, Colorado. (41 mi.)

Laramie. The original town sprouted up in the 1860s as a tent city along the Overland Trail and later grew due to its location on the Union Pacific portion of the Transcontinental Railway. Its early days were the definition of the Wild West. Laramie's first mayor resigned after three weeks on the job in 1868, bowing to pressure from three local gunmen who took over the town. After the gunmen forced settlers to turn over land claims to them, the county sheriff formed a "vigilance committee." Storming the gunfighters' favorite hangout saloon, the aptly named Bucket of Blood, the vigilance committee overwhelmed the trio and hanged them.

Expect a somewhat warmer welcome today. Laramie is a peaceable city that still retains an Old West charm with a reduced chance that you'll catch a belly full of lead at the local saloon. Downtown is full of shops a co-rider will enjoy, conveniently located near watering holes a thirsty rider will find useful.

Departing Laramie, you'll make a round-about run into western Colorado following the Lincoln Highway and a few other back roads through mountain passes and canyons.

The glory days for Medicine Bow have passed, but its role in shaping our ideas about the west is assured, thanks to a Philadelphian by the name of Owen Wister. Like many Easterners, Wister was consumed by stories he'd heard about the untamed frontier. After spending several summers here, Wister penned what is recognized as the first cowboy novel, *The Virginian,* the story of a cowboy-aristocrat who takes a difficult stand in a land war. In an enduring scene from the book, a poker player calls the Virginian an SOB, to which he replies "When you call me that, smile."

At Walcott, Route 130 begins the run south to Route 230, splitting the Snowy Range at Encampment (also referred to as Grand Encampment). While you're here, check out the reconstructed western town at the local museum (www.gemuseum.com) for a better idea of what it was like to live out here on the high plains.

You're going to love the ride over Route 70 headed west. This next 60 miles of smooth curves crosses the Continental

The Continental Divide marks the point where water flows to the Atlantic or Pacific. I suppose that holds true if you spit in one direction or the other as well.

10

Divide and Battle Mountain Pass. Route 70 ends in Baggs, Wyoming. Turn south here on Route 789 which leads straight to Craig, becoming Colorado 13. It's an easy run and it puts you in position for a great loop through central Colorado. Craig has a cluster of national motels on Route 13, just after you cross over the intersection with US 40.

Segment Five
Steamboat Springs Loop

There's nothing tricky about this route. It's a fast and fun romp through the hills of the northwestern part of Colorado, an area that doesn't see as many riders or tourists. If your bike needs a little blowing out, this might be just the place to get the job done.

Reaching Steamboat Springs is half the fun of this loop. Approaching from either di-

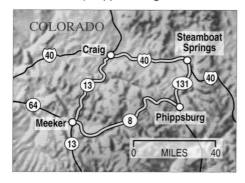

rection on US 40 is a fun run. If you're making a cross-country run on US-6, a turn north on Route 131 will bring you into town by way of Oak Creek. There are less expensive lodging options here than what you'll find in Steamboat Springs. If you're arriving on a dual-sport, an intriguing way to reach town would be by way of Route 129, which branches off of Route 70 in south-central Wyoming. It's a 30-mile stretch of hard pack and probably passable by a street bike but washboard portions of the surface would be better handled by a dual-sport.

Beyond Craig, the curves on US 40 diminish, so turn south on Route 13 for a fast resupply of scenic sweepers. By and large, you'll have the route to yourself. In Meeker, turn east on County Road 8, which passes

Federal highways like US 40 offer a scenic, laid-back experience compared to the interstates that plow through the mountains.

through sub-alpine meadow, rangeland, and forests of the western foothills. Six- to eight-thousand-foot foothills, that is. When Route 8 reaches the national forest boundary, the road surface alternates between dirt and gravel. Any street bike could handle this section of road, but if you're not comfortable with it, I'll describe an alternate route.

Over the county boundary, Route 8 becomes Route 132. Same road, just keep going. In time, Route 132 ends on Rural County Road 19. Turning left and heading east here marks a return to pavement in an isolated and utterly gorgeous area. RCR 19 meets Route 131 for the return to Steamboat Springs.

For the gravel-shy, continue south from Meeker on Route 13 to Rifle and turn east on US 6. You can catch all of Route 131 north.

Southern sections of this road take best advantage of the elevation changes as the road ascends the first 35 miles to the plateaus that supply the Yampa River. The road settles down for a bit before returning to its twisty ways through Oak Creek.

Route Details – 204 miles

➤ From Steamboat Springs, Colorado, ride west on US 40 to Craig. (42 mi.)

➤ Ride south on Rte 13 to Meeker. (48 mi.)

➤ Ride County Road 8 east to Phippsburg (portions are gravel). (83 mi.)

➤ Return on Rte 131 north to Steamboat Springs. (31 mi.)

The Green River has cut through millions of years of rock, exposing one of the richest fossil deposits found anywhere in the world.

Segment Six
Craig, Colorado, to Grand Junction, Colorado

This segment connects to Grand Junction, Colorado, by way of Dinosaur. Located at the western edge of Colorado, Dinosaur Na-

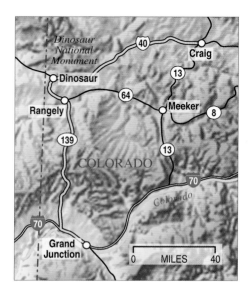

tional Monument marks the point where a large trove of fossils was discovered in 1909 (www.nps.gov/dino). Based on research at the site, paleontologists have concluded that dinosaurs and other animals were washed into the area during large-scale flooding events and buried under a heavy layer of sediment. In addition to fossils, the area is also known for the canyons carved by the Green and Yampa Rivers.

Route 139 south of Dinosaur runs through

Route Details – 179 miles

➤ From Craig, Colorado, follow US 40 west to Dinosaur. (88 mi.)

➤ From Dinosaur, follow Rte 64 south to Rangely. (20 mi.)

➤ Take Rte 139 south to Grand Junction. (71 mi.)

Douglas Pass, a scenic ride down the western edge of the state and a convenient way to get to Grand Junction. When you reach the top of the pass, you will enjoy the views in all directions—an excellent picture-taking opportunity. Following the pass, the road straightens again until you reach Grand Junction. Markers along the route describe petroglyphs and paintings left by the Fremont and Ute civilizations on the nearby rocks and sandstone cliffs.

Grand Junction marks the endpoint for this segment. The city is located in the fertile Grand Valley where agriculture and cattle-raising are the two main activities. Grand Junction has become a popular destination for mountain bikers and has developed a reputation as Colorado's wine-making center.

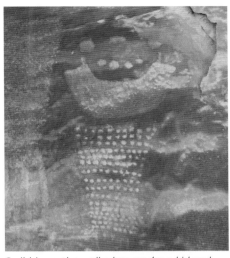

Scribble on the wall when you're a kid and you're in trouble. Let it age a few thousand years, it's art.

Independence Monument is a 450-foot-high sandstone tower in the heart of Colorado National Monument in western Colorado. It stands alone and apart from other formations, thus it is "independent."

10

Here's the Green River Overlook in Canyonlands. Leave the hose running in the backyard for a few hundred million years and look what happens.

Segment Seven
Arches Loop

10

Southwestern Colorado contains beautiful red rock country on par with eastern Utah. This loop explores both states and visits two of the best-known national parks: Canyonlands and Arches.

Starting from Grand Junction, Colorado, expect empty highway, sweepers and expansive views on your ride down Route 141 to start this trip. Turn west on US 491 and north on US 191 to reach the entrance to Canyonlands National Park.

Canyonlands preserves a multi-hued landscape shaped by erosion into innumerable canyons, mesas, and buttes by the Colorado River. Canyonlands is one of the last great undisturbed areas of the Colorado Plateau. This geological province possesses remarkable landscapes, revealed through cliff profiles that show the result of millions of years

of erosion by the action of wind and rain. The drive through the Needles Visitor Center is just one perspective. Head north on US 191 and turn into Dead Horse Point State Park where the views are even more dramatic.

But wait, there's more. Another drive north on US 191 brings you to Arches National Park. This preserve just north of Moab contains more than 2,000 sandstone arches and other strange rock formations. Like Canyonlands, Arches is the product of millions of years of erosion. A different combination and sequence of eroding forces took place here though, resulting in the arch and fin formations present in today's park. Both parks are worth exploring for the better part of a day, so make a plan to ride out and overnight in Moab, then return to Grand Junction the next day.

Route Details – 403 miles

➤ From Grand Junction, Colorado, take Rte 141 south to Dove Creek, Colorado. (156 mi.)

➤ Follow US 491 north to Monticello, Utah. (24 mi.)

➤ Ride US 191 north to Rte 211. (15 mi.)

➤ Follow Rte 211 to Canyonlands National Park and return. (80 mi. round trip)

➤ Continue north on US 191 to Arches National Park. (45 mi.)

➤ Take Rte 128 north to US 6. (42 mi.)

➤ Return to Grand Junction via US 6. (41 mi.)

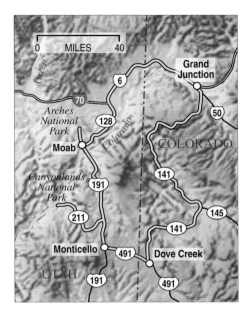

Riders follow roads that twist and turn to follow paths between the canyons in Arches National Park

Segment Eight
Million Dollar Loop

If you have time to make just one excursion through Colorado, this loop is a wise investment. Fort the most part, the route follows the San Juan Skyway, traversing the heart of five million acres of the San Juan and Uncompahgre National Forests.

Riding its full length will take you over high mountain passes, through historic towns, past fields filled with wildflowers, and rocks weeping with waterfalls. In the fall aspens color the landscape a brilliant yellow. It's no wonder that *Sunset Magazine* wrote, "The San Juan Skyway . . . possibly America's greatest fall-color drive . . . its Aspen views are alternately breathtaking and intimate."

Route 550 south of Montrose is famously known as the Million Dollar Highway. Whether that refers to its cost to build or the views, no one is sure. I'll wager on the views. The route starts flat, but begins to pick up interest around Ridgway. And it doesn't stop improving. You get to Ouray and right out of

town, the road earns its nickname. Hugging close to the mountain, Route 550 begins to buck and kick like a fussy mule through tight valleys. It feels like the hills are leaning in on you. Below Silverton, the road changes character again, riding the broad shoulders of the mountain peaks, revealing panoramic vistas that look so perfect you'd think they were Photoshop'd.

Then you reach Durango. It's fun just saying the name Durango, it sounds so quintessentially Western. When you announce your vacation plans at work, tell your co-workers, "Yeah, I'm gonna saddle up the old paint and head up to Durango." They'll look at you with a new-found respect, I guarantee. However, bear in mind that may not extend to spitting your tobacco in the conference room trashcan.

It's worth hanging out here in Durango for a couple of days for at least two reasons. One is the Durango and Silverton Narrow

US 550 may have cost a million dollars a mile, but they didn't spend it on guardrails. Watch where you're going!

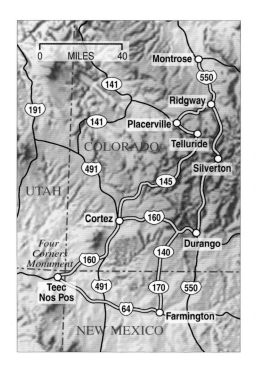

Route Details – 285 miles

➤ At Montrose, Colorado, take US 550 south to Durango. (107 mi.)

➤ Follow US 160 west to Cortez. (44 mi.)

➤ Turn north on Rte 145 and follow to Placerville. (83 mi.)

➤ Follow Rte 62 east to Ridgway. (24 mi.)

➤ Return to Montrose via US 550 north. (27 mi.)

Extension – 205 miles

➤ From Durango, Colorado, Follow Rte 140 south (becomes Rte 170 in New Mexico) to Farmington, New Mexico. (44 mi.)

➤ Follow US 64 west to Teec Nos Pos, Arizona. (68 mi.)

➤ Take US 160 east to Four Corners Road. (6 mi.)

➤ Visit Four Corners and return to US 160. (2 mi. round trip)

➤ Continue on US 160 east to Durango, Colorado. (85 mi.)

10

Gauge Railroad. The line here was constructed between 1881 and '82 from Durango north to haul freight, ore, and passengers. It represents something truly rare—an authentic slice of the Old West. The railroad has remained in continuous operation since its founding nearly 130 years ago, using the same steam-powered locomotives and rolling stock that have always operated on this line. The run to Silverton is an all-day excursion that includes a tour of the gold mine and a guided tour of Silverton.

The other reason to stay another day in Durango is your proximity to Four Corners. In a day's time, you can make an easy 200-mile run to the Four Corners Monument and back. As you may know, Four Corners is the only point where four states come together at one point; while you're this close, it's worth the extra day.

Continuing on the San Juan Skyway, the ride up Route 145 is near the equal of US 550 for its curves and views, and it's empty. The route passes over Lizard Head Pass and then Telluride (www.telluride.com). The town's early mining riches created a boom that drew thousands of residents, and a few scallywags. Butch Cassidy and his Wild Bunch cut their teeth here, robbing the San Miguel National Bank here in 1889. When the ore played out, it was white gold that came to the rescue. Situated in a box canyon on the windward side of the San Juan Mountains, Telluride gets its share of fine, powdery snow, attracting skiers (and a new class of scallywags: snowboarders).

Segment Nine

Grand Junction, Colorado, to Colorado Springs, Colorado

This segment connects three loop rides in the southwestern corner of the state via US Rte 50, which figures prominently in many cross-country rides, especially the portion we'll ride. The climb to 11,000-foot Monarch Pass on US 50 is widely acclaimed by riders, and for good reason. The ascent is perfectly sloped, just enough to stay on the

Once paved only to the halfway mark, a project to blacktop the remainder of the road up Pikes Peak should be completed, or nearly so, in 2012. Paved or not, any roadworthy bike can make the climb.

High altitudes means highly variable weather. Ride through the rain at the summit and you'll probably reach clear skies in a mile or two on the other side.

throttle and keep your suspension packed. With two lanes to the top, you'll never be slowed by a pokey truck or RV. Arriving at the summit, you will find a large gift shop, which makes the perfect spot for a break while you enjoy the views.

Many towns in Colorado were settled by one of two groups: miners or ranchers—except Colorado Springs. This town, situated in the shadow of the front range of the Rockies was originally known as "Little London" and noted for its civilized attractions, the opera house, fine dining, and exceptional lodges. Situated in the rain shadow east of the mountains, Colorado Springs enjoys a mild climate with warmer winters and cool summers.

Pikes Peak, located just to the west of the

city, is the most-visited mountain in North America and second only to Mount Fuji worldwide in number of visits. It is the easternmost of the "fourteeners," making it a popular landmark for folks arriving from the east. Your reward for the time it takes to reach the summit is a 360-degree view that stretches from the Midwestern plains in the east to hundreds of miles of rugged peaks to the west and north.

You can reach the summit in two ways, by your bike or by a cog railway (www.pikes-peak.com/Attraction/23.aspx). The ride up Pikes Peak can be a challenge. The 19-mile climb is certainly passable on your bike, but it can be hard on the powertrain, especially if you're riding two-up and have to pace yourself behind a slow moving car. If you have any questions about your bike's suitability or your capability, you may be better off taking the railway to the top.

Whether on your way to or from Pikes Peak, pay a visit to the Garden of the Gods, a paradise for creative landscape photographers. Tall red spires rise against a backdrop of snowy mountaintops and azure blue skies. Even better, it's free.

10

Route Details – 303 miles

➤ From Grand Junction, Colorado, take US 50 east to Poncha Springs. (186 mi.)

➤ Follow US 285 north to Buena Vista. (24 mi.)

➤ Ride US 24 east to Colorado Springs. (93 mi.)

This section of unpaved road paralleling US 24 near Buena Vista, Colorado, was once part of the Colorado Midland Railroad. Today this hard-packed surface welcomes riders on any style of bike.

Segment Ten

Colorado Springs, Colorado, to Boulder, Colorado

Denver was pissed. The year was 1888 and the Cascade and Pikes Peak Toll Company had just completed a road to the top of their nearby fourteener, draining tourists and dollars from the local Denver economy. Not to be outdone, Denver's mayor proposed a road to the top of Mount Evans, a peak that dominates the western skyline and tops Pikes Peak by a little over a hundred feet. By the 1960s the entire route to the top had been paved, making this the highest paved road in America (top world honors go to the 16,000-foot Ticlio Pass in Peru).

This last segment of the tour visits Mount Evans, and follows a series of mountain peak byways to close the loop on this Rocky Mountain journey.

This segment heads west on US 24 to Woodland Park, picking up route 67 north, a twisty and scenic route around the metropolitan area just over the hills to the east. Evidence of wildfires is notable throughout the area with charred remains of pine trees dotting the landscape along with the occasional remnants of a home destroyed by wind-whipped blazes. In Deckers, turn north on Route 126 at the split, following the TO 285 sign. Look for a gaggle of bikes hanging out at the Bucksnort Saloon just east of Pine on South Elk Creek Road in Sphinx Park (thebucksnortsaloon.com). Routes 126 and 67 are a favorite of area riders and the Bucksnort is their unofficial rally point.

Turn north on US 285 for a short spell, then north on Route 73, the Evergreen Highway, then Route 74 headed north from the town of Evergreen. Look for Squaw Pass Road, Route 66 just north of town and turn left to head west. This road runs into Route 103 which loops around to Route 5, the paved road leading to Mount Evans (www. mountevans.com). If you have ADD, you'd better get medicated before you try to ride this road to the top. The views are nothing short of stunning and with no guardrail to keep you and the road in sync, it's a long way down if you fail to pay attention to what you're doing. As you near the summit, the road narrows, the pitch gets steeper and the switchbacks become very tight. Don't care for heights? I'd suggest you give it a look-see on Google Street View before you commit to the ride to the top. At the summit, a short quarter-mile walk will take you the last 130 feet to the very top of the mountain.

Route 103 ends on US 6/I-70 in Idaho Springs. Examine a good map closely and you'll see that you can ride the old alignment of US 6 east, if you choose. It's a short stretch of interstate until US 6 splits off and you may not feel it's worth the effort after so many great miles. There's more to come. The coda to this 3,000-mile journey is Route 119, part of the Peak-to-Peak Highway. Traffic falls off quickly after you pass the casinos and turn for Central City a short way into the run and the return to Boulder passes through the rocky hills that define the city's western skyline.

Route Details – 202 miles

➤ From Colorado Springs, Colorado, take US 24 to Woodland Park. (20 mi.)

➤ Take Rte 67 north to Deckers. (24 mi.)

➤ Take County Road 126 north to US 285. (25 mi.)

➤ Follow US 285 north to Rte 73. (7 mi.)

➤ Ride Rte 73 north to Evergreen. (9 mi.)

➤ Ride Rte 74 to County Road 66, Squaw Pass Road. (5 mi.)

➤ Follow Squaw Pass Road (becomes Rte 103) to Mount Evans Road. (18 mi.)

➤ Ride Rte 5 to Mount Evans summit and return. (30 mi. round trip)

➤ Continue on Rte 103 to US 6 at Idaho Springs. (14 mi.)

➤ Follow US 6 to Rte 119. (7 mi.)

➤ Ride Rte 119 to Boulder. (43 mi.)

10

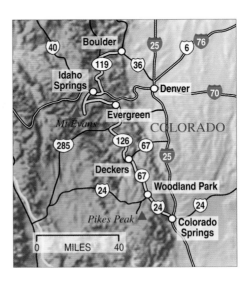

11 DESERT SOUTHWEST

The roads described in this chapter explore large portions of the American Southwest in two loops covering more than 4,000 miles. In the eastern loop we'll visit ancient Indian cultures, Old West outposts, and the mystical shapes of Monument Valley, all connected by the most famous roads in the region. The western loop encompasses the region's grandest national parks, including Grand Canyon, Zion, Bryce, Yosemite, and Death Valley. And just wait till you get to those canyons in Southern California. Those roads are, like, for real. Dude.

In the decades since Hollywood regularly entertained us with tales of cowboys and Indians, the lasting images from that era were more than cowboys sitting around campfires and shootouts on dusty cow town streets. What have been burned into our collective consciousness are sepia-toned memories of the desert landscape. The silhouette of the saguaro cactus standing watch over a quiet desert at dusk. The mystery of abandoned settlements and stories told in petroglyphs. The exquisite enormity of the Grand Canyon, island mesas and towering rock formations that reveal the incalculable power of nature, and the scale of geologic

Jackass Ron's. A purveyor of fine cutlery, starting at only $10. Think he sells Ginsu?

If you need some time to rest and reflect, the Desert Southwest is the perfect place to find solitude.

Trails leading from the main road invite you to explore off the beaten path, but only with the right kind of bike. And provisions.

11

time. The Southwest has a way of putting us in our place in both space and time. It makes us feel small.

The deserts and mountains have sustained civilizations of varying sizes over thousands of years. Their success or failure to adapt to changing conditions, such as population growth, droughts, and encounters with other Indian cultures, has intrigued scientists and archaeologists for decades. The most notable group in this region, the Anasazi, built grand cities into the sides of sheer cliffs, supporting a civilization that flourished from 1200 B.C. to around AD 1300. Soon after this time, the Anasazi abandoned their cliff dwellings and migrated hundreds of miles, gradually integrating with other cultures like the Hopi and Zuni. Researchers think that understanding the factors that caused this group to "disappear" will help us better understand the effects of rising global temperatures and changing weather patterns on today's society.

The Southwest contains a greater concentration of big name national parks than perhaps anywhere else in the United States.

There really is a bike in this picture. See if you can find it. It's easy to lose yourself on the many great roads in Utah.

Grand Canyon, Zion, and Yosemite constitute something of a holy trinity of national park sites, but there are dozens of others scattered in between. Canyon de Chelly, Anasazi, Wupatki, and Chaco Canyon are just several of dozens of sites that preserve the remnants of ancient civilizations. Bryce Canyon, Sequoia, and Kings Canyon have less name recognition than the big three but are just as spectacular and unique.

Any ride through the desert requires some special consideration. Folks joke all the time about the desert's dry heat—"it ain't the heat, it's the humidity." But your bike doesn't know that. When it pukes its guts at high noon or snaps a throttle cable on some deserted back road, your only option may be walking for help ten, twenty miles, or more. You won't be laughing then, either. Keep a couple of extra water bottles in your gear, just in case.

So what is the best time of year to tour

Utah 12 is both technically challenging and a remarkably beautiful must-ride, if you are anywhere near this part of the country.

here? That's a tricky one. The loops in this chapter cover an extraordinary range of elevations and landscapes, from 10,000-foot mountain passes to 282 feet below sea level, where temperatures during any given day will differ by as much as 60 degrees. Spring and fall present the most pleasant touring through much of the region, but you'll want to check on the mountain passes of the Sierras for the western loop. And if you plan a ride through Death Valley in the summer, you'd best start early in the day.

Connections

These tours through southern California, Arizona, and New Mexico intersect or run close to five others in this book. The Coastal Cruise is adjacent to this tour's western loop, while the Lone Star and Crossing the Heartland tours run adjacent to this tour's eastern loop. Meanwhile, the tour through Bigfoot Country runs near the portion of this tour that passes through Yosemite. The eastern loop also runs near the sub-loops described in the Rocky Mountain Way tour.

US 89 ALT between Arizona and Utah is a stunning ride.

Desert Southwest — The Eastern Loop

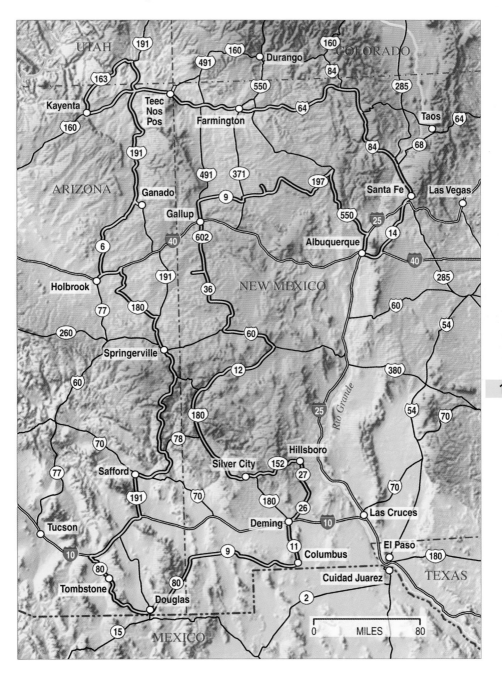

Each October, the skies of Albequerque fill with colorful hot-air balloons.

Segment One
Albuquerque to Farmington, New Mexico

Route 14 from Albuquerque, also called the Turquoise Trail, leads to Santa Fe (www. turquoisetrail.org). Turquoise, a blue-green precious mineral, is commonly found in jewelry produced by Southwestern tribes, dating back to AD 900. The Cerrillos (little hills) have yielded many treasures. Gold, lead, and turquoise all drew prospectors, leading to the establishment of towns along this path. The discovery of rich coal seams led to an inevitable boom—and subsequent bust. Some towns faded away to nothing while others, like Madrid, were discovered anew by artisans and craftsmen.

The Turquoise Trail ends in Santa Fe (www.santafe.org), one of the country's

Spectacular photo opportunities present themselves continually throughout the Southwest.

Motorcycle Journeys Through North America

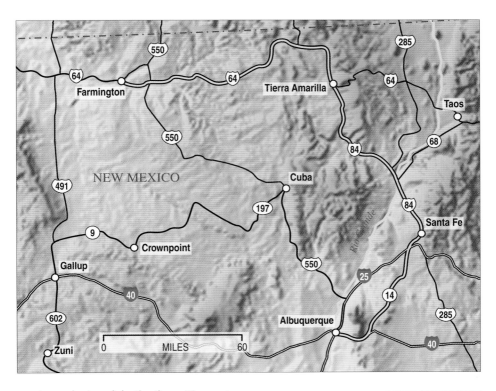

most popular travel destinations. It's easy to understand why. The city boasts the influence of thousands of years of overlapping cultures, with dozens of historic sites and museums, distinctive Pueblo and Mission architectural styles, a vibrant arts scene, and abundant natural beauty. While you're here, museums like the Palace of the Governors (www.palaceofthegovernors.org) and the New Mexico History Museum (www.nmhistorymuseum.org) offer you a glimpse into the combinations and clashes of civilizations that led to today's city. You're also close to the Bandelier National Monument, an ancient home of the Ancestral Pueblo People (www.nps.gov/band) and Los Alamos National Laboratory, one of the most widely recognized research laboratories in the world.

Route Details – 272 miles

➤ From Albuquerque, New Mexico, travel north on Rte 14 to Santa Fe. (55 mi.)

➤ In Santa Fe, follow US 84 north and west to Tierra Amarilla. (93 mi.)

➤ Ride US 64 west to Farmington. (124 mi.)

11

As you venture farther north on US 285 and US 84, the landscape will change slowly from high desert to green plateaus. The intersection with US 550 on the way to Farmington marks a connection point to the Rocky Mountain Way tour at Durango. An overnight stop in Farmington will provide you with ample lodging choices and services.

You can't help but feel awestruck by the formations that define Monument Valley.

Segment Two

Farmington, New Mexico, to Holbrook, Arizona

Route Details – 394 miles

➤ From Farmington, New Mexico, follow US 64 west to Teec Nos Pos, Arizona. (55 mi.)

➤ Ride US 160 north to Four Corners Road. (6 mi.)

➤ Follow Four Corners Road to the monument and return to US 160. (2 mi. round trip)

➤ Return on US 160 south to US 191. (28 mi.)

➤ Follow US 191 north to US 163. (26 mi.)

➤ Turn west and south on US 163 through Monument Valley to US 160. (65 mi.)

➤ Ride US 160 east to US 191. (41 mi.)

➤ Follow US 191 south to Ganado, Arizona, to Hubbell Trading Post. (99 mi.)

➤ Return north on US 191 to Burnside. (5 mi.)

➤ Ride Indian Rte 15 south to Indian Wells. (33 mi.)

➤ Follow Indian Rte 6/77 south to Holbrook. (34 mi.)

This loop makes a turn south into Arizona, stopping first at the Four Corners Monument. Having your picture taken at the spot where Colorado, Utah, New Mexico, and Arizona touch has been a vacation staple and rally location for decades. Survey purists argue that the monument isn't in the exact spot where the four states touch. And? You could be off by ten miles out here and no one would care.

Monument Valley is best approached from east to west(www.navajonationparks.org). The orange-red sandstone buttes that rise above the desolate plains define the west for many people. Scenes of sagebrush flats giving way to craggy cliffs and solitary rock pillars dominated films about the west and created indelible images of solitude that still fire the imagination. This is one of those few places on earth that retain a powerful sense of mysticism and majesty and will make the ride on US 163 through the valley a classic that you'll remember for the rest of your life.

From the intersection of US 163 and US 160 in Kayenta, turn east on US 160, then south on US 191. The land here is flat, bar-

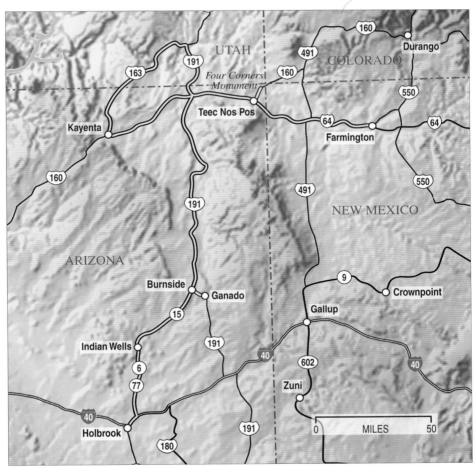

The Wigwam Motel in Holbrook, Arizona is a fun reminder of the lengths motels and restaurants will go to gain a traveler's attention and dollars.

ren, and dry. On occasion a small monolith of rock—a miniature Monument Valley—will appear on the horizon in stark contrast to everything that surrounds it. Distances are deceiving here. A formation that appears to be just ahead can take ten minutes to reach.

Canyon de Chelly is a unique national park, sustaining a living community of Navajo people (www.nps.gov/cach). The park is Navajo Tribal Trust land, managed jointly by the Park Service and the Navajo Nation. The canyon is one of the longest continuously inhabited areas of North America, its distinctive architecture, artifacts, and imagery having enjoyed remarkable preservation. Follow the south rim drive and enjoy the over-

looks. As you survey the green canyon floor, it's fun to think about what it would be like to have been raised here. Imagine having this for a playground!

Contact between advancing pioneers and Indian cultures often concluded with devastating outcomes for the latter. But there were a few confluences that worked to the benefit of everyone. The Hubbell Trading Post is one good example. John Lorenzo Hubbell established this post in 1878 to serve the Navajo Nation, but his role was more than that of a local proprietor. Hubbell demanded consistency and quality in the craftmanship of local rugweaving and silversmithing, a trait that led to wide recog-

This iconic shot of Monument Valley can be found along US 163 a few miles south of Mexican Hat, Utah.

Motorcycle Journeys Through North America

Canyon de Chelly is one of the longest continuously inhabited landscapes in North America and continues to serve as home to members of the Navajo tribe.

nition, higher demand, and better returns for local artisans. Members of the Hubbell family continued to operate the post until 1967 when it was sold to the National Park Service. It is operated today by a non-profit park association that continues the high-quality service established by the Hubbells.

I'm sure you're familiar with the cliche that entering a particular park or building is like "stepping back in time" but often it just doesn't ring true. A building filled with arti-facts is just a museum. The fact that the Hubbell Trading Post continues to serve an unchanging role makes your time-traveling experience feel much more real. The post is filled with hand-dyed and woven rugs and other works, their intricate designs and pat-terns representing important elements of Navajo culture. Often, a weaver sits at a loom working on a piece, completely oblivi-ous to onlookers and focused only on the work at hand.

Return to our loop, follow US 191 north, backtracking to Burnside, then head south and west on Indian Route 15 to Indian Wells. IR 6 joins IR 15 and heads due south to a point just east of Holbrook. Outside the Na-vajo Reservation, you may notice the route number change to Route 77.

Planning Note: Four Corners is a short photo-op stop, but plan to spend some time in your visit to Monument Valley and Canyon de Chelly. Travel services don't line the roads here, so don't do too much improvisation without some idea of where you'll land for the night. If you spend extra time around the valley, the half-way point in Kayenta has a good selection of lodging. The distance be-tween Kayenta and the next cluster of travel services at Chinle is 100 miles.

The Painted Desert and Petrified Forest reveal evidence of an ancient environment that was much wetter and greener than today's hot, dry desert.

Segment Three
Holbrook to Safford, Arizona

Holbrook, Arizona, is located along historic US Route 66, which is known more for its one-of-a-kind tourist traps, restaurants, and motels than for the driving experience. One of its more memorable motels is found here. Don't call it a tee-pee, or a room, or a cabin. It's a wigwam. The Wigwam Motel, built here in 1950 by Chester Lewis, was modeled on the original Wigwam Motel in Horse Cave, Kentucky, and is one of three surviving examples. Lewis licensed the name and

model from the original designer, Frank Redford, under an unusual agreement. Each room, er . . . wigwam, was equipped with a coin-operated radio, ten cents for thirty minutes. Every dime collected was sent to Redford as payment.

The Wigwam Motel remains in the Lewis family and continues to welcome visitors. Classic cars situated around the property make it look as though folks are still rolling in from the Mother Road to bed down for the night. The sign atop the motel asks, "Have you slept in a wigwam lately?" On a trip like this, that's an important question. You might want to put that on your To Do list for this journey.

The Petrified Forest and Painted Desert, just east of town, are the first stop on this segment. At one time, vast forests covered the region, providing habitat for early forms of dinosaurs and crocodile-like creatures called phytosaurs. Periodically, fallen trees and other ground debris would be covered

> ### Route Details – 285 miles
> - ➤ Take I-40 east from Holbrook, Arizona, to Petrified Forest Road. (25 mi.)
> - ➤ Follow Petrified Forest Road south to US 180. (29 mi.)
> - ➤ Ride US 180 east to Saint Johns. (39 mi.)
> - ➤ Follow US 191 (formerly US 666) to Safford. (192 mi.)

11

by volcanic ash rich in silica. Dissolved by groundwater, the silica migrated into the wood, eventually forming quartz crystals that replaced the organic matter. In other words, the trees acted like molds. The varied colors of the trees and the surrounding badlands are from different minerals such as iron oxide and manganese that were depositied along with the silica.

If the visual delights of the painted desert aren't enough to stir you, the ride will. The mid-portion of this route follows the Coronado Trail but you might know it better as the Devil's Highway (formerly US 666). Diabolical is an apt description. With more than 450 switchbacks, many marked 10 mph, the 93-mile stretch between Springerville and Clifton will test you and your bike. By many measures it's the curviest stretch of road in the country. It's also lonely and has no cell phone service, so you won't be able to call for help if you run into (or run over) trouble here. Make sure you plan your day so you are riding this stretch when you are fresh, fully fueled, and have plenty of sunlight left. You definitely don't want to ride this section of road in the dark.

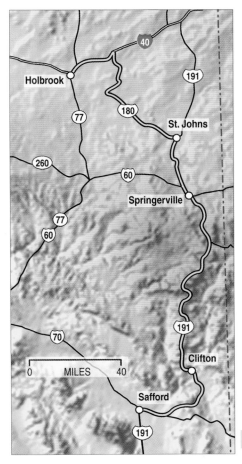

11

Segment Four
Safford, Arizona, to Douglas, New Mexico

The route from Safford to Douglas is a shorter ride than most, allowing plenty of time for visits to Tombstone and Bisbee.

Like the stone towers of Monument Valley, the name "Tombstone" immediately conjures up visions. Through the mind's eye, you instantly see the scene played out in so many westerns—the town marshal squaring off against Squint-Eyed Biff or some other badass in front of the saloon. Only in Tombstone, it really happened. On a frequent basis. Victims who didn't survive were toted up to Boot Hill where the epitaphs engraved on their stones were in part the reason the town survives today. Daily reenactments of famous events like the Gunfight at the O.K.

Poor old George Johnson could have benefitted from modern DNA analysis in criminal investigations. It's likely he's not the only innocent party buried on Boot Hill.

11

Corral draw a steady crowd of tourists. It's cheesy, but that's half the fun.

The other stop along the way is the rejuvenated town of Bisbee. Old Town Bisbee is home to a thriving cultural scene and is noted for its architecture, including Victorian style houses and an elegant art deco courthouse. Bisbee was laid out before the automobile, resulting in a European feel to the streets. Between the gunfights at Tombstone and the cafés, shops, and galleries in Bisbee, it's easy to while away an entire day.

Route Details – 154 miles

➤ From Safford, Arizona, take US 191 south to I-10. (32 mi.)

➤ Follow I-10 west to Rte 80. (48 mi.)

➤ Ride Rte 80 south to Tombstone. (24 mi.)

➤ Continue on Rte 80 south through Bisbee to Douglas. (50 mi.)

11

Bisbee, Arizona, is a thriving art town with many narrow streets and alleyways that are fun to explore on and off the bike.

Segment Five
Douglas, Arizona, to Silver City, New Mexico

Route Details – 293 miles

- ➤ From Douglas, Arizona, ride Rte 80 north to Rodeo, New Mexico. (57 mi.)
- ➤ Follow Rte 9 east to Columbus, New Mexico. (88 mi.)
- ➤ Take Rte 11 north to Deming. (33 mi.)
- ➤ Follow Rte 26 north to Nutt. (29 mi.)
- ➤ Pick up Rte 27 north to Hillsboro. (30 mi.)
- ➤ Follow Rte 152 west to Santa Clara. (49 mi.)
- ➤ Take US 180 west to Silver City. (7 mi.)

The first part of this segment through southern Arizona and New Mexico is a good opportunity to get in touch with yourself. That means the road is flat and straight enough that you can almost navigate with your knees.

The landscape of the Chihuahuan Desert is so bleak and barren it looks empty, but a closer inspection reveals many different types of plants and animals. In dry times, the terrain is dominated by creosote bushes, honey mesquite, and the soaptree yucca. But when the rains come to the desert, wildflowers carpet the land, appearing as if by magic.

Jackrabbits and cottontail rabbits are common here, as are kangaroo rats and other small rodents. Porcupines and skunks

11

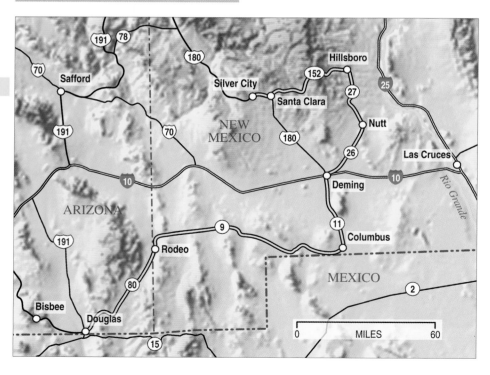

US 180 is a relatively unknown and underrated route through eastern Arizona and western New Mexico. It runs from the Grand Canyon to Hudson Oaks, Texas.

are frequently seen. Prey that's easy to spot and catch draws hawks, buzzards, and coyotes. Snakes? Oh yeah, there be snakes here. In the nearby mountains, you'll find deer, bear, sheep, and even migrating parrots.

The road north of Deming finally starts to provide a little interest as long, wide undulations in the land eventually give rise to small hills. Route 152 from Hillsboro west is a hoot. Staggering through Gallinas Canyon like a drunken cowboy, this road will wear out your arms and shoulders over the next 45 miles.

Silver City is a fine place to rustle up some grub and spread your bedroll out for the night. Folks here have made many improvements to the downtown area that make it a pleasure to visit—a fitting end to a long day's ride.

Road Tip – Planned Stops

When planning a long ride, look for places along your route where you can pause for a day or more every three to five days. Even if you're spending your days out riding in the area, coming back to a familiar location each night provides a mental break that keeps you fresh on a long trip. It also adds a little flexibility in your schedule in case you encounter a bad weather day or mechanical breakdown.

11

Segment Six
Silver City to Gallup, New Mexico

Here's a thought. Rather than going any-where right away, pull out the map and check this out. You're in Silver City, New Mexico, and that puts you not so far from that kickin' piece of US 191 you rode earlier on this loop. You could . . . and this is just a suggestion . . . hang around for an extra day and run the Coronado Trail in reverse. If you run up US 180, you can pick up Route 78 across the border to US 191 near Morenci and run the tastiest part of The Beast up to Springerville (for gas), then return to Silver City. That's a long day's run, about 350 miles, but for another shot at that road, it's probably worth it. Like I said, just a thought.

Continuing on our main loop, head north toward Gallup. Most of US 180 in this seg-ment is a pleasurable ride through the Gila National Forest. It's considerably more green than yesterday's alkali flatlands. This area is a major migratory path for birds, and a popu-lar destination for birdwatchers.

Gallup, New Mexico, is located in the heart of Native American tribal lands with Navajo, Hopi, Zuni, and other tribes residing nearby. Gallup is near Window Rock, the

US 191 leads to some awesome riding, characterized by many as the best road in the southwest.

Route Details – 314 miles

➤ From Silver City, New Mexico, follow US 180 west and north to Rte 12. (92 mi.)

➤ Take Rte 12 east to Datil. (74 mi.)

➤ Pick up US 60 west and ride to Quemado. (44 mi.)

➤ Take Rte 36 north to Zuni. (73 mi.)

➤ Follow Rte 602 into Gallup. (31 mi.)

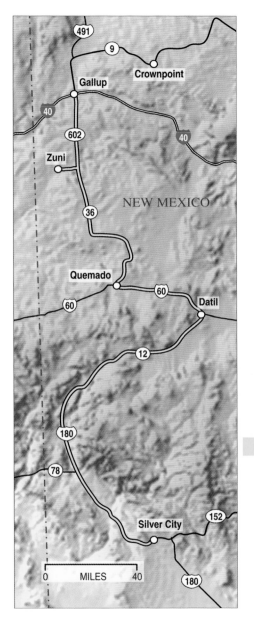

seat of government for the Navajo Nation and the location of the geological formation which lends the town its name.

Window Rock features a statue dedicated to Navajo code talkers who played an important role transmitting messages in World War II. Transmitting instructions and plans by radio had become commonplace, and so too, had enemy eavesdropping. Encryption schemes became a key to operational success, but they were frequently broken. The Japanese attack on Pearl Harbor created an even greater need for secure communication. Following the attack, Philip Johnson, son of a missionary to the Navajos, read about the U.S. Army's use of the Comanche language to transmit instructions. Raised among the Navajo, Johnson was fluent in the language and understood its complex grammatical structure. Recognizing its potential as an unbreakable code, Johnson approached the Marine Corps and, after successful demonstrations, a corp of Navajo speakers was recruited. Navajo code was used during World War II, the Korean War, and until the early years of the Vietnam War. It was never broken by the enemy.

11

Segment Seven
Gallup to Albuquerque, New Mexico

This segment of our trip closes the loop running 211 miles through an arid and largely featureless portion of the state. Whether you choose to ride this segment as described or make a break for Albuquerque directly on Interstate 40 may depend on your bike's affinity for dirt roads. All the roads in this segment are paved; however, the most interesting feature, Chaco Canyon, is found at the end of a 25-mile run on a dirt road to the site of the national park—fine for a dual-sport, but your street bike may not think too kindly of you.

Leave Gallup heading north on US 491. A short ride on divided highway leads to the first turn, Navajo Service Route 9. Follow Route 9 to Crownpoint, turning north on Route 371. This is a short run, just 3 miles. You'll turn east on Route 57, also designated East Route 9, Indian Road 9, Navajo Service Road 9. Take your pick. Stick with Route 9 and you'll be good. After Route 9 leaves Navajo territory, it becomes Route 197.

If you're able to cover the ground, the side trip to Chaco is worth the effort. The southern approach to Chaco begins where Route 57 splits off from Route 9, about 13 miles af-

> **Route Details – 232 (270) miles**
>
> ➤ From Gallup, New Mexico, take US 491 north to Navajo Service Rte 9. (15 mi.)
>
> ➤ Follow NSR 9 east to Crownpoint. (40 mi.)
>
> ➤ North on Rte 371 to East Rte 9. (3 mi.)
>
> ➤ East on Rte 9 to County Road 57. (14 mi.)
>
> ➤ Optional: North on County Road 57 to Chaco Canyon National Park. (38 mi.) round trip
>
> ➤ Continue east on East Rte 9 (becomes Rte 197) to Cuba, New Mexico. (77 mi.)
>
> ➤ Follow US 550 south from Cuba to Albuquerque. (83 mi.)

11

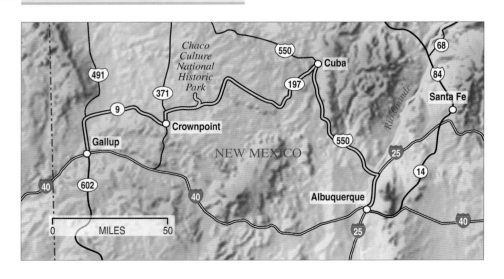

Abandoned settlements can be found throughout the Southwest. You have to wonder what it was like here when it was occupied.

ter the turn onto Route 371. For 400 years, between AD 850 and 1250, Chaco Canyon was a prosperous crossroads serving peoples throughout the Four Corners area. Chaco was a center for trade, ceremony, and government unlike anything before or since. The distinctive architecture of this canyon settlement feature multi-story buildings that re-

quired planning, organized labor, and engineering to build. The Chacoan culture had developed well beyond hunting and gathering to be able to combine architectural design, geometry, landscaping, and astronomical alignments into the creation of a public architecture that amazes visitors a thousand years later.

11

Point your bike toward the Desert Southwest so the next bike that stops here to take a photo will be yours.

Desert Southwest — The Western Loop

*This second loop within our Desert Southwest journey begins and ends in
Phoenix, Arizona, covering some 2,500 miles. We'll visit the grandest of the
national parks: Grand Canyon, Zion, Bryce, Yosemite, and Death Valley. And,
near the end of this loop, we'll move from these monuments of natural beauty
to the land of make-believe: Las Vegas.*

11

< A trail through Sequoia National Park reveals the beauty of this southern Sierra gem.

Phoenix to Grand Canyon Village, Arizona

The stretch from Phoenix to Grand Canyon is only 300 miles, but considering what lies between these two points, it could take you a couple of days to make the trip. There are at least a half dozen places you'll want to visit on the first segment of this loop.

After leaving Phoenix, Arizona, going west on US 60, favorable riding conditions appear quickly as you turn north on Route 89. The stretch above Prescott to Cottonwood on 89 ALT through the Black Hills is world-class rid-ing. Tuzigoot National Monument is the first stop, just off 89 ALT in Clarkdale, Arizona. The Tuzigoot Pueblo was built starting around AD 1000 by the Sinagua, a people who specialized in agriculture and trade. At the height of their civilization, their trade routes spanned hundreds of miles from their central location.

Montezuma's Castle requires a detour away from Route 89 ALT, but you've run the better portion of that for now and the castle is a real spectacle. A short walk leads you to this remarkable 10-story high-rise apartment building set into a cliff. This is one of the best preserved cliff dwellings in the southwest. No one knows why the Sinagua abandoned the structure in the 1400s. It was probably due to a combination of factors. New tribes were entering the area and clashes were becoming more frequent. Any lengthy drought would also have caused the inhabitants here to move to a more sustainable area.

The next stop along the route is Sedona. This area has boomed with tourists in recent years, drawn to the red rocks that surround the area. If you have time for just one thing here, sign up for a Pink Jeep tour (www.pinkjeep.com). The tour is an off-road expedition through the gullys and gulches of Sedona's scenic backcountry, a ride that's almost as much fun as the road from Sedona to Flagstaff.

Route 89 ALT north of Sedona climbs Oak Creek Canyon to Flagstaff, an elevation gain of about 2,500 feet. The landscape around Flagstaff is high desert, often much cooler, and frequently wetter than the lower re-

Route Details – 321 miles

- ➤ From Sun City West, Arizona, follow US 60 west to Wickenburg. (32 mi.)
- ➤ Follow US 93 north to Rte 89. (7 mi.)
- ➤ Ride Rte 89 north to Rte 89 ALT in Prescott. (52 mi.)
- ➤ Follow Rte 89 ALT to Rte 260 in Cottonwood. (46 mi.)
- ➤ Take Rte 260 to I-17. (14 mi.)
- ➤ Go north on I-17 to Exit 289 for Montezuma Castle. (2 mi.)
- ➤ Ride to Montezuma Castle and return to I-17. (5 mi. round trip)
- ➤ Continue north on I-17 to Rte 179. (11 mi.)
- ➤ Ride to Sedona, on Rte 179. (15 mi.)
- ➤ Continue on Rte 89 ALT into Flagstaff. (30 mi.)
- ➤ In Flagstaff, pick up US 89 north to Rte 64. (51 mi.)
- ➤ Follow Rte 64 to Grand Canyon Village. (56 mi.)

11

This prehistoric cliff dwelling, called Montezuma's Castle, was built by the Sinagua peoples 100 years before the Aztec ruler Montezuma was born. But facts don't deter a memorable name.

gions. If you make the climb up 89 ALT in June, don't be surprised if you find snow in Flagstaff!

North of Flagstaff are two approaches to the Grand Canyon. US 180 makes a direct run to the south rim where park facilities and lodging are located. A second approach, continuing north on US 89 to Cameron and then Route 64 west into the Grand Canyon National Park, passes the Sunset Crater, Walnut Canyon, and Wupatki National Monuments. All three are worth a visit, even a brief one. Walnut Canyon and Wupatki feature preserved dwellings and the history of local Indian cultures, while Sunset Crater is the site of a large volcano.

Approaching Grand Canyon from this direction means you'll have the full ride along East Rim Drive to view the canyon. If you plan to stay here, make your reservations well in advance. A year ahead of time is not too early.

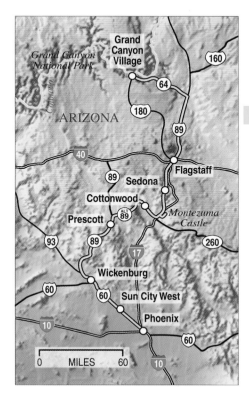

11

The Grand Canyon is on everyone's Bucket List of places to see. And for good reason.

Segment Two

Grand Canyon Village, Arizona, to Springdale, Utah

US 89 ALT passes through Marble Canyon where the sheer high cliffs stand in contrast to the table-flat land you're riding through. The route picks up some curves as you enter Kaibab National Forest.

If you've been to the south rim of the

Grand Canyon before, consider skipping it and paying a visit to the north rim this time. However, it's not exactly right off the road. You'll drive about forty miles south from Jacob Lake on 89 ALT to reach the north rim.

Like Grand Canyon, Bryce, Arches, Canyonlands, and dozens of other parks in the southwest, Zion National Park is situated on the Colorado Plateau, a land formation that was raised as much as 10,000 feet from the height at which it was formed. As rivers worked to return to their original depth, they cut remarkable canyons throughout the region. When you look at the cliffs of Zion, you're seeing nine different periods of geological history and looking back 150 million years in the development of the earth. The rock layers between Bryce Canyon to the east, Zion, and the Grand Canyon to the west form what's known as the Grand Staircase. The bottom layer of rock at Bryce is the top layer of rock at Zion. And the floor of Zion Canyon likewise is the top level of rock at the Grand Canyon.

The flora and fauna found in Zion are remarkably plentiful and diverse. Habitat zones range from the sparse vegetation of moisture-starved desert to lush meadows that follow the Virgin River through this deep slot canyon. The contrast between towering cliffs and green valley floor, all surrounded by a vast desert landscape, enhances Zion's timeless beauty.

The volume of traffic through the narrow canyon prompted park officials to ban private vehicles through the park floor and replace them with propane-powered shuttle buses. This arrangement has dramatically improved the park experience and it's just about as convenient as riding through on your own. You're free to hop off at any stop, explore as you like, and catch the next shuttle.

Route Details – 246 miles

- ➤ From Grand Canyon Village, ride east on Rte 64. (52 mi.)
- ➤ Turn north on US 89 to US 89 ALT at Bitter Springs, Arizona. (59 mi.)
- ➤ Follow US 89 ALT to Kanab, Utah. (93 mi.)
- ➤ Go north on US 89 to Rte 9 at Mt. Carmel Junction. (17 mi.)
- ➤ Ride west on Rte 9 to Zion National Park in Springdale. (25 mi.)

Outside the park in Springdale you'll find plenty of lodging options, but like Grand Canyon, you'd be advised to book ahead. Zion is Utah's most popular park, and once you get away from the immediate area, there aren't many options.

Zion National Park and the surrounding area are filled with great roads.

Utah 12 is quite possibly the most scenic and entertaining road in the Desert Southwest. It connects Bryce Canyon and Capitol Reef, both impressive national parks.

Segment Three
Springdale to Richfield, Utah

Route Details – 345 miles

➤ Ride east on Rte 9 to US 89. (25 mi.)

➤ Continue on US 89 north to Rte 14. (23 mi.)

➤ Follow Rte 14 west to Rte 148. (23 mi.)

➤ Follow Rte 148 north to Rte 143. (8 mi.)

➤ Take Rte 143 east to Panguitch. (32 mi.)

➤ Follow US 89 south to Rte 12. (7 mi.)

➤ Ride Rte 12 east to Rte 63 at Bryce Canyon. (14 mi.)

➤ Follow Rte 63 to Bryce Canyon and return to Rte 12. (8 mi. round trip)

➤ Continue on Rte 12 to Torrey. (110 mi.)

➤ Take Rte 24 to Capitol Reef Visitor Center in Fruita. (11 mi.)

➤ Continue on Rte 24 west to Rte 119. (74 mi.)

➤ Follow Rte 119 west to Richfield. (10 mi.)

Now that you've gotten warmed up with Grand Canyon and Zion, you'll appreciate the diversity of the next set of parks that are found along this segment of the tour. By the time you're done, you'll have a greater appreciation for the wonders that have been preserved by our national park system. On this segment you'll visit Cedar Breaks, Bryce Canyon, and Capitol Reef National Parks.

Retrace your steps briefly on route 9 and turn north again on US 89. There is a sequence of roads here that will take you by all three parks and provide an unforgettable ride in the process. Off 89, turn west on Route 14 to Route 148, following signs for Cedar Breaks. Following your visit to the park, turn east on Route 143, south on US 89 at Panguitch, then east on Route 12 to Bryce. Route 12 covers some of the most rugged portions of the Colorado Plateau and leads to Route 24. Turn east to visit Capitol Reef, then head west on Route 24 when you're ready to move to the next part.

The distinctive features of Bryce Canyon are the hoodoos—columns of varying widths that are clustered throughout the park's natural amphitheaters. Formed by the interaction of erosion and freeze-thaw cycles of water, hoodoos consist of soft sedimentary rock topped by a harder, more erosion-resistant stone. The mineral in the different layers of rock give the hoodoos their characteristic bands of different colors and widths and totem-pole shape. These otherworldly pinnacles, up to 200 feet high, with their red, white, and orange colors create a visual feast for the eyes.

To the north and east, Capitol Reef is a 100-mile-long wrinkle in the earth's crust. The land here is described as a waterpocket fold, which was formed in sandstone layers as they were eroded by water, resulting in colorful cliffs, spires, domes, monoliths, canyons, and even arches. You might say that Capitol Reef is a "greatest hits" collection of the formations you'll see in all the other parks. Except those crazy hoodoos.

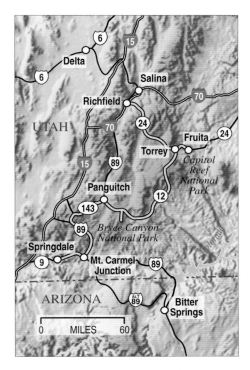

It tickles the imagination to consider what combination of geology, composition, and erosion has contributed to the unique hoodoo formations in Bryce Canyon.

11

Segment Four
Richfield, Utah, to Bishop, California

If civilization came to an end while you were on this portion of the journey, you wouldn't know about it until you got to Bishop. Maybe you wouldn't care. It's stark, serene, and largely empty of people.

US Route 50 has developed a reputation as the loneliest road in America. Ironically, the subsequent rush of folks eager to cross the "loneliest road" has caused the title to shift to US 6. You'll want to have a plan when you cross this section of road. It ain't for princesses or girlie-men.

Cedar Breaks displays formations similar to Bryce Canyon but in a less developed form.

US Route 50 in Nevada is referred to as the Loneliest Road in America. Ironically, this title has increased traffic along the route.

First, 526 miles is a long slog between start and stop points. I realize this. However, some folks just like to burn through the slabs. So, for them, allowing one day between Richfield and Bishop makes sense. On the other hand, this segment doesn't have to be done all at once. Ely, Nevada, is located near the halfway point on this leg at 243 miles from Richfield. Ely is the only town of any consequence you'll encounter for a long, long time. Pass this by and you're making the commitment to cross the state. Think about that if you get a late start.

Gas is another issue. A serious one. Top off in Hinckley, Utah, before you launch onto US 6. It's 146 miles to Ely from this point. From Ely, it's another 164 miles to the next reliable gas stop in Tonopah, Nevada. Maybe

Route Details – 526 miles

➤ From Richfield, Utah, follow Rte 118 north to Rte 24. (10 mi.)

➤ Continue on Rte 24 to Salina. (9 mi.)

➤ Follow US 50 west to Delta, Utah. (70 mi.)

➤ Take US 6/50 west to Ely, Nevada (gas up or top off). (153 mi.)

➤ Continue on US 6 west to Bishop, California. (284 mi.)

11

you'll get lucky and find something in between, but it isn't guaranteed. You'll find services more frequently on the road to Alaska than along this part of Route 6.

The entrance to Yosemite is so grand, it feels like you've entered a valley that has been lost in time.

Segment Five

Bishop to Yosemite, California

Before you leave Bishop for Yosemite Park, check the condition of Tioga Pass on Route 120. Here's what the Park Service says about Route 120: "Clearing of Tioga Pass begins on or about April 15 of each year and usually takes between one to two months." There's a good chance you won't be riding this road until mid-June. It's worth the wait.

For the endurance you had to muster to cross Nevada, Route 120 and many of the roads to follow are an awesome payback.

Top the gas tank off at Lee Vining before you turn west on Route 120. It's 140 miles from Bishop to Yosemite's main lodge and there is no gas available in the park. Lee Vining is the halfway point to the park, so

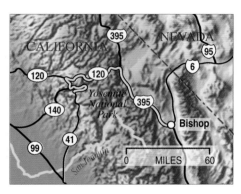

Route Details – 148 miles

➤ From Bishop, California, take US 395 north to Rte 120. (64 mi.)

➤ Ride Rte 120 west to Rte 41, Big Oak Road. (60 mi.)

➤ Follow Rte 41 into Yosemite National Park. (10 mi.)

➤ Circle Rte 140 through the Yosemite Valley. (14 mi. round trip)

Get to Tioga Pass Road too early and you'll need something other than a motorcycle to cross it.

you'll have plenty to get in, visit the park, and leave.

Yosemite is one of the most photographed and written-about places on earth. The attention is well deserved. Arriving at the entrance to Yosemite is a memorable moment, like the first time you peer over the rim at the Grand Canyon. When you enter Yosemite through Big Oak Tunnel, you feel like you've discovered that secret portal that transports you to a planet lost in time. You'll find a thriving, fertile valley surrounded by towering granite cliffs, elegant waterfalls,

and giant sequoias. Get off the bike and spend some time on a ranger-led hike through some of the park's vast 1,900 square miles that'll take you beyond the two or three square miles that everyone sees.

Like Grand Canyon and Zion, make a plan that will allow you to secure lodging here in advance if you plan to stay at facilities in the park. There are more options here outside the park than others if you are making plans on the fly. On Route 41 south of the park, Yosemite West has a cluster of motels, as does Fish Camp.

11

Ever heard of Kings Canyon? This beautiful park contains inspiring scenery, but exists in the shadow of its better-known neighbor to the north, Yosemite.

Segment Six

Yosemite to Mojave, California

With a little advanced routing in your GPS program, you can pick your way around the Fresno area with a quicker series of back roads than I describe here. This route beyond Fresno requires a little research to follow exactly, but it will put you on some of the finest southern California canyon roads.

The roads in this segment pass by Kings Canyon and Sequoia National Parks. Considering their proximity to Yosemite, it's no surprise these parks experience a "visitor shadow" created by the popularity of their northern neighbor. Kings Canton ranked 101st while Sequoia placed 75th on the list

of annual visitors. (I know you're wondering . . . Aniakchak National Monument on the Alaskan Peninsula, and accessible only by air, is the least visited park facility, logging 14 visitors in 2009. The Blue Ridge Parkway is highest with almost 16 million visitors.)

One relatively easy route to Mojave (described here) follows Old Stage Road, Jack Ranch, and Route 155 to Lake Isabella. From here, the run south on Route 438, known locally as the Bodfish-Caliente Road, is a blast. This puts you on Route 58, not too far from Mojave, and ready for a run across Death Valley.

Route Details – 379 miles

➤ Depart Yosemite on Rte 41 south to Fresno, California. (91 mi.)

➤ Follow Rte 180 east to Rte 198. (52 mi.)

➤ Take Rte 198 south to Exeter. (73 mi.)

➤ Follow Rte 65 south to Ducor. (31 mi.)

➤ Take Avenue 56 to Fountain Springs. (7 mi.)

➤ Take Old Stage Road to Jack Ranch Road. (17 mi.)

➤ Follow Jack Ranch Road to Rte 155. (6 mi.)

➤ Follow Rte 155 east to Lake Isabella Boulevard. (28 mi.)

➤ Ride south on Lake Isabella Boulevard (becomes County Rte 483, Bodfish-Caliente Road) to Rte 58 at Caliente. (38 mi.)

➤ Ride Rte 58 east to Mojave. (36 mi.)

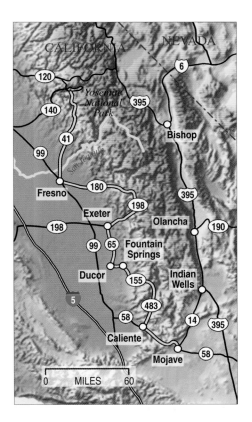

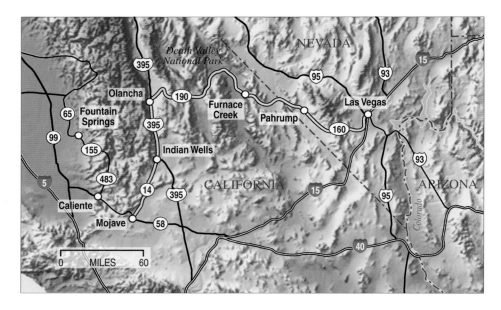

Segment Seven
Mojave, California, to Las Vegas, Nevada

This segment marks a decision point in this loop, depending on the time of year you're here. If you're riding through the southwest between fall and spring, the road through Death Valley will be hot but manageable. Summer is a different matter. With air tem-peratures regularly reaching 120 degrees and ground temperatures near 200, Death Valley is no place to ride. You're better off making a direct run back to Phoenix by way of Routes like 247, 62, 72 and US 60.

Death Valley's heat is created by its unique

A riding group poses for a shot in Death Valley. Judging by their clothing, it must be the dead of winter.

11

The mountains surrounding Death Valley create a thermal "cap" that regularly elevates temperatures on the valley floor to well above 120 degrees.

shape and location. In many ways, it's like a natural convection oven. The valley is located east of four mountain ranges so it receives very little rainfall. On average, Death Valley receives less than two inches of rain per year, far less than most desert areas. In some years only trace amounts or no rain at all have been recorded. The lack of moisture and clear skies mean the sun's rays shine brighter and hotter here than other places. Heat is trapped in this basin, 282 feet below sea level, and the heated air is recirculated by the mountain ranges on each side.

Despite the forbidding climate, the basin has a long history of human activity and settlement that continues today. Mining in the valley has experienced numerous boom-and-bust cycles, with the last borax mine closing in 2005. Stop by the Furnace Creek Visitor Center to learn about colorful characters like Death Valley Scotty, who claimed his nearby castle was built with gold from his Death Valley mine. Ride to Dante's View for a perspective more than 5,000 feet above the basin floor.

The remainder of this ride leads to Las Vegas, an entertaining town whether you are a player, a partyer, or just enjoy people-watching. If you're one of the latter, you've struck the motherlode here.

Route Details – 311 miles

➤ From Mojave, California, follow Rte 14 north to Indian Wells. (54 mi.)

➤ Follow US 395 north to Olancha. (44 mi.)

➤ Ride Rte 190 east to Furnace Creek, California. (99 mi.)

➤ Continue on Rte 190 (becomes Ash Meadows Road in Nevada) to Pahrump, Nevada. (54 mi.)

➤ Take Rte 160 south to Las Vegas. (60 mi.)

11

Many people feel the Red Rocks of Sedona possess a mystical, spiritual quality. The beauty of contrasting colors in the sky, rock, and trees may have something to do with that.

Segment Eight
Las Vegas, Nevada, to Phoenix, Arizona

The last segment of this tour follows a simple route passing by the Hoover Dam on the return to Phoenix. A five-year construction project has been completed, rerouting US 93 over a 2,000-foot bridge about one-third mile from the dam. This eases what had become a burdensome trip. With Route 93 running over the dam, heightened security restrictions meant most vehicles were searched before they were allowed to pass, creating monumental backups. Traffic now bypasses the dam over the new Colorado River Bridge. Watch for a turnoff to lead you down the old section to the visitor center.

The Colorado River had long been eyed as a potential source of hydroelectric power and irrigation waters; the project to construct a concrete dam took place here during the Great Depression between 1931 and 1936. It was the largest project of its kind ever attempted, and in some cases new construction techniques had to be developed. The result was a structure considered one of the crowning engineering achievements of

The remnants of a broken dream, the buildings of Santas Claus slowly decay along US 93 in northwestern Arizona.

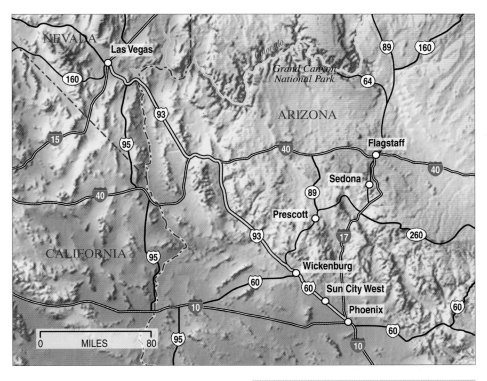

the 20th century. Standing more than 700 feet from base to crest, the gravity-arch structure weighing 6.6 million tons holds back the 247 square-mile reservoir called Lake Mead. Hydroelectric production at the dam generates about 4 billion kilowatt-hours of power each year, enough to serve 1.3 million people. A guided tour will give you an insider's look at this engineering marvel.

This loop route and its companion loop in the eastern Southwest are filled with examples of lost dreams, folks who came west to pursue riches to be extracted from the ground, or the revenues that could be extracted from the pockets of vacationers. Some towns have been able to reinvent themselves. Other towns were caught in a downward spiral with disappointment leading to decline, then abandonment. Santa Claus, Arizona, is an interesting example of

Route Details – 311 miles

➤ Depart Las Vegas, Nevada, on US 93 south to Wickenburg, Arizona. (283 mi.)

➤ Follow US 60 east to Sun City West, Arizona. (28 mi.)

11

the latter, originally conceived in the 1930s and built in 1937 by Nina Talbot, a local real estate agent who sought to use a Santa theme to attract interest in this deserted, and some would say god-forsaken, parcel of arid, infertile land. Although it didn't succeed in helping sell the local real estate, the small town did establish itself as a tourist attraction for a couple of decades. The last operating businesses in town were closed by 1995 and today it has become another member of the Highway of Broken Dreams.

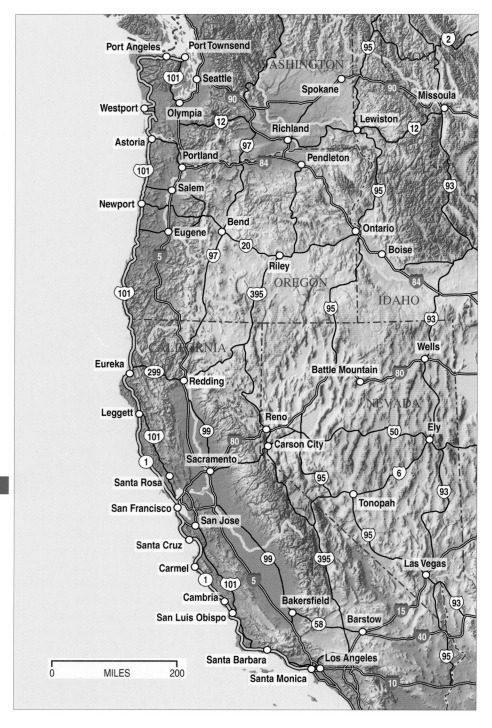

Motorcycle Journeys Through North America

12 COASTAL CRUISE

This coastal ride follows the course of US 101 and California's Highway 1 for more than 1,500 miles along the Pacific highlands and shoreline. Beginning in the seaside town of Port Townsend, Washington, your ride will take you from the lush, evergreen interior of the Olympic Peninsula along the rugged Washington and Oregon coast, through northern California to San Francisco. World-class riding continues on the Pacific Coast Highway around Big Sur, ending near the most recognizable landmarks in southern California: Santa Monica, Beverly Hills, and Hollywood. This tour is designed to be ridden over a six-day period, the better to explore the occasional side road, a chance to stand in the surf, watch seals sun themselves on the rocks, or linger at a seaside café.

Few roads in the world are known as well as the duo of US Route 101 and California's Pacific Coast Highway. And for just reasons. Mile for mile there is no other tour on the North American continent that covers as much breathtaking coastline, laced with entertaining, fun-to-ride roads.

But while that shoreline remains the fixture of this tour, everything else shines around it. Beginning in scenic Puget Sound,

you'll round the Olympic Peninsula of Washington state, a region of just a few hundred miles that nonetheless boasts some of the greatest geographic and climatic diversity on the continent: a rocky coastline dotted with driftwood that gives way to verdant rainforest, high alpine meadows, and treeless, snow-capped summits. Towns built on fishing and timber blend with affluent coastal enclaves and back again. Beaches alternate

The Pacific Coast Highway offers its most dramatic displays through Big Sur, an area where the Santa Lucia mountains rise abruptly from the coastline.

The Monterey Aquarium houses the Kelp Tank, a one-of-a-kind display. A wave machine circulates raw seawater, introducing nutrients into the water that California Giant Kelp require to thrive.

rolling across the iconic Golden Gate Bridge into the City by the Bay, you can easily spend days enjoying San Francisco's diverse lifestyle in a hundred different ways: sampling dim sum from steam carts in the largest Chinatown outside of Asia; feeling the wind in your face, not from a bike, but from the side of a cable car flying down Market Street; or surveying the famous city skyline from the top of Coit Tower or a boat on the bay.

between seals and sunbathers. Silent, ancient redwoods that mark meaningful time in hundred-year spans stand as ageless coastal sentinels taking scant notice of your passage.

San Francisco is a destination unto itself, anchoring the middle of this journey. After

What lies farther south captures the essence of the California experience: white sands and high surf, the soaring cliffs of Big Sur, and the tony seaside escapes of the rich, famous and infamous, like Monterey, Carmel, and San Luis Obispo. Beach life here has

The closer you look at this picture, the more road and curves you see. That's what makes the Pacific Coast Highway part of an unforgettable motorcycle journey.

a distinctly different feel than other sunny climes. The surfer-cruiser lifestyle made famous through movies and music remains a staple of daily life. Combine that laid-back attitude with a well-known west coast predilection for new age philosophies, trend-setting cuisine and fashion, a splash of celebrity, and a dash of eccentricity, and you've got a recipe for some people-watching that will rival the riding.

With temperatures moderated by the Pacific Ocean, you can comfortably follow this route at the height of summer. While this corresponds to the driest time of the year for the coast, outfitting for this trip should include a good set of raingear. You'll call on it less frequently in the second half of your ride as you leave the rain-soaked northwest and enter the drier California climate. Fog, however, will be ever present. And that can make for a cool ride.

Southern California rock band The Eagles captured the essence of life here as they sang about a "peaceful, easy feeling." In a quiet moment, as you reflect on your ride, you'll probably find yourself using those exact same words to describe your trip along America's Pacific coast.

A ride down the West Coast will take you through the Avenue of Giants, one of the best ways to appreciate the true scale of California's unique redwoods.

Connections

This route either shares roads with or runs near three other tours in this book. US 101 and Rte 20 in Washington state make up the early part of the Evergreens and Canyons tour, while US 101 connects Rte 299 and Rte 36, two main routes in the Bigfoot Country tour.

12

What road trip, by bike or by car, would be complete without a good old drive-through-the-Redwood photo?

Segment One
Port Townsend to Westport, Washington

Begin your coastal tour by following Route 20 for a short distance out of Port Townsend to Discovery Bay. You'll make the right turn to follow US 101 north, then west, then south around the Olympic Peninsula.

The Olympic Peninsula is marked by three distinct regions: the rocky Pacific coastline, a rugged interior filled with glaciated mountains, and a rare temperate rainforest. Park the bike and take a little time in each region to enjoy the diversity of flora and fauna. Out of Port Angeles, make a detour on Hurricane Ridge Road to reach the visitor center for stunning views of the Olympic range.

As you wend your way around the peninsula, you'll want to have your raingear handy. This area is the wettest in the continental United States, receiving more than 150 inches of rain per year. Luckily, the driest time coincides with the summer riding season, but you'll still encounter many days of light precipitation and fog.

A town like Forks, Washington (www.forkswa.com), located at the mid-point of the peninsula, doesn't usually trip your attention radar. It looks like almost any other small town you'd encounter on your journey through Washington state's evergreen forests. That all changed in 2005 when Stephanie Meyer, a first-time author, published a book in 2005 entitled *Twilight*. The success of the books and movies about teen vam-

Residents in Aberdeen, Washington, recognize their association with grunge music pioneer Kurt Cobain through a memorial park and statue near a bridge where Cobain once hung out.

12

US 101 through old growth forest in the Olympic Peninsula is beautiful even in the rain. Have good raingear for your trip through the Pacific Northwest.

pires and romance, set in Forks, Washington, brought instant attention to this declining logging town.

A run of about 25 miles out of Forks brings you to the Pacific coast. You'll smell the salt air and see fog rolling up and over the roadway well before you catch a glimpse of water through dense undergrowth. But you know it's there, making it all the more rewarding when you catch a glimpse of the first break in the trees and a pullover where you can gather your first documented evidence. Pull into Ruby Beach for a dramatic view of islets just off a beach filled with tens of thousands of driftwood logs, remnants of the region's era of timber harvesting.

Toward the end of this portion of the route, you'll roll through Aberdeen, Washington, known more widely as the birthplace and hometown of Kurt Cobain. Cobain, along with Krist Novoselic, founded the grunge rock band Nirvana in Aberdeen in 1985 and quickly became identified with the Seattle music scene. The band rocketed to fame, a reward which perhaps Cobain wasn't prepared to handle. Cobain died of a self-inflicted gunshot wound just nine years later. After years with no formal recognition, dedicated Nirvana fans have coaxed the town into honoring its most famous son with signage and, most recently, the dedication of a small park near one of Cobain's favorite hangouts, featuring an 8.5-foot-tall guitar.

The last part of the run takes you down Route 105 to Westport, a small town of just a couple thousand folks along Grays Harbor. Westport is home to a large commercial fishing fleet but it also has enough travel amenities to make it a good overnight stopping point. A small aquarium at the dock is stocked with local fish and the boardwalk is a popular area for afternoon walks and a fresh seafood meal.

12

Route Details – 231 miles

➤ From Port Townsend, ride west on US 101 to Forks, Washington. (102 mi.)

➤ Continue south on US 101 to Aberdeen. (109 mi.)

➤ Ride west on Rte 105 to Westport. (20 mi.)

Segment Two
Westport, Washington, to Newport, Oregon

From Westport, make the trek to US 101 by Route 105 heading south to Raymond. If you have a few minutes to spare, there's a head-scratching little stop just a bit off the beaten path. It's not every day you get to check out the final resting place of a Pickled Pioneer. Let me explain.

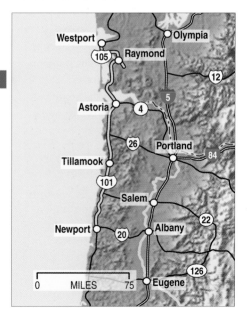

A lonely hill along Washington Route 6 marks New Canaan, though that name has been lost with the passage of time. In 1855, this was the new promised land as envisioned by Dr. William Keil, leader of a Missouri religious community known as the Bethelites. Dr. Keil and his son Willie made plans to assemble a wagon train and transport their entire community to the Great American West. Alas, four days before the trip's beginning, Willie succumbed to malaria.

Determined to have his son fulfill the dream of the journey, Keil built a lead-lined coffin and after placing his son in it, filled the coffin with Golden Rule whiskey (Unofficial motto: "When embalming fluid ain't handy, it'll do."). Literally sauced, Willie's casket was hauled west with the rest of the group. Word of this leapt ahead of the wagon train. Reports say that hostile Indian groups would allow the group to pass unharmed in exchange for a peek at pickled Willie.

When the group reached the area, Willie was laid to rest on the hill here in New Canaan. As it turned out, the settlers found the area a bit damp for their taste, so they relocated to Oregon and were responsible for founding the town of Aurora. Willie stayed behind. The weather didn't bother him a bit.

Returning to US 101 in Raymond, turn south following the road as it weaves between mountains, marshes, meadows, and waterside. The route crosses into Oregon through the Lewis and Clark National Historic Park, marking the point where the intrepid explorers found the West Coast. Unable to find a Starbucks, a member of the explorer's party dubbed the area Cape Disappointment. Or, he could have been dismayed that no boats were standing by in the harbor to whisk them back to civilization. Accounts vary in the retelling.

A pretty trip down US 101 awaits as you make your way south of Astoria, riding along the Oregon coast. Here, the road hews closely to the coast, frequently offering glimpses of the ocean along with the occasional pullout or parking lot. Route 101 bends around Tillamook State Forest before drawing away from the water to pass through Tillamook. While you're here, stop by the famous Tillamook Cheese Factory for

Route Details – 236 miles

➤ Out of Westport, Washington, follow Rte 105 south to Raymond, Washington. (33 mi.)

➤ Follow US 101 south to Rte 6. (1 mi.)

➤ Ride south on Rte 6 to Willie Kiels site marker and return. (11 mi. round trip)

➤ Continue on US 101 south to Newport, Oregon. (191 mi.)

a breather. Sample the cheese (free) and check out the cheesemaking process (also free). They make 167,000 pounds of the stuff every day, so try all you want. They'll make more. (www.tillamook.com)

Seafood lovers will enjoy a stopover in Newport, Oregon, home to the succulent Yaquina Bay oyster. Newport is also regarded as the Dungeness crab capital, too. The Yaquina Head Lighthouse just north of town is the tallest on the Oregon coast (93 feet) (www.yaquinalights.org). Its vantage point offers stunning views of the Oregon coast and the town of Newport below.

12

California may be a populous state, but there are many miles of open, freewheeling highway to cruise.

Segment Three
Newport, Oregon, to Eureka, California

Arguably the most scenic segment of US 101 lies between Newport and Eureka. Here Route 101 runs right to the edge of the coast, providing you with many unobstructed views of the Pacific Ocean. And the riding ain't half bad either! Expect to run through patches of fog so dense you can barely make out your front fender. A mile or two later, you'll leave the fog curtain and enter brilliant sunshine.

The Pacific coast is renowned for its remaining stands of virgin redwoods. You can't help but feel awestruck by the size and majesty of these giant works of nature. Living an average of 1,200 to 1,800 years, coastal redwoods are the largest living trees on earth, with many reaching well over 350 feet. That's the equivalent of a 32-story building.

Although redwoods can grow in other climates, it is only here along the coast that they can grow to such amazing heights. Un-

Route Details – 314 miles

➤ From Newport, Oregon, follow US 101 south to Eureka, California. (314 mi.)

This beautiful historic home is in downtown Eureka, California

der ordinary circumstances, trees reach their maximum height based on how effectively they can pump moisture to the top of the tree. A redwood can absorb water from the constant fog through its needles, a strategy that allows it to grow higher here than anywhere else.

Standing at the base of a redwood, it's hard to really appreciate how tall these trees are. That's what makes the skylift and the Trees of Mystery a fun stop (www.treesofmystery.net). It's a tourist trap, for sure. There's a token free museum, a gift shop filled with gewgaws and trinkets that your nieces and nephews, kids, and grandkids will love. The real reason for stopping is the one-third mile lift ride that rises 571 feet to a point that gives you an unobstructed view of the landscape and the majestic redwoods that soar above everything else.

The stopover for this segment is Eureka. Be sure to venture through Eureka's old town, filled with Victorian homes including the Carson Mansion, one of the world's most ornate residences and certainly the most photographed feature in town.

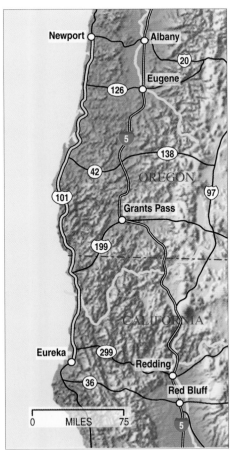

12

Segment Four
Eureka to San Francisco, California

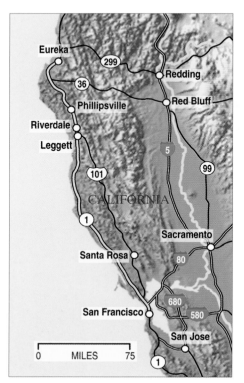

On your way down 101, detour through the Avenue of the Giants on SR 254, a road that runs parallel to 101 for about thirty miles (avenueofthegiants.net). You'll enjoy an up-close look at these remarkable specimens and find plenty of photo ops and short hikes. Rockefeller Forest encompasses 10,000 acres of old-growth redwoods, including the Champion Coast Redwood at 370 feet.

By the time you get to Leggett, you'll be departing US 101 to take up Highway 1 south. Here it's referred to as the Shoreline Highway; later it takes on the familiar moniker of the Pacific Coast Highway. It might take longer than a day's ride to cover this stretch, not because of traffic but just because there are so many enticing small towns, boardwalks, scenic vistas, parks, and other features to take in.

Consider staying over at San Francisco, the end point for this segment, for a day or two

Redwoods National Park also includes dozens of miles of unspoiled, undeveloped coastline.

12

Big Sur is a prominent feature along the Pacific Coast Highway. Pictured here is the famous Bixby Bridge.

to enjoy a small sampling of what this world destination has to offer. If this is your first time in The City by the Bay, here's a short list of ideas:

- Visit Fisherman's Wharf and Ghirardelli Square—two of the most popular downtown attractions.
- Grab a boat to Alcatraz—and make sure to get your tickets in advance.
- Ride the cable cars—they're known as the city's rolling landmark and they're the best way to move around downtown
- Take the curves on Lombard Street—just make sure you account for the steep decline as you manage the brakes.

Route Details – 311 miles

- ➤ From Eureka follow US 101 south to Rte 254, Avenue of the Giants. (33 mi.)
- ➤ Go south on Rte 254 to US 101 at Phillipsville. (28 mi.)
- ➤ Take US 101 south to Riverdale. (27 mi.)
- ➤ Follow Rte 1 south to San Francisco. (223 mi.)

12

- Walk the Golden Gate Bridge—A fun afternoon activity on what is probably the world's most recognizable bridge.

Cliff House has existed here in several different forms since 1863. Here it is pictured in its mid-1950s form on a postcard.

Segment Five
San Francisco to Cambria, California

Many credit Southern California as the place where America's love affair with cars took root. One reason for that might be California's Highway 1. It's more than just a scenic drive. The Pacific Coast Highway connects many of the elements that have made famous the West Coast lifestyle.

When you think of Highway 1, a dozen images come to mind all at once: cruising

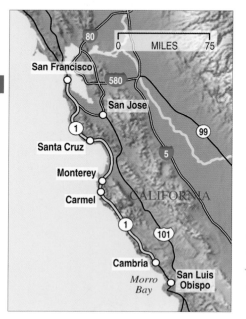

along a twisty, sunlit ribbon of asphalt that clings tenuously to a craggy coastline, revealing one dramatic view after another. Waves pounding the rocks a hundred feet below as you hit one perfect apex after another. Small beachside towns filled with art studios, surf shops, and hole-in-the-wall eateries with menu entries you've never heard of, like arugula. (Okay, you've heard of it. But have you eaten it? It's not bad, actually.) And that perfect temperature. Day after day, the thermometer points to "Just Right for a Ride."

Departing San Francisco, the road flirts with the coast on and off to San Gregorio Beach where it opens into a limitless view of ocean and sky to the right, and to the left, rounded hills of muted browns and greens.

Thousands of acres of state forest, agricultural zones, and preserves provide a buffer from encroaching urbanization of California's cities along Highway 1 in all but a few areas. Traffic varies from non-existent to moderate excepting a stretch between Santa Cruz and Monterey where Route 1 becomes heavily trafficked. The road leads into Monterey, a popular destination for travelers of all modes.

Monterey is a city of firsts in California

(www.monterey.org), originally serving as the capital of the territory, known as Alta California when it was possessed by Spain and later, by Mexico. The region included all the territory that today we call California, Nevada, Arizona, Utah, along with parts of Colorado and Wyoming. As the first port of entry for overseas goods in California, Monterey became a center of commerce.

Most people recognize Monterey for its role as a commercial fishing and canning center, immortalized in the works of John Steinbeck. Pacific fisheries collapsed in the 1950s leading to the demise of the industry and a slow transition to tourism. And that's where we find Monterey today. Fisherman's Wharf and Cannery Row are popular destinations. The Monterey Bay Aquarium is built on the site of a former sardine cannery. Its signature displays are two massive tanks that feature Pacific marine and aquatic life (www.montereybayaquarium.org).

Once you ride through Monterey and make it south of Carmel, the road to Cambria is everything you could wish for in a memorable motorcycle ride. Rugged mountains sheltered this part of the coast from early development, so Highway 1 connects

Route Details – 236 miles

➤ Follow Rte 1 (Pacific Coast Highway) south to Cambria, California. (236 mi.)

to no major commercial centers for the next hundred miles. You'll experience almost nothing but road, sea, and sky, in innumerable twisted, winding combinations.

Point Sur is a notable stop along the way. Built in the late 1800s, this lighthouse is open to the public with tours on Wednesdays and weekends. From the point, you can enjoy dramatic views of the coastal highway. A little farther south is the Bixby Canyon Bridge, another historic stop along the highway. Built in 1932, the bridge opened travel to the Big Sur area and has since enjoyed frequent appearances in car commercials, television, and movies.

Hold up for the day in Cambria. Regarded by many as one of California's prettiest towns, Cambria is framed by towering pines and shimmering seas. Downtown is filled with locally owned stores, and restaurants run the gamut: homestyle cooking, seafood, Mexican, Californian, fine dining—you name it.

12

The iconic Golden Gate Bridge looks even prettier at night.

The Pacific Coast Highway near Point Mugu, California. Roads like the PCH and US 101 are national treasures for motorcyclists as much as national parks.

Segment Six
Cambria to Santa Monica, California

America was founded as an egalitarian society, meaning that we regarded one another as equals, a sentiment you'll find in most of the riding community. It's not what you ride,

it's *that* you ride, as the saying goes. There are a few exceptions though, a fact you'll realize as you make the next stop on our tour.

In 1919, publishing magnate William Randolph Hearst wrote to San Francisco architect Julia Morgan to request help in designing "a little something" for his 250,000-acre estate situated on the western shoulders of the Santa Lucia Mountains near San Simeon, just north of Cambria on Route 1. The collaboration that began to build comfortable camping accommodations resulted

> ### Route Details – 233 miles
>
> ➤ Continue on Rte 1 (Pacific Coast Highway) south to Santa Monica. (233 mi.)

in an estate with 165 rooms and 127 acres of gardens, terraces, pools, and walkways.

The level of opulence is staggering. Anything you look at is the finest of the fine. From the scale of the buildings to the intricate details in the finish, it is hard to imagine a residence of such grandeur—or the type of person who might inhabit it. As George Orwell said, "All animals are equal but some animals are more equal than others."

Portions of the castle remained unfinished, as Hearst's failing health finally diminished his interest in the project. In 1957 the Hearst Corporation donated the grand estate to the state of California to preserve and open to the public. Several different tours of the estate are offered, some designed to showcase the grandeur and spectacle of the main building, others providing a more intimate look at Hearst's private quarters. You can easily spend a day here, so take a day off from riding to explore and enjoy the fruits of Hearst's incredible appetite for the stupendous.

From Cambria south, Highway 1 begins to venture into the more highly developed areas of southern California. The route joins

The San Ysidro post office is the rally point for the most southwestern point in the Four Corners Rally.

with US 101 in San Luis Obispo, and then separates again a dozen miles later at Pismo Beach. Stair-stepping down the coast, Highway 1 runs through Lompoc, a place you'll remember if you travel this way during the height of the summer season.

Thanks to the moderating influences of the ocean, Lompoc (pronounced LOM-poke), enjoys a consistent climate year-round. This makes it well suited for growing flowers for cutting and for seed. Travel through here between early June and mid-August and you'll

Perhaps your trans-continental journey will begin on the West Coast. These riders are collecting a bit of water from the Pacific to take to the Atlantic.

12

find fields awash in every color you can imagine, as the flowers reach their peak. A large portion of Lompoc's flower valley is located directly along Highway 1.

The last stretch of Highway 1 on this tour rejoins US 101 again at Las Cruces for a run along the coast into the Los Angeles metro area. Surf's up along this section of the California coast, home to landmarks like Marina del Ray, Venice Beach, the Santa Monica Boardwalk, and dozens more well-known coastal communities. While you're here in the L.A. area, you're in a good position to visit favorites like Hollywood or cruise around Beverly Hills.

A local favorite road is the Angeles Crest Highway. Designated Route 2 on your map, this road heads approximately northeast out of the greater L.A. area through the San Gabriel Wilderness ending near I-15 at Cajon

Junction. If you've ever read a motorcycle test ride in a national glossy bike magazine, chances are it was tested on the Angeles Crest. But before you go, check to make sure it's open (www.dot.ca.gov/cgi-bin/roads. cgi). Angeles Crest is beautiful, but fragile. It

The Santa Monica Pier was constructed in 1909 and later evolved into the classic amusement park and recreation area it is today. The pier is managed by a non-profit group dedicated to protecting and maintaining it for all who are or remain young at heart.

was built across some of the most unstable land in the world. The road is routinely closed for months at a time for repairs due to mud slides, forest fires, quake damage—you name it.

Before you head off on the next part of your journey, the best place to wrap up this tour is to spend some time at Muscle Beach and the Santa Monica Pier. Muscle Beach began in the 1930s as an outdoor recreation center of sorts, with a collection of acrobatic equipment provided by the city. It's a tradition that continues today, with local citizens who routinely put on acrobatic performances.

Nearby Santa Monica Pier remains a popular destination for locals and tourists alike (www.santamonicapier.org). From the 1900s to mid-century, piers like this one were found up and down the coast, many providing the type of amusements you'll find here today: arcades, a carousel, rides, and carnival games. As times changed and tastes shifted, many piers fell into decline. Strong Pacific storms claimed some; urban renewal projects were the demise of many others. Santa Monica's pier was very nearly demolished in 1972. Concerned residents formed an association that would preserve the pier and lead to its restoration.

Road Tip – The Hidden Key

Your keys? Where are they? Say, what was that jingling sound you heard when you looked over the breakers a few minutes ago? *Uh oh.* Find a spot on your bike where you can hide a spare key. I wrapped one in electrical tape to disguise it then hid it under the gas tank which, on my bike, is bolted in front and hinged in the back. I keep a nut driver in an unlocked pocket in case I need to remove the bolts. No one would know what that's for (except you), and I don't have to worry what'll happen if my keys go missing. Find a similar spot on your bike and you'll enjoy peace of mind that if your keys are lost your vacation doesn't have to end.

It's the perfect place to rest for a spell. To ponder the seeming limitlessness of the Pacific Ocean. To observe and enjoy the wonderful eccentricities of southern California's colorful, diverse citizenry. To play back all the images you've stored and memories you've made on this trip. And to wonder if you shouldn't mount your bike, turn it north, and ride it all over again.

12

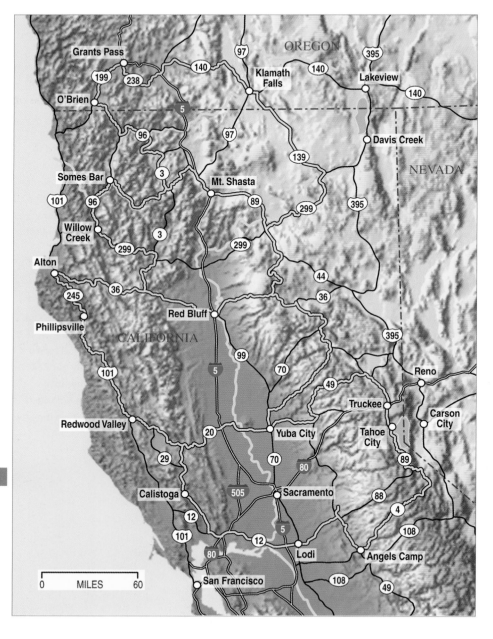

Motorcycle Journeys Through North America

13 BIGFOOT COUNTRY

This tour can be completed in ten days to two weeks and covers about 2,200 miles in the upper half of northern California and into southern Oregon. It includes a mix of well-known roads like the Avenue of Giants and Route 36, along with other local favorites such as Routes 299, 89, and the Quincy-Laporte Road. The tour is laid out in a series of intersecting loops that will guide you to the best roads northern California has to offer, along with an incredible range of experiences unique to the Golden State.

Digging through some old papers recently, I found a list I'd made that described a perfect motorcycle tour. Grand views. A diversity of people and cultures. Good . . . no, great food. An assortment of enjoyable and unusual things to do. Access to cities and beaches (my wife's requirements). Awesome roads, lightly traveled—or better yet, empty. Remote stretches where the human influence can neither be seen nor heard. Temperate weather.

As I thought about this perfect motorcycle vacation, I realized—that's northern California. It's all there. In a state that's world famous for its vastness and beauty, the

northern portion of the state is a genuine mecca for motorcyclists. Shaped by the volcanic Cascades and the soaring Sierra Nevadas, most of the roads through this part of the country must deal with sharp elevation changes which means two things: switchbacks and grand views.

Though the lower end of the region is anchored by urban centers, portions of the upper half remain isolated and untamed. The entire west coast is a beach. And the range of professions here engender a varied and engaging culture. Some make their living by time-honored methods, such as ranching and prospecting, while others cultivate

California Route 4 runs through Ebbetts Pass, a delicious mixture of pavement and scenery.

California Route 36 does this for about 140 miles from the coast to Redding.

Motorcycle Journeys Through North America

Bumpass Hell is the spot where Kendall Bumpass discovered just how hot the hot springs are here.

world-class wines, or are engaged in the manufacture of radio telescopes designed to communicate someday with E.T.

Compared to other parts of the motorcycling universe, like the Badlands or Beartooth or Deal's Gap, northern California is less well known. Maybe that's because there is no one label that defines the area or one particular road that stands out above all others. In this part of the state, almost any road you pick is a good one. More open road for you and me.

While many people associate California with a desert climate, the northern portion enjoys a more temperate climate. That means the region is best experienced from the late spring to early autumn, with June through August being the preferable months. Temperature changes can be significant and snowfall in higher elevations can occur at any time. Extra layers are a must. Just in case.

Connections

Bigfoot Country shares a few miles of road with the Coastal Cruise tour and is in close proximity to Desert Tracks as well as Evergreens and Canyons.

Redwoods grow only along the coast where ocean moisture promotes a more or less continuous source of fog.

Segment One
Lodi to Yuba City, California

At 360 miles, the first section of this northern California tour is packed with great roads, varied terrain and lots of things to see and do. Run hard and you can cover it in a day, but the better plan is to take your time and make two days of it.

The story of modern California often begins with the Gold Rush. The first part of the tour today is near the area where in 1848, James Marshall found shiny flakes in the tailrace at a lumber mill. Testing revealed its true nature. News of Marshall's discovery spread quickly, setting off a scramble that in just a few short years drew more than 300,000 gold rushers to the region. San Francisco, a tent settlement with about

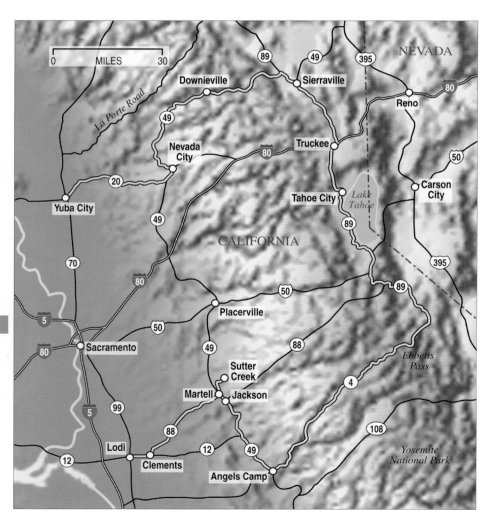

13

1,000 residents in 1848, exploded to 25,000 residents by 1850. The influx created an incredible and nearly instant demand for housing, transportation, and other services that quickly transformed the region. Although a few fortune seekers made out well in the early days, the people who profited most were the tool makers. Marshall, who made the original find, died in poverty decades later in Kelsey, about five miles from the site of his discovery.

Sutter Creek is one of the areas that benefitted from the gold rush growth and even today, the historic downtown area gives off a vibe reminiscent of the heady days of the mid-1800s, so drop the kickstand and spend a little time roaming the streets. There are a dozen or more ways to explore Gold Country

Route Details – 364 miles

➤ From Lodi, California, follow Rte 12 east to Clements. (12 mi.)

➤ Ride north on Rte 88 to Martell. (26 mi.)

➤ Ride north on Rte 49 to Sutter Creek. (2 mi.)

➤ Turn south on Rte 49 to Angels Camp. (32 mi.)

➤ Ride east on Rte 4 to Rte 89. (76 mi.)

➤ Follow Rte 89 north to Sierraville. (99 mi.)

➤ Go south on Rte 49 to Nevada City. (78 mi.)

➤ Follow Rte 20 west into Yuba City. (39 mi.)

California Route 89 near Monitor Pass. Ride this way for fun.

heritage between Sutter Creek and Jackson. You can arrange for a personal walking tour (www.gabbysgoldrushtours.com), or explore on your own following suggestions from Sutter Creek's published self-guided tours. (www.suttercreek.org/seasonaltours). Check out the Knight Foundry, one of the earliest and one of the few remaining water-powered machine shops.

Just down the road is Jackson, home of what many consider the Mother Lode of California gold. The road you're traveling, Route 49, is the route that many prospectors took as they swarmed into gold country (www.historichwy49.com). The Kennedy Mine (www.kennedygoldmine.com) in Jackson plunges more than a mile below the earth's surface. The area is also known for four massive wooden wheels, each more than fifty feet in diameter, referred to as the Kennedy Wheels, which were used to move the mine

Angels Camp is the setting for Mark Twain's famous tale about a jumping frog.

tailings, preventing them from polluting local waters. They ran continuously from the early 1900s until 1942; two of the four remain intact.

Lake Tahoe is a popular spot to put the bike on the kickstand and hang out for a few days.

Discovery of gold at Sutters Mill set off a rush that helped settle the west and bring California into the Union ahead of other western territories.

Almost every town along Route 49 is associated with the gold rush, but Angels Camp is famous for reasons of its own. In 1865, a then little known writer published a story set in Angels Camp. The story, *The Celebrated Jumping Frog of Calaveras County,* centered around a wager made by a fictional character named Jim Smiley. The story's author was Mark Twain and its success introduced him to the nation. Today, folks in the area celebrate Twain's story with a frog jumping contest at the Calaveras County Fair in late May.

Route 4 climbs over the Sierra Nevada mountains through the Pacific Grade Summit. Where it crosses Ebbetts Pass at more than 8,700 feet, it is northern California's highest road. Past Mount Reba, Route 4 reverts to goat trail status (narrow, unmarked pavement) and is not plowed in the colder months. Passage from June through October is usually reliable. At the intersection with Route 89, continue straight ahead toward Lake Tahoe on Route 89 north.

Tahoe offers something for everyone. Itching to hit the tables for a little run with Lady Luck? Just wander across the state line to the north shore where all the action Nevada can offer awaits you. A well-rounded plan might include water skiing, horseback riding, and a cruise around the lake on the Tahoe Queen (www.tahoesouth.com). Or gain a more complete perspective from a helicopter tour of the mountains and lake (www.helitahoe. com)

Out of Tahoe, Route 89 continues to skirt through Sierra Nevada mountain communities. A bite at the Round Up Café in Sierraville offers a chance to take a load off and enjoy the alpine climate of the region.

Perhaps the best preserved Gold Rush town is yet to come. Nevada City's entire downtown is listed on the National Register of Historic Places and includes more than 90 storefronts and Victorian homes (www. nevadacitychamber.com). The town is fortified by green hills that ring the perimeter and the city borders the Tahoe National Forest. If you were to stop riding and set up housekeeping here, no one would be surprised. It's that pretty.

13

Riders attack the curves on Route 36 through northern California.

Segment Two
Yuba City to Red Bluff, California

Segment Two is another long stretch of great riding. In fact, two of the most famous roads in the region are included in the itinerary for this section. Route 20 is a convenient route to the west coast, traversing the fertile farmland of the Sacramento Valley, one of the most productive agricultural regions in the world. Past the intersection with Route 16, the interest begins to pick up as Route 20 enters hill country on its way to US 101 in Redwood Valley.

After the Grand Canyon, the giant redwoods of the northern California coast may draw the most stark and humbling contrast between nature's incredible accomplishments and our own pitiable achievements. Standing at the base of a tree 30 feet around and nearly 400 feet tall has a way of making you feel, well, puny.

The Avenue of the Giants (www.avenueofthegiants.net) reinforces that feeling, and then some. This 30-mile route parallels US 101 between Phillipsville and Pepperwood, weaving through a forest of trees so massive, you could imagine the giant from *Jack and the Beanstalk* peering around any of these incredible specimens. Stop at the Humboldt Redwoods State Park to get the most from your experience. An easy hike from the visitors center will allow you to encounter the trees up close, including what's left of the Dyersville Giant, once the world's tallest tree. Many of the world's tallest trees are found here. Top honors cur-

Route Details – 387 miles

➤ From Yuba City, California, take Rte 20 west to Redwood Valley. (113 mi.)

➤ Turn north on US 101 and ride to Exit 645, Avenue of the Giants (Rte 245). (92 mi.)

➤ Tour the Avenue of the Giants, rejoining US 101 near Pepperwood. (30 mi.)

➤ Ride US 101 north to Rte 36 in Alton. (14 mi.)

➤ Follow Rte 36 east to Red Bluff. (138 mi.)

13

rently belong to "Hyperion," a 379-foot specimen in Redwood National Park.

Route 36 runs for almost 140 miles between US 101 and Red Bluff. It is frequently lauded as one of the best roads for motorcycling in California by folks who have ridden every corner of the Golden State. Considering the competition, that's saying something. Route 36 features head-twisting scenery and drapes over every hill as if it were laid gently into place. It's smooth, fast, and fun and for the most part, it's all yours. A portion of the western third narrows to goat track for a few miles before getting seriously twisted up between Bridgeville and Plantina. From there, Route 36 roller coasters up and down small elevations all the way into Red Bluff.

Redwood Forest. Home of the Keebler Elves.

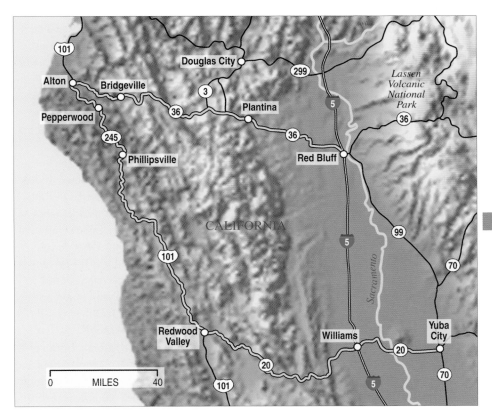

13

Lassens Peak is the southernmost active volcano in the Cascade range. Lassen and Mount St. Helens are the only two Cascade volcanoes to erupt during the 20th century.

Segment Three
Red Bluff to Mount Shasta, California

At 170 miles, the run between Red Bluff and Mount Shasta is an easy day's run, but there are a couple of interesting stops along the way that make it a full day.

Heading east out of Red Bluff on Route 36, the character of the road couldn't be

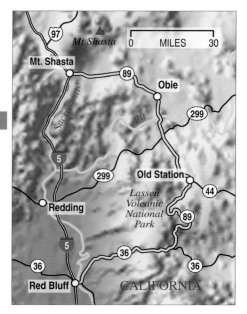

more different than the road you came into town on. The section of 36 east of Red Bluff is flat and dry. Once in a while, you'll get a glimpse of the far off horizon and the Sierra Nevadas. That's where we're headed. When Route 36 intersects Route 89, hang a left, following the sign toward Lassen Volcanic National Park. We'll stay on Route 89 for the remainder of the run. Easy, right?

Route 89 winds toward the Lassen Volcanic National Park. Other than Mount St. Helens in Washington state, Lassen is the only other volcanic peak in the Cascades range to erupt in the last 100 years. Lassen is also the snowiest spot in California. What do you think is a lot of snow? Fifty inches? A hundred? Lassen receives an average of 600 to 700 inches of snow each year. In some years, as much as 1,000 inches have been recorded. That's 83 feet of snow!

As a geothermally active area, Lassen offers trails that feature all manner of bubbling pools, hydrothermal vents, and boiling mud pots. One of the largest is Bumpass Hell. This

Route Details – 173 miles

➤ From Red Bluff, California, follow Rte 36 east to Rte 89. (46 mi.)

➤ Ride Rte 89 north to Mount Shasta. (127 mi.)

site takes it's name from Kendall Bumpass, a cowboy who stumbled across the area in the 1860s. Stepping on what he thought was solid ground, Bumpass broke through a thin crust, scalding his leg badly. When he brought a newspaper reporter to the area to show what happened, he broke through again. Same leg. This time, it had to come off.

The ring of volcanic mounds and the lack of major urban centers means that you won't find a lot of radio stations or other manmade electrical signals in the area. That makes this area a perfect spot to observe electromagnetic waves from the sky and it's why you'll find a large collection of radio telescopes in Hat Creek. The Hat Creek Radio Observatory (www.hcro.org) is jointly operated by the University of California Berkeley and the SETI Institute. SETI is a privately funded organization focused on the search for extra terrestrial intelligence. Work continues on construction of the Allen Telescope Array, a collection of satellite dishes that can work together like one large dish. This tool will allow radio astronomers to scan thousands of nearby stars for signals that indicate the presence of intelligent life. Stop by on your way through for a free tour and some unique photo opportunities.

This segment ends near Mount Shasta, another member of the Cascade range. At 14,179 feet, Shasta is one of the tallest mountains in California, falling just a few hundred feet short of Mount Whitney in the Sierras. Shasta stands in stark contrast to the surrounding landscape, rising abruptly out of the valley floor. Its sudden appearance on the horizon has been noted by more than one literary observer including naturalist and author John Muir, who on first sighting the peak wrote "When I first caught sight of it over the braided folds of the Sacramento Valley, I was fifty miles away and afoot, alone and weary. Yet all my blood turned to wine, and I have not been weary since." Sounds like the perfect way to end a day's ride.

Hot flowing lava created these tubes, which were later used by native Americans as a stronghold when the cavalry tried to roust them out of their homelands.

13

Segment Four
Mount Shasta, California, to Medford, Oregon

This segment includes some of the most sce-nic and isoloated sections of road in the re-gion. It's not that the route is difficult, it's just that if you run into trouble here, help will not arrive quickly. Make sure both you and your bike are in top shape for this ride. Do you have a tire plug kit? Please say yes.

A few back road moves will put you near Gazelle where you can begin the trek north and west on the Gazelle-Callahan Road, which slowly gains elevation as you work your way across the top of the semi-arid Great Valley and into the mountains. Route 3, turning north toward Fort Jones, offers many long distance vistas.

In Fort Jones, turn left onto Scott River Road—a narrow path that follows the Scott River. While the road runs at river level for much of its length, some portions are cut high above the valley floor, narrow consider-ably, and offer no guardrail. Stay alert through these sections.

The upper end of California is so different from elsewhere that it feels like a different state. Not California and not quite Oregon. Perhaps that's why folks in this area have been attempting to establish the State of Jefferson for decades. The greatest momen-tum for the movement occurred in Novem-ber 1941 when a group of armed Jefferson State patriots began blocking traffic on US 99, handing out copies of a Proclamation of

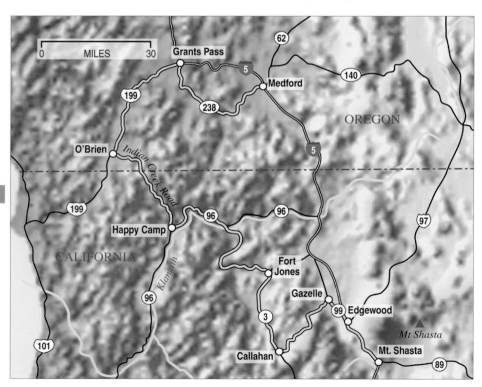

13

Independence and stating their intention to secede from California and Oregon every Thursday until further notice. A few weeks later, world events conspired against them. When the bombing of Pearl Harbor drew the United States into World War II, Jefferson State secessionists abandoned their effort and focused on the war at hand. After all, they were full-time patriots and only part-time rabble-rousers.

Indian Creek Road runs north and west out of Happy Camp through an undeveloped and immense portion of wilderness. You'll lose count of the gentle sweeping curves as you work your way toward Oregon. A return to striped pavement is the only indication that you've crossed the state line. The road changes names along the way, becoming Grayback Road, then Route 5828. Just stick with the "main" road until you reach US 199. There's only one. Follow US 199 and Route 238 into Medford to conclude this segment.

Like many Oregon cities, Medford is modern and sophisticated, with a wide choice of attractions, arts, and entertainment. It's a good spot to stop for a day or two if you need a riding break because there are many things to see and do right in the area.

Route Details – 236 miles

➤ From Mount Shasta, California, follow North Old Stage Road to Old Hwy 99. (13 mi.)

➤ Ride Old Hwy 99 to Gazelle. (8 mi.)

➤ Follow Gazelle-Callahan Road west to Rte 3. (25 mi.)

➤ Ride Rte 3 north to Fort Jones. (26 mi.)

➤ Ride north on Scott River Road to Rte 96. (31 mi.)

➤ Follow Rte 96 west to Happy Camp, California. (30 mi.)

➤ Out of Happy Camp, follow Indian Creek Road (becomes Grayback Road, then Rte 5828) north to O'Brien, Oregon. (38 mi.)

➤ Out of O'Brien, follow US 199 north to Rte 238 in Grants Pass. (35 mi.)

➤ Ride Rte 238 east to Medford, Oregon. (30 mi.)

Medford boasts a range of dining options, including Asian cuisines, Hawaiian, German, Italian, Mexican, and the Gold Winger's favorite: the endless buffet (okay, mine, too).

Mount Shasta is clearly visible across the beautiful Fall River Valley along California Route 299.

13

Segment Five
Medford, Oregon, to Mount Shasta, California

This segment, though longer than others, is a faster ride as it traverses large sections of arid high-country desert. The route departs Medford on Route 62, then Route 140. If you didn't have a chance to visit Butte Creek Mill during your stay in Medford, it's right along the way as you head out of town. Stay on Route 62 into Eagle Point and turn onto Old Crater Lake Highway. Follow Royal Avenue through town to the mill on your right.

The wheels at Butte Creek Mill have turned without ceasing, producing flours and meals for more than 130 years. Unlike mills that use a familiar wooden wheel, water pours into a 12-foot penstock, creating enough pressure to activate a series of turbines that power the heavy milling stones, which were quarried in Paris, France. After a stop in Moline, Illinois, for finishing, the stones went back to the Atlantic and tra-

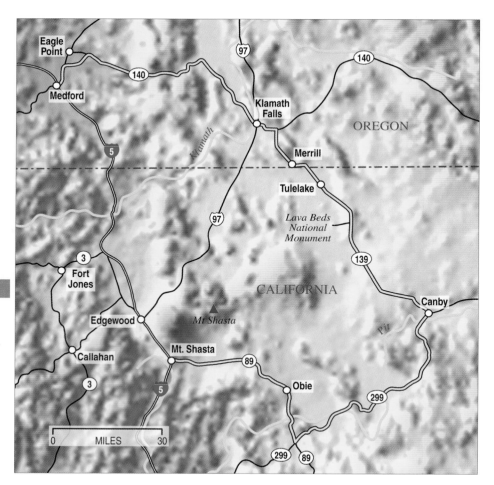

versed the dangerous Cape Horn before making their way up the coasts of South and North America to Crescent City.

Follow Brownsboro Highway out of Eagle Point to join Route 140 east toward Klamath Falls. Along this route in the mid-40s, it wouldn't have been unusual to see a balloon floating placidly from west to east. Many folks pondered the origin and nature of these strange sightings but only a few knew the truth. The balloons originated from Japan and carried up to 1,000 pounds of explosives. In a six-month period from late 1944 to early 1945, Japanese fire bombs were launched by the hundreds, using the jet stream to reach the North American continent. While the bombs were largely ineffectual, one bomb killed a group of six on a Sunday picnic when they discovered it in the woods east of Klamath Falls near Bly.

The Office of Censorship directed the U.S. press to avoid mentioning the bombs to convince the Japanese that they were having little effect. Apparently, it worked. Just six months later, operations ceased. Can you imagine keeping the lid on something like that in today's twenty-four hour news cycle? An attack like that today would cause panic in the streets, not to mention a run on bread, milk, and toilet paper.

Just south of Klamath Falls you'll discover yet another strange chapter in WWII history. Tulelake (www.tulelake.org) is the site of the largest and most controversial Japanese-American internment camp, built in response to public hysteria over the Pearl Harbor attack. Tens of thousands of American citizens of Japanese descent suspected of being alien spies were collected in one of ten such centers. Many were forced to renounce their American citizenship and were deported after the war. The site at Tulelake has

Riders plan their next move on the seductive, serpentine roads of the Golden State.

been preserved to tell their cautionary tale and to help us understand just how easily our liberties and rights can be lost.

The return route toward Shasta passes Lava Beds National Monument, which features more than 700 lava tube caves. If you've never hiked a lava tube, take a little time to explore. Hiking trails have been built to accommodate anyone. In the early 1870s the U.S. Army mounted an expensive campaign to root out a renegade band of the Modoc Indian tribe holed up in the caves. For more than five months, the Modocs held off an army ten times their size and, as you wander the endless trails, you'll quickly realize how it could be done.

Route Details – 280 miles

➤ Ride State 62 east out of Medford, Oregon, to Rte 140. (7 mi.)

➤ Follow Rte 140 east to Rte 39 in Klamath Falls, Oregon. (74 mi.)

➤ Take Rte 39 (becomes Rte 139 in California) south to Rte 299. (73 mi.)

➤ Follow Rte 299 south to Rte 89. (67 mi.)

➤ Go north on Rte 89 to Mount Shasta, California. (59 mi.)

13

Segment Six
Mount Shasta to Red Bluff, California

As you begin to work your way back toward the central part of the state, segment six might best be described as the "Shut Up and Ride" leg of this journey. A high percentage of the 310 miles that make up this segment are paved single-track roads through the remote Shasta and Trinity National Forests.

The route revisits a few miles of road we've previously seen, departing at Callahan toward Cecilville. This next 65 miles between Callahan and Somes Bar is frequently single-track with rough sections, but rideable by anyone.

While signs of civilization are scattered, you'll run across remote outposts from time to time. If you've ever thought you might like to take up kayaking, but weren't sure how to get started, the answer lies here along the banks of the Salmon River. Pay a visit to the Otter Bar Lodge (www.otterbar. com) for a high-touch, hands-on kayaking experience. You'll not only learn from some of the most proficient paddlers in the world, you'll also enjoy comfortable lodging and five-star menus.

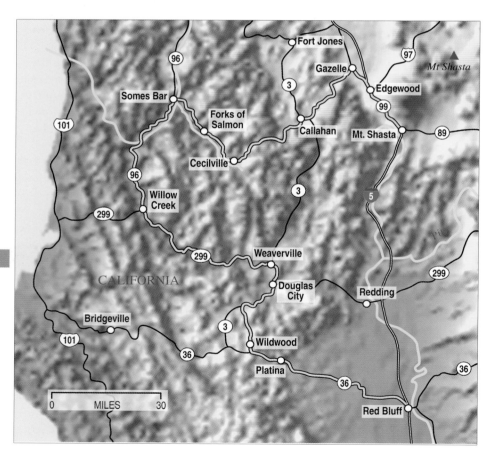

13

Rider Dave Hartley sizes up Sasquatch at a rest stop in Willow Creek, California. Willow Creek is recognized as the leading research center surrounding the legend . . . er, I mean "origins" of Bigfoot.

Route Details – 310 miles

➤ From Mount Shasta, California, follow North Old Stage Road to Old Highway 99. (13 mi.)

➤ Ride Old Highway 99 to Gazelle. (8 mi.)

➤ Follow Gazelle-Callahan Road west to Rte 3. (25 mi.)

➤ Ride Rte 3 north to Callahan-Cecilville Road. (2 mi.)

➤ Follow Callahan-Cecilville Road to Cecilville. (30 mi.)

➤ Take Cecilville Road north to Forks of Salmon. (18 mi.)

➤ Ride Salmon River Road north to Rte 96 at Somes Bar. (18 mi.)

➤ Follow Rte 96 south to Willow Creek. (45 mi.)

➤ Out of Willow Creek, take Rte 299 south to Douglas City. (62 mi.)

➤ Ride south on Rte 3 to Wildwood Road. (20 mi.)

➤ Take Wildwood Road south to Rte 36. (17 mi.)

➤ Follow Rte 36 east into Red Bluff. (52 mi.)

At Forks of Salmon, it's time to turn left and continue along the Salmon River Road, heading toward Somes Bar. Here, you'll join Rte 96 and begin your return.

You can't ride through country this remote without thinking about the legend of Bigfoot, the supposed ape-man that is frequently spotted in this region. Reports of the hairy proto-man evolved from Indian lore citing the presence of a Sesquac or "wild man" in the dense and remote forests of the Pacific Northwest. As an impressionable youngster, I entertained ideas of leaving home with a friend to find the Bigfoot. We made many plans and material lists needed to observe and capture the dreaded beast, but in time we realized that our meager funds and a fondness for mom's cooking would keep us safely at home.

Even if Bigfoot is a hoax, it hardly matters to the folks in Willow Creek. Bigfoot is big business here and the folks of Willow Creek lay claim to the title of Most Bigfoot Sightings with a considerable degree of civic pride. Three large statues of the ol' Hairy One are situated around town, along with a museum dedicated to Bigfoot sightings.

The return to Red Bluff requires a few hours ride on just a couple of roads. Route 299 joins Route 3 in Weaverville and splits just below Douglas City. Stick with Route 3 at the split and then left on Wildwood Road. At the end of Wildwood Road turn left on Route 36 for the last 50-mile run to Red Bluff.

13

Segment Seven
Red Bluff to Yuba City, California

Route Details – 207 miles

- ➤ Out of Red Bluff, California, follow Rte 36 east to Rte 89. (51 mi.)
- ➤ Follow Rte 89 south to East Quincy. (64 mi.)
- ➤ In East Quincy, ride west on La Porte Road to Lower Honcut Road. (75 mi.)
- ➤ Follow Lower Honcut Road to Rte 70. (5 mi.)
- ➤ Ride Rte 70 into Yuba City. (12 mi.)

Compared to days past, the route between Red Bluff and Yuba City is an easy 210-mile stretch of pleasant valley roads in the foothills of the Sierras.

The main feature of this route is the Indian Valley, a picturesque and fertile mountain meadowland surrounded by alpine forests. Villages like Canyondam, Greenville, and Indian Falls are great spots to stop and take in a little small town atmosphere.

La Porte Road, as well as Oroville-Quincy Road, are two examples of great riding of-

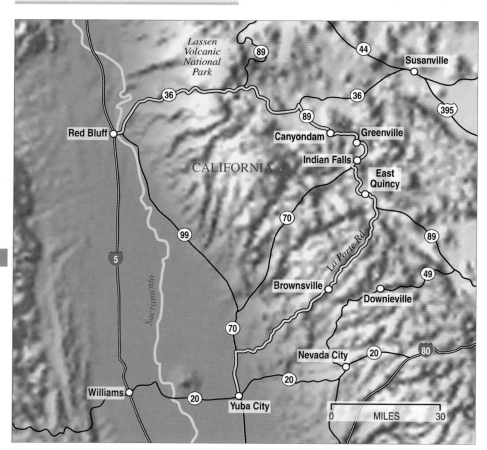

13

It doesn't matter what kind of year-round rider you are, this road won't be hosting traffic of any kind until the snowplows finish their job.

fered here that are favored by local riders. Keep an eye on your speed, especially in the turns. While La Porte is fun to ride, it's not uncommon to encounter gravel spills in places that matter little to four-wheelers, but a whole lot to us on two wheels.

If you plan to tour this area before June or after September, it's not a bad idea to check on road conditions before you head out. The higher elevations receive snow measured in feet, and roads across the higher elevations are frequently closed. The folks at the Indian Valley Visitor Center can point you in the right direction (www. indianvalley.net). If the road between Quincy and La Porte is closed, you can follow Route 89 to the Route 49 junction and return to Yuba City via Nevada City.

Road Tip – Remote Riding

When riding in remote areas like northern California, it's important to make sure your bike is in top operating condition. Carry a tire plug kit and some means of inflation at all times. A personal locator is not a bad idea either. The SPOT Personal Tracker works by satellite and is designed to keep family and friends apprised of your whereabouts and will help you contact emergency services if you get into trouble. When you're out here, hours from the closest cell tower or small town, a tracker offers you some peace of mind. Of course, Sasquatch might be willing to lend a hand.

13

Segment Eight
Yuba City to Lodi, California

The last segment of this northern California adventure makes a tour of the famous Napa Valley, home to one of the state's best known industries—wine making. More than 90 percent of American wine is of California vintage and were it a country of its own, California would be the world's fourth largest producer. That's a lot of vino.

You've been riding hard for the past week, so consider spending a little time relaxing in Calistoga. This small, well-preserved western town is at the northern end of wine country and prides itself on a relaxed atmosphere. Thanks to plentiful underground heat, Calistoga is also known as the spa capital of northern California. Downtown boasts a

couple dozen spas and massage therapy centers standing by to work out the kinks you've accumulated over the past couple thousand miles.

Few folks realize it, but Calistoga is home to another "Old Faithful" geyser, just north of town. Along with its counterpart in Yellowstone, this geyser is one of only a few in the world that erupts on a regular schedule, about every thirty minutes, day and night.

Following Route 29 down through Napa Valley (napavalley.com) is like cruising through the California aisle at your favorite wine shop. Countless rows of perfectly manicured vines stretch across this narrow valley, bounded by low, brown hills. The area's rep-

The roads that run along the valleys between ranges in California often look just like this. It's hard to pick a bad route.

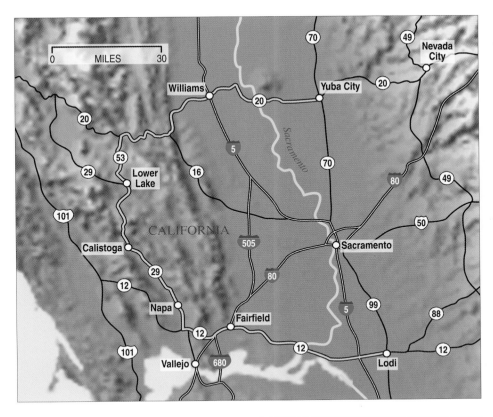

utation for fine wine dates back just a few decades. Other forms of agriculture dominated the area until the mid-1960s when Robert Mondavi split from his family's original Napa Valley vineyard, Charles Krug, to form his own. Following his lead, the number of wineries began to grow, as did the valley's reputation. Today there are more than 300 vintners in the area.

There's a lot to see here in the valley and the smart folks take to the air to get the best view. Balloon rides are a popular attraction, with several operators to choose from. Wine Country Balloons (www.balloontours.com) offers a complete experience. After helping to inflate your balloon, you'll enjoy a 60- to 90-minute tour over the valley and a gourmet meal on your return.

Route Details – 196 miles

➤ Ride west out of Yuba City, California, on Rte 20 to Rte 53. (67 mi.)

➤ Follow Rte 53 south to Rte 29 in Lower Lake. (8 mi.)

➤ Ride Rte 29 south to Rte 12. (61 mi.)

➤ Follow Rte 12 into Lodi. (60 mi.)

13

Returning to Lodi via Route 12 closes out this tour of the northern portion of the Golden State. The ride through such varied and remote country is a continuing reminder that the western United States is one of the best regions for motorcycle touring. Anywhere.

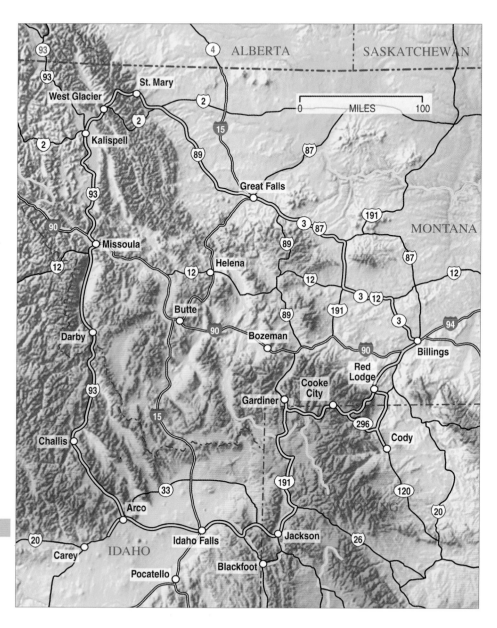

14 NORTHWEST PASSAGE

Three of the nation's most renowned national parks and some of motorcycling's most famous roads are included in this 2,270-mile grand tour through Montana, Wyoming, and Idaho. While this tour includes the big names, such as Yellowstone, the Grand Tetons, and Glacier National Park, it also uncovers the lesser-known, such as the nation's first experiments with nuclear power including (believe it or not) nuclear aircraft engines. You'll also visit Craters of the Moon, Beartooth Pass, the Chief Joseph Highway, and the Going to the Sun Highway. You'll also enjoy unknown gems, including the Salmon River Valley and the scenic Sawtooth Mountains. And no trip to this part of the country would be complete without dinner at Helen's, Home of the Hateful Hamburger.

Searching for a title for his anthology of stories, poems, and essays about Montana life, well-known western writer William Kitteredge came up with *The Last Best Place*. As a colleague, I'm both envious of Kitteredge and grateful to him because those four spare words sum up what I might take paragraphs to explain.

While Kitteredge was referring to Montana exclusively, this tour does range into Wyoming and Idaho. I hope that's okay with any Montanans who happen to read

Though it doesn't get as much press as US 212 through Beartooth Pass, the Chief Joseph Highway between Cody and US 212 has some incredible stretches of twisties.

US 93 through the Salmon River Valley in Idaho is a free-wheeling, memorable ride.

this. Your next-door neighbors share much of the beauty and wildness of your state.

Every region of the country has its scenic byways but none surpasses this region's combination of soaring mountains and limitless vistas. Oh, and they happen to be strung together by roads that evoke such a visceral riding reaction, you might just bend your handlebars. As the road lying ahead comes into view, anticipation swells. Countless sweeps and turns return such a pleasurable riding experience, you want to dig into your seat, lean harder, and ride faster.

Traversing eastern prairie lands is an entirely different experience when you tour by bike. Four-wheelers are heavy and stable enough that you don't feel the effects of high crosswinds, save for an occasional gust. On a bike, you'll frequently find yourself holding a straight line only by leaning the

Date taken: June 21st. Bring your thermals. And some very good sunglasses.

bike well into the breeze. Just when you think you're stuck in that position permanently, relief comes. The road drops into a crease in the earth and you fall into another world, just like Alice. The winds fade as you dip below the lip of the canyon and the sun regains its strength. Golden fields give way to green forests. And this is where the people are. Small towns hover in the crevices here, protected from ceaseless Chinook winds.

Mountains and prairies eventually give way to the volcanic plain where Earth's crust bubbles and spews, forming geysers, fumaroles, and mud pots that hint at the heat just below the surface. Remnants of volcanic flows turn the landscape into some-thing so alien you can easily visualize what it might be like to land on another planet.

But here, in a region laced with the roads we riders crave, the joy of following the pavement pales in comparison to the grandeur of the mountain ranges—the Tetons, Absarokas, Beartooth, and Sawtooth ranges, and of course, Glacier National Park. John Muir, the famous conservationist named Glacier "the best care-killing scenery on the continent." The Blackfeet Indians named it the Backbone of the World. When you're standing at an overlook with verdant alpine valleys framed by 10,000-foot snow-capped monoliths, there's no reason to argue with them.

In the prime riding season of midsummer,

Turn left for an excellent ride through the Sunlight Basin, stay right for an epic run through the Beartooth. Decisions, decisions!

US 2 runs just to the south of Glacier National Park. It's an easy detour to ride up to St. Mary on US 89 and run through the park from east to west. You'll encounter less traffic on this approach through the park.

14

Motorcycle Journeys Through North America

St. Mary Lake frames the eastern portion of Glacier National Park.

dusk arrives late here in the higher northern latitudes, as if the sun itself is reluctant to see the day end. That gives you all the more time to enjoy the after-ride, recounting the day's adventures with your riding companions on the terrace at a local watering hole. Here in the golden sunlight of late evening

you come to fully understand what Kitteredge meant. The Last Best Place. That's exactly where this journey has brought you.

Ride here in July and August. If you arrive a month on either side of the height of summer you'll want to stay keenly attuned to current and forecasted weather. Bring layers.

Connections

The Northwest Passage tour connects to the Evergreens and Canyons tour by way of US 12 over the famous Lolo Pass. You're also not far from the Badlands tour by way of US 14 through the Bighorn Mountains. The Rocky Mountain Way tour through Colorado can be joined by following US 191 south out of Wyoming to US 40. The beginning of the Canadian Rockies loops isn't far away either; just catch US 89 north and cross into British Columbia.

Afoot and light-hearted,
*   I take to the open road,*
Healthy, free, the world before me,
The long brown path before me,
*   leading wherever I choose.*

*   —Walt Whitman,* Song of the Open Road

14

Segment One
Great Falls to Red Lodge, Montana

Often when a town grows into a city, traffic and noise and a palpable sense of urgency replace the charm once defined by quiet neighborhoods and streets lined with mom-and-pop shops and restaurants. That hasn't

Route Details – 279 miles

> ➤ From Great Falls, Montana, follow Rte 3 south to Billings. (219 mi.)

> ➤ In Billings, pick up US 212 south and follow it to Red Lodge. (60 mi.)

happened in Great Falls (www.gfcvb.com). Tidy, tree-lined streets invite you to enjoy an evening stroll where anyone will nod a warm greeting. Even a downtown festival in full swing feels subdued. Folks around here would never think of whoopin' and hollerin' like they might at a comparable Texas shindig.

The grand loop through this part of the region departs Great Falls on Route 3, a signed state road that runs exclusively to Billings, Montana's largest city. There's no half-hour

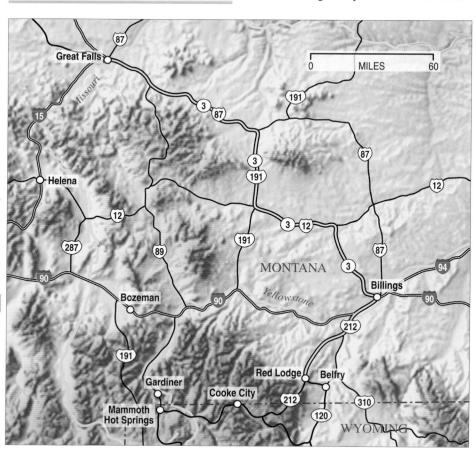

It was a crazy idea, building a road through the Beartooth Wilderness. But we can be thankful someone did.

slog to get through urban traffic here in Great Falls. Five minutes and you're on the outskirts of town headed into the rolling, grassy hills and long flat plains of the high prairie. Occasionally the horizon is broken by small renegade hills or isolated mountain ranges, remnants of geological events unrelated to the formation of the Rockies to the west.

Route 3 runs directly through downtown Billings and ends on I-90, which is co-signed with US 212. It's a short run on I-90 west when 212 departs southwest toward Red Lodge, the conclusion of segment one.

It's apparent immediately upon entering Red Lodge that tourists are welcome here. Of course, that's what we are, so that's a good thing. Colorful and varied restaurants and shops line the main street at the foot of the Beartooth Mountains. You'll find no shortage of lodging. Plan to stay for an extra day because the next segment loops back into town before heading on to the next destination.

Segment Two
Cody Loop

I am confident to claim, without fear of contradiction, that Beartooth Highway is one of the most exciting and memorable motorcycling roads you'll find in the continental United States. US 212 climbs over a mile in elevation from Red Lodge, making it one of the highest-elevation roadways in the country. The terrain that plays out in every direction is so remote, it remains virtually untouched and appears today much as it

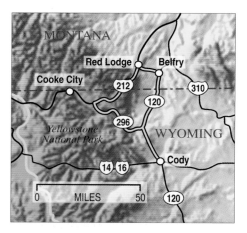

Route Details – 176 miles

➤ From Red Lodge, Montana, ride US 212 west to the Chief Joseph Highway (Rte 296) junction. (51 mi.)

➤ Follow the Chief Joseph Highway (also known as Sunlight Basin Road) to Rte 120. (46 mi.)

➤ Ride south on Rte 120 into Cody. (16 mi.)

➤ Departing Cody, ride north on Rte 120 to Belfry. (47 mi.)

➤ Ride west on Rte 308 to Red Lodge. (16 mi.)

did to early American natives who frequented the isolated and game-filled valleys between the peaks. The first dozen or so miles out of Red Lodge pass unremarkably and you begin to fear, "Is this it?" Then, when the road hits the side of the mountain and has no room to wander, the fun begins.

The road begins a relentless ascent on the eastern range, barely clinging to the mountain in spots. Patches of fresh pavement and guardrail frequently indicate areas that have been rebuilt following landslides. Just a few miles into the switchbacks there is a large overlook area where it's finally safe to pull over and admire the views you've been chasing for the past half-hour. Riders strike up casual conversations, checking out bikes and comparing Beartooth with other famous roads around the globe. I've frequently heard riders describe Beartooth as "riding on top of the world" and after passing the summit at over 11,000 feet, I understand why.

You've ridden the best stretch of Beartooth when the time comes for the Chief Joseph Highway, a 36-mile run between US 212 and Route 120, pointing toward Cody. CJH frequently equals the Beartooth Highway for splendid views, but it's easier to relax and enjoy both the ride and the scenery. The road is less technical, so you won't have to think quite as hard about hitting the apex and setting up for the next corner every few hundred yards.

The story of Cody, Wyoming, is centered around its namesake, William "Buffalo Bill" Cody. Old Bill was not the sort of fellow you could pin down long to one endeavor. At age 14, he was struck by gold fever in Colo-

Portions of the Chief Joseph Highway are known as the Sunlight Basin Road.

rado and became a "Fifty-Niner," then worked for the Pony Express, served in the Civil War, became a trapper, wagonmaster, stagecoach driver, and possibly a hotel manager. But he gained worldwide and enduring fame for his Wild West-themed shows, which transfixed generations of Americans and popularized many of the notions and ideals that were later reinforced by movies and television. I guess you could say Buffalo Bill invented and popularized the mythology of the Old West (en.wikipedia.org/wiki/Wild_West_Shows).

Bill Cody was not only a legendary promoter, he was also a visionary, founding his town here in the northwest corner of Wyoming to serve as a welcoming point for tourists arriving by train from the East. Although folks arrive from all over today, Bill's legacy has endured and prospered. Downtown, the Irma Hotel (www.irmahotel.com) serves travelers just as it did when Cody built it more than 100 years ago. By far the most authoritative source for information about the area is the Buffalo Bill Historical Center at the west end of Sheridan Avenue (www.bbhc.org) where the price of admission will provide access to multiple exhibits about

Cody, Yellowstone, Western Art, the Plains Indians, and an extensive collection of antique firearms.

Stay over in the evening between June and August and you'll have a chance to enjoy amateur rodeo night when young riders attempt to make a name for themselves in a bid to eventually join the pro rodeo circuit. You'll also want to mosey out a short distance on US 16 just west of town to the Old Town Trail, where there is a collection of 26 Old West buildings dating from 1879 to 1901, some from Cody's founding. The collection includes the cabin used by Butch Cassidy and his Hole-in-the-Wall Gang and the River Saloon, which still features bullet holes in the floor, no doubt the result of one too many aces tucked up the sleeve.

Head back to Red Lodge by retracing your path on Route 120. Belfry Highway is the prettier option going north and it gives you the choice to make a straight return to Red Lodge, or go back over the Chief Joseph Highway and through Beartooth Pass. Option A, the direct route, is an easy 60-mile ride over the wide open basins of northern Wyoming, while Option B is about twice as long. But more than twice as fun.

14

The Beartooth Mountains loom large in the background over the Lamar River Valley in northwestern Wyoming.

Segment Three
Red Lodge to Gardiner, Montana

I hope you don't mind riding the Beartooth again. This segment takes you over the range once more, this time continuing to the northeast entrance of Yellowstone National Park. Due to its remote nature, you'll encounter no delay entering the park from here.

Near the entrance, Cooke City is one of the western mining towns that sprung up in the late 1800s and still survives today supported

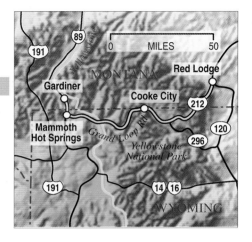

by the tourist trade. The area caters to an avid winter activity season. When the roads close to four-wheel traffic, they open to snowmobiles. Can you imagine whipping a snowmobile around some of the runs on Beartooth? Better not powerslide too far to the cliff side; the consequences would be severe.

The Northeast Entrance Road skirts along the top of Yellowstone. This part of the park is characterized largely by rolling hills and meadows where you'll frequently encounter herds of bison, mule deer, or pronghorn, North America's fastest land animal. (Their top speed is an impressive 60 mph, faster than some bikes I've owned.)

Yellowstone, America's first national park, is also one of its largest. Yellowstone is part of the Snake River Basin geological formation and it is slowly sliding over a stationary hotspot below the earth's crust. If you look at a map of the region, you can clearly see the track of the North American continent as it slides from northeast to southwest. Someday, not that you or I will see it, the area we know as Yellowstone will be geothermally dead and all the hotspots will have migrated to North Dakota. I guess that and Lawrence Welk's birthplace will give folks two reasons to visit North Dakota. Good for them.

This segment stops in Gardiner, Montana, which makes a good launching point for spending a day or two to explore the park. To make the most of your time here, visit the National Park Service website (www.nps.gov/yell). Or, just show up, and make it up as you go along. Do keep in mind as you traverse the roads here in the park that deer, elk, bears, bison, and dozens of other creatures pay little attention to roads and frequently wander across at will. Don't be surprised to round a corner and find an adult bison bull staring down an SUV.

Gardiner is perched at the northern entrance to Yellowstone along the river. It's a

Route Details – 121 miles

- ➤ Out of Red Lodge, Montana, ride US 212 west to Cooke City. (65 mi.)
- ➤ Continue on US 212 into Yellowstone National Park to Grand Loop Road. (32 mi.)
- ➤ Turn right, following the Grand Loop Road to US 89 near Mammoth Hot Springs. (18 mi.)
- ➤ Ride US 89 north to Gardiner. (6 mi.)

subdued alternative to West Yellowstone, a larger and busier travel center. The Absaroka Lodge (www.yellowstonemotel.com/), built right along the river, offers clean, comfortable accommodations with a view of the Yellowstone River and the downtown area. Food and other diversions are within easy walking distance.

Living in an area like Sunlight Basin makes you wonder if you'd ever get any work done. It's just too pretty not to stare at.

Gardiner, Montana, to Idaho Falls, Idaho

Route Details – 243 miles

➤ From Gardiner, Montana, follow US 89 south to Teton Park Road. (118 mi.)

➤ Ride Teton Park Road south to US 89 at Moose, Wyoming. (21 mi.)

➤ Follow US 89 south through Jackson. (14 mi.)

➤ Turn west on Rte 22 (becomes Rte 33 in Idaho) west to Victor, Idaho. (23 mi.)

➤ From Victor, follow Rte 31 to Swan Valley. (22 mi.)

➤ Ride US 26 west to Idaho Falls. (45 mi.)

When you see iconic western photos with snow-capped mountains reflected in the crystal clear waters of a lake or stream, there's an above average chance you're seeing a picture snapped in Grand Teton National Park. This segment runs through western Yellowstone and runs the length of Grand Teton, ending in Jackson, Wyoming.

The mountain ranges we've ridden through thus far have all been beautiful, but the Tetons are especially striking. Their sudden rise from the valley floor is often said to be their most outstanding visual feature. This is due largely to their youth. Among the Rocky Mountains, the Teton range is one of the youngest. The peaks of these mountains

Helen's Corral. Home of the Hateful Hamburger. Pick up one of their family-friendly T-shirts. You'll know what I mean when you see it.

above their base of 5,000 to 7,000 feet have yet to be worn to soft foothills by the forces of erosion.

The Jackson Hole Valley has blossomed as a full-scale, trendy travel destination in the last decade. It's beautiful, and pricey. Enjoy the day at Teton and the streets and shops in Jackson. I don't normally make a note of the price for travel services, but I feel it's only fair to point out that Jackson is expensive. If your budget allows you to splurge on deluxe accommodations, this is your place. Run-of-the-mill hotel rooms here at national chains easily top $220 per night. If you'd rather spend the $160 difference elsewhere, turn west and head to Idaho Falls where the same room at the same hotel chain averages $60. Wyoming route 22 and Idaho 31 are scenic, easy-riding routes. From Swan Valley, it's a short 40-mile run to Idaho Falls. From Jackson, it's about 90 miles.

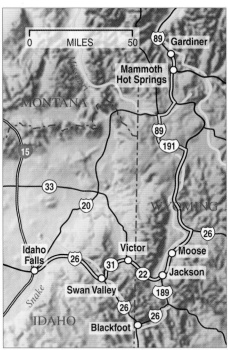

14

< Yellowstone is famed for its boiling springs and geysers like Old Faithful, but other parts of the park preserve vast expanses of western wilderness.

Segment Five
Idaho Falls, Idaho, to Missoula, Montana

In 1951, usable electricity was generated for the first time from nuclear power. This was at the Experimental Breeder Reactor, part of Idaho National Labs (bit.ly/EBR-1). Today, the EBR is open to the public for tours where you'll see exactly how nuclear-powered electricity is generated. The site features four reactors and control rooms and more. The most unusual exhibit is the one you'll see as you enter the parking lot.

To one side of the lot are two hulking mechanical behemoths that look like something built at Burning Man out of found metals. These are actually the prototypes of nuclear aircraft engines.

The concept of aircraft nuclear propulsion was pursued by the Army shortly after the close of World War II. The idea was that a nuclear-powered aircraft could stay aloft for weeks or months at a time, creating a strategic air advantage. Fortunately, the concept never got off the ground and was made obsolete by long range ballistic missiles.

Arco, Idaho, is situated a few miles west

> ### Route Details – 388 Miles
> ➤ From Idaho Falls, ride west on US 20 to Arco, Idaho. (70 mi.)
> ➤ Follow US 93 south to Craters of the Moon National Monument. (19 mi.)
> ➤ Ride US 93 north to Challis, Idaho. (100 mi.)
> ➤ Continue on US 93 north to Missoula, Montana. (199 mi.)

of the lab at the crossroads of two former stagecoach routes. Arco was the first town lighted by atomic energy in the mid-1950s. In town, turn south on US 93 to find Craters of the Moon National Park.

In geological years, the lava flows at Craters have just barely cooled. The youngest flow here is just 2,000 years old. Located in the Snake River Basin, Craters is part of the same volcanic chain that powers Yellowstone. The landscape here is so rugged and alien, NASA has used it as a simulated lunar landscape for astronauts. The loop drive running through the park offers you an upclose view of this strange ground, but the best view is from a cinder cone. A hike to the top of Inferno Cone will give you an unobstructed view of the lava fields and the high desert landscape beyond.

We haven't spoken much about the riding since arriving in Idaho Falls, but it's about to take a turn for the awesome. Arco marks the southern gateway of the Lost River Valley and the run up US 93 to Challis may be as enjoyable as any run you've made to date.

A man-boy, a panel of switches, and a nuclear power plant. This spells trouble.

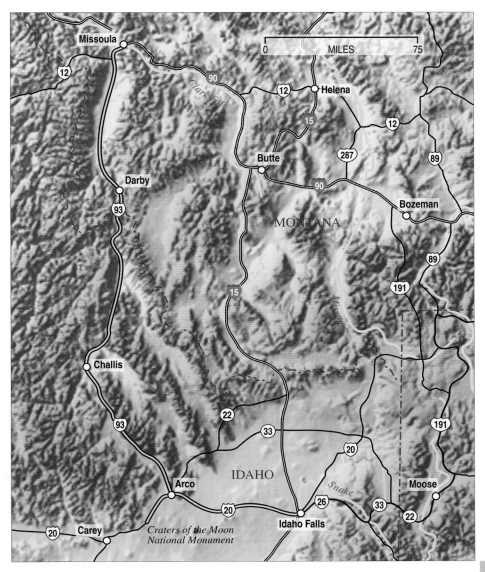

Route 93 winds over and around rolling green pastureland dotted with shacks that remain from the original homesteaders who settled this land in the 1850s. To the right, the Lost River Range dominates the eastern sky and includes Idaho's tallest peak, Mt. Borah (12,662 feet). Challis makes a convenient stopping point along this segment.

Route 93 north out of Challis becomes prettier still as it is joined by the Salmon River and enters the Salmon River Valley. Services become sporadic along this section of road, especially north of Salmon. Darby is a good spot to stop for a late lunch and then you can finish the run into Missoula.

14

Segment Six
Missoula to West Glacier, Montana

US 93 from Missoula to Kalispell is well-trav-
eled but not crowded. It doesn't compare to
the ride you enjoyed in the previous segment, but there are a few spots worth mentioning that make welcome stopping points.

First is the National Bison Range, one of
the oldest wildlife refuges in the nation. The
refuge was created to support a population
of American bison and is home to a small
herd of about 500 animals. The open grasslands of the Bison Range make it an excellent
spot to observe other Montana wildlife including pronghorn, mule deer, and the
occasional black bear.

Nearing Kalispell, US 93 curves around
Flathead Lake. If you had a mind to paddle
it, Flathead would take some time to circum-

navigate. Covering some 200 square miles,
Flathead was carved out by glacial action
and is fed by two mountain-born rivers. If
you fall in, you'd best know how to swim.
Flathead is 300 feet deep.

Following the busy streets of Kalispell,
West Glacier is a welcome relief. This western entrance to Glacier National Park remained nearly inaccessible until the Great
Northern Railway reached this location in
1893. Following the designation of Glacier
as a national park in 1910, tourist traffic
grew steadily and businesses increased
around the entrance to support them. It's
not overwhelming, though. West Glacier is
still a relaxing place to stop before heading
through the park.

US 89 on the east side of Glacier National Park, headed south toward
Browning, Montana, is a spectacular piece of road.

Route Details – 156 miles

➤ From Missoula, Montana, continue north on US 93 to Kalispell, Montana. (121 mi.)

➤ Follow US 2 east to West Glacier, Montana. (35 mi.)

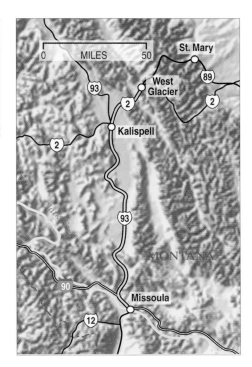

When the town was first established, the area was known as Belton. After it was re-named in 1949, the train station and historic inn across the street retained the former name. The Belton Chalet (www.beltonchalet.com) continues to serve travelers today with cottages and nicely appointed rooms that seem reasonable given their unique and his-toric nature. Dining on the outdoor deck, en-joying crisp mountain air and the extended twilight of high summer, is the perfect end to the riding day.

The Grand Tetons are made more spectacular by their sudden rise from the otherwise flat terrain of the surrounding area.

Segment Seven
West Glacier to Great Falls, Montana

Segment Seven marks the last leg of this northwestern tour. It's understandable to think that you've seen it all by the time you turn onto the Going to the Sun Highway.

> **Route Details – 206 miles**
>
> ➤ From West Glacier, follow the Going to the Sun Highway to St. Mary, Montana. (50 mi.)
>
> ➤ Follow US 89 south to Great Falls. (160 mi.)

You've been on the road for a week or more, and you've seen some of the most spectacular sights the continental U.S. can offer. What could top the peaks of the Beartooth Range? Or be more dramatic than the rise of the Tetons? What could be a more wondrous spectacle than acres of bubbling pools and cauldrons bathed in vivid comic book colors? There's just one thing, and that is Glacier National Park.

Going to the Sun Highway was completed in 1932 and excepting a tour by helicopter,

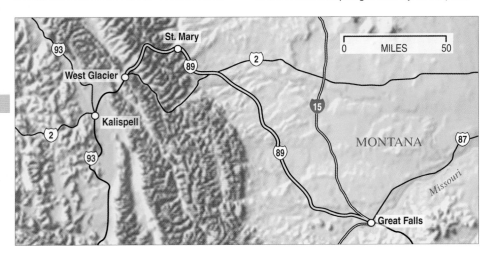

it's the best way to enjoy a tiny sliver of the stunning beauty of this world heritage site. Don't worry about riding this road in a hurry. A steady stream of summer tour traffic will prevent that, but it's just fine. There's too much natural eye candy to absorb here to pay much attention to the ride. But at one of the many overlooks, it's fun to look back over the stretch of road you've just traveled to appreciate the engineering and work involved in creating this throughway. Logan Pass marks the Continental Divide and the highest point on the road, but the Triple Arches overlook may offer the best view of the line of peaks that run above the Canadian border.

St. Mary marks the departure point from Glacier and begins your return to Great Falls via US 89. It's hard to believe that after covering more than 2,000 miles, this journey is drawing to a close. There is great riding yet to come on US 89 as it descends the hills for the high prairie, but the peaks that loom over St. Mary Lake make for a fitting final scene. The memories you gather from this journey will last a lifetime.

Road Tip – Shakedown Run

Adding a bunch of gear to your bike just before a long trip is tempting, but not a good idea. As you figure out how things are supposed to work, you're not giving full attention to your ride. Always perform a shakedown run with anything new you add. New seat, new GPS, new tires. If that new seat isn't right or the new helmet you bought is not breaking in as expected, you'll have time to remedy those irritating distractions before you hit the road.

During their brief spring and summer, the meadows of Glacier come alive with many varieties of alpine flowers.

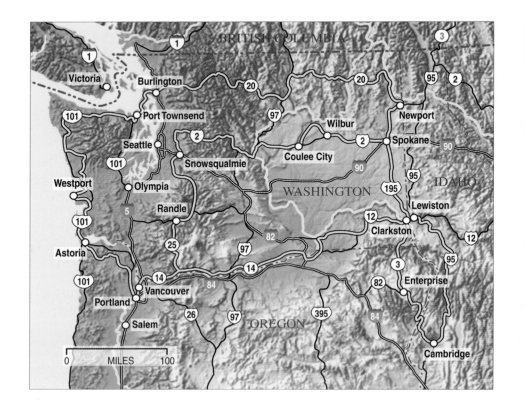

15 EVERGREENS AND CANYONS

This route maps 2,300 miles of gorgeous Pacific Northwest roads where the riding experience is exceeded only by the extraordinary scenery. You will transition from the lush, snow-capped Cascades to high and dry eastern Washington, explore Hells Canyon, the deepest in North America, then follow the Columbia River to the rugged Pacific coast. All the while you'll enjoy roads that will have you wondering whether your company would offer a relocation package to put you out here permanently. Once you spend a couple of weeks exploring the Pacific Northwest, you won't be content with anything less.

A happy combination of geological factors has created a riding environment in the Pacific Northwest unlike anywhere else in the United States or Canada. Like its northern neighbor, British Columbia, the Oregon-Washington region boasts soaring mountain ranges cloaked in forests that give rise to its nickname, the Evergreen State. Slopes and valleys are thick with pine and spruce, fir and hemlock, and the unique larch tree, a conifer that drops its needles in the fall like an oak.

Those mountains and forests wring the rain out of the moisture-laden clouds whipped up over the Pacific, regularly drenching the western coast while creating a rain shadow over the central and eastern portion of the state that results in near-desert conditions. Thus, in a matter of hours, you can ride from secluded beaches sprin-

US 101 crosses from Astoria, Oregon, into Washington state over the mouth of the Columbia River.

15

Riders gather in Baker City for the popular Hells Canyon Ride the second Friday in June.

kled along a craggy coastline, to mountains, still alive and trembling, to a high desert, softened with golden hills and laced with canyons cut by some of the mightiest rivers on Earth.

Now let's talk about the roads for a moment. Ad agencies filming car commercials love this area, which should tell you just about all you need to know. When you see a car swooping along curvy roads with dramatic views of a wide river, that's probably Route 14 along the Columbia. Roads with endless sweepers through gently rolling hills could be eastern Washington. A crazy set of switchbacks that seemingly turn in on themselves over and over again—well, that would be the Spiral Highway in Clarkston.

The region features places that are remote enough to give you a sense of solitude, but not so primitive as to lack the travel essentials. Its major cities are clean and inviting and fun to explore while the people here are intellectually curious and easily approachable. And when you're finished riding here—

Route 410 approaching Chinook Pass is clear in mid-June but there are still plenty of snowball fixin's to be found.

The road to Hurricane Ridge lifts you to an elevation where you can enjoy a long view of the Olympic Mountains.

a task that could continue long beyond the journey I've mapped—you're on the doorstep of the Canadian Rockies, northern California, and the tri-state area of Idaho, Montana, and Wyoming, all of which contain tens of thousands of miles of great roads.

Raingear should be handy, but you may not need it as much as you think. The Pacific Northwest has a reputation for rain, rain, and more rain, but when you look at precipitation maps and averages, some surprising facts come to light. The Seattle area, often depicted as wet and dreary, receives about 38 inches of rain per year on average, about two inches less than the mid-Atlantic. In the riding season, the contrast grows even larger. Between May and September, the mid-Atlantic averages 19 inches of precip while the Seattle area sees only about 7 inches. Areas right along the coast and at higher elevations receive much more rain

throughout the year, so as you travel through those areas, you'll want to pull out the gear. On average though, you're likely to find far better weather than you think, especially during the summer months.

Doesn't all this make you ready to ride? I am. Let's saddle up and see what wonders of riding await us in the emerald Northwest.

Connections

The section of US 12 east out of Lewiston into Montana is a well-known portion of motorcycling road running through Lolo Pass. If you're thinking about connecting to the Northwest Passage tour, this lightly traveled section of road is one of the prettiest in the US highway system and a great way to move from one supreme riding region to another. You're also connected to the Coastal Cruise tour, and close to the start of both the Canadian Rockies and the North to Alaska tour.

15

US 101 crosses from Astoria, Oregon, into Washington state over the mouth of the Columbia River.

Segment One
Portland, Oregon, to Westport, Washington

The first segment of this tour begins in Portland, Oregon, an attractive, progressive city situated near the confluence of the Willamette and Columbia Rivers, bounded by the Coast Range to the west and the Cascades to the east. Downtown Portland thrives with a large business and retail district that is fun to explore by bike or by foot. Folks here are very conscious of their natural surroundings and are involved in many outdoor activities. Portland is easily accessible from around the country by air, and motorcycle rentals are offered locally.

Head northwest out of town on US 30 to Scappoose and once there turn left on the Scappoose–Vernonia Road heading west. You'll join Route 47 and turn right toward Mist, Oregon. Near Mist, bear left on Route 202. Many of the roads you'll travel through this region began as Indian paths, trails

Route Details – 191 miles

➤ From Portland, Oregon, ride north on US 30 to Scappoose. (21 mi.)

➤ Follow the Scappoose-Vernonia Hwy northwest to Pittsburg. (21 mi.)

➤ Ride Rte 47 to Mist. (12 mi.)

➤ Take Rte 202 (Nehalem Hwy) to Astoria, Oregon. (46 mi.)

➤ Ride US 101 north to Raymond, Washington. (58 mi.)

➤ Follow Rte 105 to Westport. (33 mi.)

15

blazed by settlers, or roads built for logging. As a consequence, most routes squiggle their way across the terrain, a real plus if you're exploring them on two wheels.

Route 202 reaches the mouth of the Columbia River at Astoria. Turn north on Route 101 and shortly you'll cross the bridge into Washington state. Follow signs to Cape Disappointment State Park for the first of many great photo ops you'll have on this journey. The Cape is home to the oldest lighthouse on the west coast, perched on a cliff some 200 feet above the shore.

Westport, Washington, is a good stopping point for your first day's ride. You'll be near the water in an area with many lodging choices. After settling into your room, ride down to the Westport Light and Westhaven State Park. The wide beach here stands in contrast to the rocky coastline along most of the route, and it's a favorite of beachcombers and kiters.

The burgers at Fat Smittys are not only large, they're also high in fiber.

Traveling around the coastal areas of Washington state, you'll become very familiar with the protocols of ferry crossings.

Segment Two
Westport to Burlington, Washington

Today's ride takes us around the Olympic Peninsula. There's a lot to see and an early start will afford you extra time to wander through the best of Olympic National Park.

Head out of Westport on Route 105, then rejoin US 101 in Aberdeen. As 101 heads north, it turns inland a little. If you want to stay close to the shore, you can explore routes like Route 103 or 109. These are not through-routes, so you'll need to return to 101 to continue the northward trek.

US 101 skirts the western boundary of Olympic National Park. The Olympic Peninsula is a unique geographic province that is part rainforest and part rugged mountain terrain. It also holds large lowland lakes and cascading rivers. You can access just about every part of the park as you circle the peninsula. One of the most unusual areas of the park is the Hoh Rain Forest. It's uncommon for a rainforest to exist in an area where temperatures are moderate. You'd normally

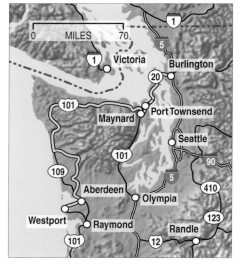

expect this type of landscape in a tropical climate. Tree species that grow here reach extraordinary heights for their type and everything is covered with flora that thrives in a humid environment, especially ferns and mosses. Another popular stop in the park is

Olympic Park boasts an enormous range of landscapes and climates, from dramatic coastlines and rain forests to alpine meadows and snow-capped peaks.

The Sol Duc River rambles through the shadows of towering old trees in Olympic Park before spilling into a moss-covered ravine.

Hurricane Ridge on the northern boundary of the park. This short ride brings you from lowlands covered with old growth forests to the treeline, where firs give way to open meadows. On a clear day, the views of the Olympic Mountains and the Strait of Juan de Fuca are spellbinding.

Following your visit to Olympic, continue around the peninsula on Route 101 to Maynard. From this point you'll catch Route 20 heading east through Port Townsend. Catch the ferry here over to Whidbey Island, then the mainland. Whidbey Island is the largest island in Puget Sound. If you are thinking you'd like to make a tour of the Puget Sound area, this is a good basecamp. It's a short ride up Route 20 to the ferry at Anacortes, which loops around several islands and then docks in Sidney, B.C.

This segment ends in Burlington, Washington. Your journey for the next couple of days will stick to Route 20, a scenic route that throws just about everything at you: twisties, straights, rain, desert, mountain passes, more desert—you name it. Get a good night's sleep; you'll need it!

Route Details – 281 miles

➤ Leave Westport, Washington, on Rte 105 heading north to Aberdeen. (21 mi.)

➤ Follow US 101 around the Olympic Peninsula to Rte 20 at Maynard. (198 mi.)

➤ Then continue on Rte 20 east to Burlington, using the ferry crossing at Port Townsend to Whidbey Island. (62 mi.)

15

Segment Three
Burlington, Washington, to Lewiston, Idaho

Route 20 out of Burlington traverses the entire state, so you might call it a "greatest hits" road. The ferry ride you took to reach Burlington gave you a taste of waterside life in the state. The remainder, from here to the eastern border, will give you the full spectrum experience of a ride through Washington state. Route 20 includes hundreds of

miles of twisty sections, a great variety of scenery, and long runs of sweepers. You'll make several mountain passes, then drop into river valleys, ride by orchards, glacially-fed lakes, national forests, and just enough small towns along the way to keep you and your bike fed and fueled.

The run on Route 20 is enough to keep you occupied for more than a day as you work your way east. Somewhere around Washington Pass you'll make the abrupt transition from the wetter coastal area to the bright, sunny high plains of central Washington. It's not unusual to ride from cool 50-degree weather to temperatures 30 degrees higher with bright sunshine in just a matter of miles. Route 20 parallels US 97 north before turning east into the forest again for more twists, turns, and scenic vistas.

Route Details – 529 miles

➤ From Burlington, Washington, follow Rte 20 east to Newport. (375 mi.)

➤ Ride US 2 west to Spokane, Washington. (48 mi.)

➤ Follow US 195 south to Lewiston, Idaho. (106 mi.)

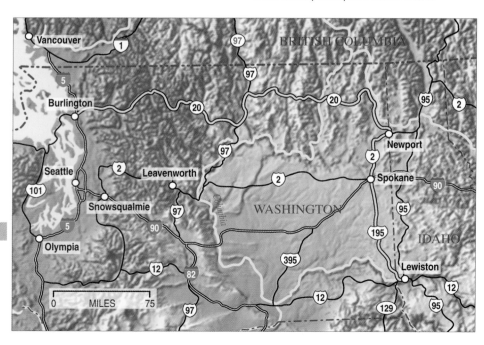

Route 20, the North Cascades Highway, woiuld be a fitting end to a fabulous cross-country route.

Given the length of the run, you'll want to look at some mid-point like Republic, Washington, as a potential stopping point. If you feel good about doing 250 miles from Burlington to Republic, I'd recommend you call ahead for a room the night before, just to make sure you have a place to stop. Republic is home to Stonerose Interpretive Center, a fossil site where you can dig for your own fossils (www.stonerosefossil.org).

The second leg of this segment runs to the state border at Newport and a decision point. Turn west on US 2 and ride to Spokane, wending through verdant hills, pastures, and meadows to Lewiston by way of US 195. The other option is to run east on US 2 and follow US 95 down through Coeur d'Alene. Both routes offer plenty of scenery and a fun ride. The first option is about 30 miles shorter and usually features less traffic.

15

Segment Four
Hells Canyon Loop

This segment will take you to some of the most spectacular riding in eastern Oregon and western Idaho, exploring Hells Canyon and the surrounding mountains. Technically, you could probably cover this in a long riding day. But I think you'll want to ride this in two parts, first following US 95 south from Lewiston, Idaho, to the area around Cambridge, Idaho, for an overnighter. This 200-mile run puts you in the perfect position for a return of equal length through what many consider the finest riding in the Pacific Northwest. That's high praise for an area rich with fantastic roads, as you've already discovered.

Prepare for this ride by making sure your bike's tires are in good condition, fluids are topped off, and everything is running smoothly. The run from here to Clarkston, Washington, will run through some extremes of temperature, and services will be

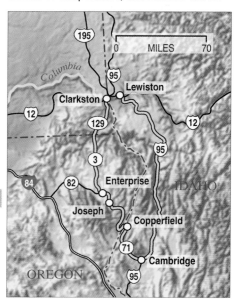

sparse. Gas is available en route in just a couple of spots, so start off with a full tank.

A ride through Hells Canyon should be on everyone's short list of motorcycle adventures. The canyon drops 5,000 feet below the western rim on the Oregon side, 8,000 feet below the Seven Devils Mountain range immediately to the east, and features some of the greatest extremes of altitude and climate you'll have the privilege of riding, coupled with outstanding views of the Wallowa Mountains. And it's great riding throughout.

Within a matter of minutes, Route 71 escapes the hustle and bustle that characterizes the urban core of Cambridge, all five blocks of it. Soon you're following a path through rugged brown hills that grow as you descend slowly toward the Snake River. It's going to get hot here, especially in the summer. Make sure you stay hydrated.

The scenery and the riding are as intense as the heat. Route 71 swoops along the Snake, crossing at the Brownlee Dam into Oregon. Route 86 joins the canyon from the west, clearing the way for your escape. If you'd feel better topping off on gas before you complete the route, stay west on Route 86 past the turn for North Pine Road and ride a couple of miles up to Halfway where you'll find gas and food.

The remaining portion of the route is as challenging as it is scenic. While national forest roads are not maintained to the same level as state roads, you'll find that Route 39 is well worth the run. Switchbacks line this route, posted from 15 to 45 mph and light traffic means you'll run up on few four-wheelers to break your rhythm.

Hells Canyon is the deepest river gorge in the U.S. with a distance of nearly 8,000 feet from nearby peaks to the floor below.

The final portion of the route from Enterprise, Oregon, to Clarkston, Washington, is a real sleeper of a road. Straight and pretty, Route 3 charms you from the outset, portending a pleasant ride through high mountain country. What's this? A sign announcing a 25 mph curve is a nice surprise. What happens next will be a magical moment that'll cap this highlight reel of riding. After bending a few more moderate turns, glimpses of a fall-off on the shoulder announce your arrival into some type of canyon area, but it isn't until you round a few more turns and then . . . *Bam,* it hits you. Trees fall away to open skies and far in the distance you'll spot the northern rim, marking an oasis of riding. Knowing that the pavement will bend and fight and twist its way across this land for the next half hour will raise the hair on your neck.

Route Details – 399 miles

➤ From Lewiston, Idaho, take US 95 south to Cambridge. (195 mi.)

➤ Follow Rte 71 west to Brownlee Dam, Idaho. (28 mi.)

➤ Follow Brownlee-Oxbow Road north to Copperfield, Oregon. (13 mi.)

➤ Ride Rte 86 west to North Pine Road (NF 39). (8 mi.)

➤ Follow North Pine Road to Joseph. (62 mi.)

➤ Ride Rte 82 north to Enterprise, Oregon. (7 mi.)

➤ Take Rte 3 (becomes Rte 129 in Washington) north to Clarkston, Washington. (86 mi.)

15

The road along the Snake River leads to more great riding through the Walla Walla Mountains.

Segment Five

Clarkston, Washington, to Portland, Oregon

US Route 12 out of Clarkston is a free-wheeling gem of a road. No major challenges, just gently rolling green hills and cultivated fields that stretch to the horizon. Near Wallula, US 12 meets the Columbia River at nearly the same point first reached by the Lewis and Clark Expedition in October, 1805. We're going to turn south on US 730. Follow this short segment of road to Umatilla, then turn north on US 385/I-82 just long enough to cross the river, exiting on Route 14. This scenic road, dubbed the

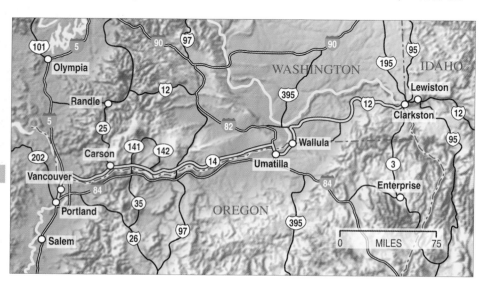

Lewis and Clark Highway, runs along the Columbia River on its journey to the Pacific Ocean, depositing us in Portland.

The Columbia River drains a 259,000-square-mile basin that includes parts of Oregon, Washington, Idaho, Montana, Nevada, Wyoming, Utah, and British Columbia. The river flows for more than 1,200 miles from the base of the Canadian Rockies to the Pacific Ocean at one of our first junction points—Astoria, Oregon. The Columbia River Basin generates a tremendous amount of hydroelectric power. More than 400 dams and structures have been built on the river, including 11 run-of-the-river dams. Altogether, the Columbia generates more than 21 million kilowatts.

The Dalles makes a good stop about two-thirds through this run. In contrast to other parts of the region that experience many days of cloud cover, The Dalles sees the sun about 300 days out of the year. While you're

Route Details – 342 miles

- ➤ From Clarkston, Washington, ride west on US 12 to Wallula, Washington. (128 mi.)
- ➤ Follow US 730 west to Umatilla, Oregon. (29 mi.)
- ➤ Cross Columbia River on I-82 heading north to Rte 14. (2 mi.)
- ➤ Follow Rte 14 west to Vancouver, Washington. (180 mi.)
- ➤ Ride US 30 south to Portland, Oregon. (3 mi.)

here, you're in the perfect position to take a day to check out a few local canyon roads. North of the river, Route 142 to Glenwood Highway and returning on Route 141 is a fun half-day run. South of town, a ride composed of Route 35, US 26, Route 216, and a return on US 197 would give you a taste of the Oregon Cascades around Mount Hood.

Oregon Route 3 heading north to Clarkston, Washington. Definitely part of an unforgettable motorcycle journey.

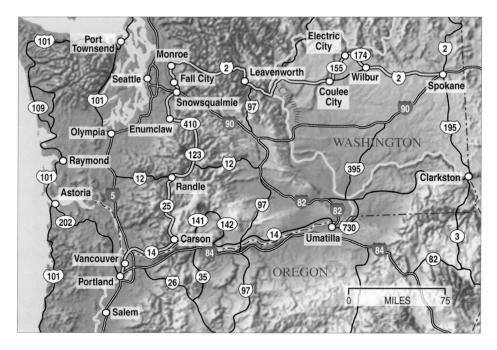

Segment Six

Portland, Oregon, to Spokane, Washington

You might call this segment the "interior tour" of the state. It serves as an optional route you can use to shortcut your tour, or to double it up for a longer run. It runs close to the urban areas of Seattle and Tacoma for those who wish to enjoy a couple of days of urban living along the coast, and it passes by some of the more famous members of the Cascade Mountains, including Mount St. Helens and Mount Rainier.

The first portion of the route picks a scenic path north through the central Cascades, by-passing much of the metropolitan area. Following Route 14 east out of Portland, turn north on Wind River Road. This connects to Forest Road 90 and eventually Forest Road 25, leading you to Randle, Washington. From time to time you can catch glimpses of

Mount St. Helens through the thick stand of forest. (For the best views of Mount St. Helens, make a day trip out of Portland up US

Road Tip – Keep the Fleece Handy

It doesn't matter where you're riding, keep a fleece jacket or thermal liner in a handy spot on your bike at all times, even in the middle of summer. Riding weather changes dramatically throughout the day in all climates, but especially as you change elevation. If you've been riding in 90-degree heat during the day, temperatures that drop into the mid-70s in the evenings will make you feel chilled, especially when riding at speed.

30 and Route 411 to Spirit Lake Highway, Route 504.)

Route 410 is the favored road to cross the Snowqualmie National Forest where you'll catch glimpses of Mount Rainier. Signs indicating 20 mph curves with 180-degree arrows foreshadow great riding to come. Take the park entrance at White River and follow the narrow twisties to Sunrise for spectacular views of the northeast face of Rainier. At 14,410 feet, Rainier towers above other mountains in the Cascade range by more than half. Like Mount St. Helens, Rainier remains an active volcano. Its last eruption was about 150 years ago.

The next section of the route runs east of the Seattle-Tacoma metropolitan area, but taking a day or two to visit the area isn't a bad idea. Seattle has an energy you can feel, whether you're cruising the streets on your bike or walking casually from one block to the next. The city has been a trendsetter in art and music for decades and is known for its great cuisine as well. Here are a few ideas that you could use to build an itinerary in the Emerald City:

- Visit the largest building in the world on the Boeing Factory Tour where you'll see 747, 767, and 777 planes in various stages of construction.
- Explore the Chittenden Locks and Fish Ladder where you can watch the boats pass and the fish migrate up and downstream through a 21-step ladder.
- Pike Place Market is Seattle's oldest and covers nine acres. It is home to hundreds of shops and restaurants including the original Starbucks.
- See the other Seattle that lies below the surface of the modern city on the Seattle Underground tour.
- Get the best perspective on the city from

Route Details – 558 miles

- ➤ From Portland, Oregon, follow US 30 north to Vancouver, Washington. (3 mi.)
- ➤ Take Rte 14 east to Wind River Road in Carson. (47 mi.)
- ➤ Follow Wind River Road north to NF 25. (36 mi.)
- ➤ Follow NF 25 north to Randle. (45 mi.)
- ➤ Take US 12 east to Rte 123. (23 mi.)
- ➤ Take Rte 123 north to Rte 410. (17 mi.)
- ➤ Follow Rte 410 north to Enumclaw. (41 mi.)
- ➤ Take Rte 169 north to Rte 18. (15 mi.)
- ➤ Follow Rte 18 north to Snoqualmie. (17 mi.)
- ➤ Follow Rte 202 northwest to Fall City. (6 mi.)
- ➤ Ride Rte 203 north to US 2 in Monroe. (25 mi.)
- ➤ Take US 2 east to Coulee City. (168 mi.)
- ➤ Follow Rte 155 northeast to Electric City. (27 mi.)
- ➤ Take Rte 174 east to US 2 in Wilbur. (21 mi.)
- ➤ Follow US 2 east to Spokane. (67 mi.)

Seattle's landmark Space Needle and the surrounding Seattle Center, home to the 1962 World's Fair.

When it's time to turn east, follow US 2 out of town. Much of US 2 is scenic and at the height of the travel season, it's a popular tour route. On the other hand, there are plenty of places to make a quick pass around anything that isn't traveling your speed. The

US 2 rolls through Leavenworth, Washington via a space-time wormhole that deposits you in Germany.

run over Stevens Pass will begin the transition into the dry climate of central Washington.

Arriving in Leavenworth is a bit of a surprise, and a testament to a town's vision and tenacity (www.leavenworth.org). You've heard the stories about small towns built around natural resources that once thrived, only to diminish and disappear when the resources played out. It's happened countless times. That same fate awaited the folks in Leavenworth in the early 1960s. Once a thriving lumber town, Leavenworth was robbed of its primary source of income when the Great Northern Railway Company diverted the railroad away from the town.

After decades of decline, the town made a last-ditch effort to reinvent itself, agreeing to

Mount Rainier presides over a crystal clear lake in the Cascade mountain range.

Route 2 in eastern Washington state runs through rolling fields with amber waves of grain. Just like in the song.

turn the town into a German hamlet in the midst of Washington State's alpine-like hills. Their efforts paid off. Today, Leavenworth is once again thriving, drawing visitors from around the globe to visit this little bit of Bavaria in the mountains near the Pacific. Although it's just a hundred miles from the Seattle area, Leavenworth is worth spending an afternoon's visit and an evening's rest.

The second portion of the route to Spokane passes by the Grand Coulee Dam. There's a reason why it's called "grand": everything about it is massive. The Grand Coulee is the largest concrete dam in the U.S., with a base between 450 and 500 feet thick, 30 feet thick at the top, and nearly a

mile in length. The Grand Coulee is the world's third largest producer of electricity, generating more power than a million locomotives. In the summer, the dam plays host to a laser light show with its face serving as the screen.

With this portion of the route completed, the only question that remains is, "What's next?" There are weeks of fine riding to the east in Idaho, Montana, and Wyoming. The high plains of north central Oregon are laced with great roads, and nearly deserted. You're just a few miles from the start of a series of rides in British Columbia. How many vacation days did you say you had? Think you can borrow against next year's?

Someone got the bright idea to bounce lasers off the Grand Coulee Dam at night to make a light show. It's a fun time.

15

Motorcycle Journeys Through North America

16   CANADIAN ROCKIES

The tours in this section are built as four mega-loops through the heart of the northern Rocky Mountains. In all, the routes mapped out here total over 3,000 miles of spectacular roads that wind through this vast and beautiful wilderness. Prepare for some of the most remote riding and unspoiled scenery you'll ever encounter.

British Columbia's motto is "Splendor sine occasu" or "Splendor Without Diminishment." It's an apt descriptor. Whether you spend a couple of days on a single loop or a couple of weeks exploring British Columbia, you'll come away with a new appreciation of the mantra "So many roads, so little time." It's no exaggeration to say that you could spend a lifetime touring the high country in Canada's spectacular western province and still feel there was more to explore.

Here's a typical afternoon: You've just ridden through a verdant river valley framed by majestic, rugged, snow-capped peaks so beautiful your teeth ache. The road ambles through endless forests, sometimes demanding your attention when it curls up next to a river or climbs a pass. Mostly it just acts as a pavement shaman, leading you on a lifetime ride. Guess what? There's another road ahead just like it. And another. Just hold your camera above your head, anywhere, and click: postcard.

When you look at a topo map, the clue to B.C.'s beauty is readily apparent. There's hardly a level spot in the entire province. If

Canada Route 16 north of Jasper National Park. Mount Robson in the background is the highest mountain in the Canadian Rockies.

16

Father and son riders Doug (right) and Greg Gilmer promise you're gonna like riding in British Columbia. Trust them.

it's not mountainous, it's valley. If it's not valley, it's water. Only the far northeastern corner of the province touches the boundaries of the Great Prairie and about the only way in there is by air.

Owing to the high latitudes and high elevations, mid-summer is the best time to tackle the routes through this region. In these climes, summer means long days of sunlight and moderate temperatures. Snow is possible at higher elevations, although summers don't see the soaking rains of late autumn and winter.

Riding here doesn't demand the same level of preparation as the full ride to Alaska, but you do want to observe a few precautions. For example, those snacks you keep in your saddlebags for an impromptu roadside picnic? Bring them into your room at night or you're likely to find your bags shredded in the morning, courtesy of a hungry bear.

Make sure you have provisions to repair a tire. A tow to a fix-it shop might cost as much as your bike is worth. For detailed planning, get a copy of *The Milepost* (www. themilepost.com) for the most comprehensive, accurate, and up-to-date information on travel services in the area.

Each loop in this section runs longer than most tours. With few diversions, becoming absorbed by the scenery and searching for the perfect photo op, it's easy to cover 350 to 400 miles or more in a day's ride. There really are no best spots to start or stop. Get on the road and ride 'til your eyeballs just can't pack any more scenery into your brain. For lodging, however, be sure to do your homework in advance. It's one thing to miss a room in Vancouver, but if you can't find one farther north, you'll be sleeping with the wolves.

One option to riding your bike to British

16

< Provincial Highway 3A is part of the International Selkirk Loop, a scenic byway that encompasses British Columbia, Washington, and Idaho.

The Icefields Parkway through Banff and Jasper National Parks offers countless scenic views and a great ride.

These riders explore the area around Hyder, Alaska. It's still a haul to get there, but riding to Hyder is a faster way to reach Alaska by bike than any other route.

Motorcycle Journeys Through North America

Even if you don't have time to ride far into British Columbia, easily accessible parks like Yoho are worth the ride. You can reach Yoho in less than a day's ride from the U.S. border at Eureka, Montana.

Columbia is flying and renting. Motorcycle rentals are available in Vancouver as well as Kamloops, a central location for three of the four loops. If your aim is to maximize your riding time in the northern Rockies, a fly-and-ride program might be a better option than riding your own bike up. And when you consider the time spent getting to and from the area, with on-the-road hotel expenses, renting a motorcycle might not be as expensive as you think.

Connections

Portions of the Canadian Rockies tour share roadway with the North to Alaska tour. You're also in close proximity to the Evergreens and Canyons tour and the Northwest Passage tour.

16

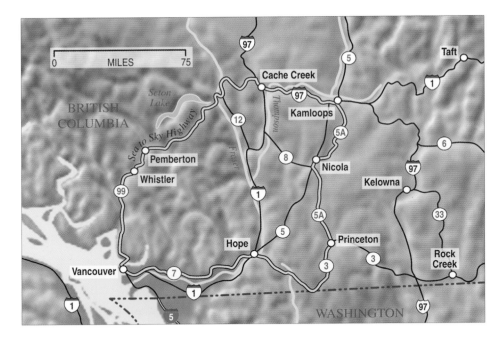

Segment One
Vancouver Loop

The Vancouver Loop might be called a "B.C. Sampler" because it's easy to reach, can be ridden comfortably in a couple of days and gives you a great sampling of what the larger British Columbia region has to offer.

The loop begins in Vancouver, a showcase of architectural drama and multi-cultural cool. What began as a typical Canadian outpost of trappers and traders has grown to one of North America's most ethnically diverse, self-aware, modern cities (www. tourismvancouver.com). Vancouver's variety of neighborhoods each with its unique appearance makes it a popular filming location (with the exception of settings that require palm trees or cactus). Nearly any street or neighborhood in the city looks like a model lifted from somewhere else. The weekend night market in Chinatown feels as authentic

as its Hong Kong counterparts. Chic SoHo-style Yaletown represents blocks of warehouses now converted to trendy shops and restaurants.

It's easy to get lost in Vancouver's charms, but we came here to ride, so let's head out. Route 99, the Sea-to-Sky Highway, begins the loop in dramatic fashion, clinging to cliffs that border the Salish Sea and Minaty Bay before disappearing into the coastal mountains that lead to Whistler, site of the alpine events of the 2010 Winter Olympics (www.whistlerblackcomb.com).

Once you pass this area, the traffic begins to thin, especially past Pemberton. Topping off here wouldn't be a bad idea. Portions of Route 99 are rough and broken, but you won't care. The sight of soaring mountains more than makes up for the bumps on the

16

road. Pull into the overlook at Seton Lake for a magazine-cover-worthy photo of your bike against a backdrop of crystalline, blue waters reflecting the rugged peaks.

After riding in relative isolation, it can be a shock to reach Route 97 for the ride into Kamloops and run into traffic—especially during summer and the high touring season as this is one of the main routes running to Dawson Creek and the Alaska Highway. It's summer and high touring season. The good news is that you're headed in the opposite direction.

Kamloops lies near the confluence of the north and south branches of the Thompson River (www.tourismkamloops.com). Kamloops' location in the rain shadow of the Coast Mountains means the area enjoys a sunny, semi-arid climate that is similar to the dry portions of eastern Oregon and Washington with fewer extremes of temperature than some areas of the Northwest. It makes a good base or rallying point for rides throughout the region and a stopover for this loop.

Turn south out of Kamloops on Provincial Highway 5A, the Princeton-Kamloops Highway. The road curves seductively over round brown hills. It's a ride that will remind you of

Route Details – 556 miles

➤ From Vancouver, British Columbia, follow Rte 99, the Sea to Sky Hwy north to Cache Creek. (211 mi.)

➤ Ride south on Rte 97 to Kamloops. (52 mi.)

➤ Follow Rte 5A south out of Kamloops to Princeton. (115 mi.)

➤ Follow Rte 3 west to Hope. (83 mi.)

➤ Follow Rte 7 to Vancouver. (95 mi.)

southern California, minus the heat, traffic, smog, and highway one-upsmanship of the local squids. The road follows the sparkling waters of Shumway, Trapp, Napier, Stump, and Nicola Lakes. If I were a road, I'd want to follow them, too.

At Nicola, Route 5A merges into Route 5, a divided highway that is lightly traveled and offers spectacular vistas. Route 5 ends just outside of Hope, but I recommend that you leave Route 5 south of Nicola and continue on Route 5A to Princeton. From there take Route 3 west to Hope, then pick up Route 7 for a meandering ride back to Vancouver or take Route 1 for the fastest return.

Vancouver, British Columbia, is a culturally diverse city with world-class cuisine and a non-stop nightlife.

16

This rider is hugging the Vermillion River in Kootenay National Park, located in southeastern British Columbia.

Segment Two
Yoho Loop

The Yoho Loop is about a three-day ride along the southern portion of B.C. Out of Kamloops, the route begins on a quiet stretch of Route 97 heading south toward Kelowna. Traffic picks up at the junction with Route 97A, then falls off again as you turn east on Route 33. This is spectacular riding country. Evergreen forests stretch as

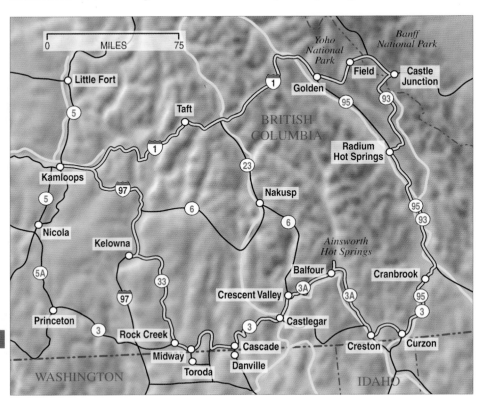

far as you can see, broken only by a nearly empty highway that wends through the high country to Rock Creek. Turn east on Route 3 heading toward Kettle Valley.

Route 3 dips south, almost touching the U.S. border at Midway. There's a border crossing here from Washington, a tiny outpost where your entry to Canada would likely go faster than at larger stations. Look for Toroda, Washington, on the map and follow Customs Road north. The same is true farther east at Danville, Washington, on Route 21, which crosses into Almond Gardens, British Columbia. A short jaunt north on Route 41 leads to Route 3.

Castlegar, situated along the Columbia River, is a logical stopping point for the first part of this loop. It's a 285-mile ride from the starting point in Kamloops, and stopping here will ensure that you're able to fully enjoy both the road and the sights in the next part of the loop. Departing Castlegar, follow Route 3A, a turn you'll find after crossing the Columbia River.

On the road from Maligne Lake in Jasper National Park.

Route Details – 928 miles

➤ From Kamloops, ride south on Rte 97 to Kelowna, British Columbia. (104 mi.)

➤ Follow Rte 33 south to Rock Creek. (83 mi.)

➤ Follow Rte 3 east to Castlegar. (105 mi.)

➤ Turn northeast on Rte 3A to Balfour. (49 mi.)

➤ Ride north on Rte 31 to Ainsworth Hot Springs and return. (20 mi. round trip)

➤ From Balfour, ride southeast on Rte 3A to Creston. (56 mi.)

➤ Ride Rte 3 east to Rte 93 just east of Cranbrook. (72 mi.)

➤ Continue on Rte 93 to Radium Hot Springs, British Columbia. (84 mi.)

➤ Follow Rte 93, the Banff-Windermere Parkway to Castle Junction, Alberta. (65 mi.)

➤ Follow Rte 1 to Field, British Columbia. (33 mi.)

➤ Continue on Rte 1 to Kamloops. (257 mi.)

Walcott Quarry, located in the Burgess Shale deposit near Field, British Columbia, is famous for its rich deposits of fossils.

Emerald Lake is the largest of Yoho National Park's 61 lakes and its primary tourist attraction. The remarkable color of the lake is created by fine particles of glacial sediment suspended in the water.

16

These riders are pausing for a rest and a photo op on Highway 93 in western Alberta before entering Banff National Park.

The ride north along route 3A through Kootenay Lake and the surrounding region is worth the run if you come here for nothing else. At Balfour, turn north briefly on Route 31 and run up to Ainsworth Hot Springs. Water temperatures in the pools here run 95 to 100 degrees F, a stark contrast to the waters of Kootenay Lake which are easily 40 degrees cooler. Return to Balfour and cross to the other side of the lake on a toll-free ferry.

Now here's something you won't see every day. Coming down the east side of the lake on 3A, you'll pass by the Glass House of Boswell (www.roadsideamerica.com/tip/1519). For a few bucks you'll be taken on a guided tour of this home, built in 1952 by a retired undertaker who employed his collection of a half-million embalming fluid bottles to "indulge a whim of a peculiar nature." Yea, I'll say. Creepy to think about but fascinating to look at. And the home has a great view of the lake, too.

Route 3A continues south, reconnecting with Route 3 at Creston. Turn east again on Route 3. At Curzon, Route 95 joins Route 3 and once again, makes a major turn, this time turning to the northeast, passing Moyie Lake. At one time, Moyie bustled with silver and lead mining and was considered Canada's most important source for these elements. Reminders of the mines are present in the concrete foundations and tailings that once hummed with activity.

Today, the primary attraction is Moyie Lake and the provincial park located along its shore (www.env.gov.bc.ca/bcparks/explore/parkpgs/moyie_lk). Strap a tent on the back of your bike or bring your camper along to enjoy Canada's excellent provincial and national park system. Not only are they affordable, you'll also enjoy the amenities that many offer, and you'll meet a lot of friendly Canadian folks who will be eager to hear about your ride.

A few klicks east of Cranbrook, Route 95 is joined by Route 93 as Route 3 ends. Con-

16

tinue on Route 93/95 north, following the Kootenay and Columbia Rivers and a series of lakes. Follow Route 93 when it diverges from Route 95 at Radium Hot Springs. Route 93, the Banff-Windermere Parkway, enters Kootenay National Park just east of town through a road segment blasted through solid rock. Much of the highway features brilliant green forest on one side and a solid rock wall on the other, with little traffic and incredible mountain vistas. At Castle Junction, Alberta, Route 93 joins Route 1, the Trans-Canada Highway. Follow Route 1 west as it splits from Route 93 just north of Lake Louise. The next stop is just 15 miles ahead..

Field lies on the boundary between Alberta and British Columbia and hosts the visitor center for Yoho National Park (www.pc.gc.ca/pn-np/bc/yoho). Yoho is home to sev-

eral natural and man-made attractions and is the perfect base for exploring them. Among the attractions is Lake O'Hara. Another is the glittering blue-green water of Emerald Lake, ringed by snow-capped mountains and pristine alpine forests, one of the most popular sites to visit. If you'd like to do this, plan your visit in advance. Access is restricted to a park-owned bus system and tickets sell out months in advance (Lake O'Hara Reservation Line: 250-343-6433).

The topography of British Columbia makes it none too friendly for laying railroad track, and yet, this was essential to opening the western frontier for development. The first tracks through this area ran at a grade of 4.5 percent. That doesn't sound like much, and if you were riding it on your bike, you wouldn't think anything of it. For a train

From Lake Louise to Jasper, Route 93 is called the Icefields Parkway. It is a stunning ride featuring dramatic mountain vistas, massive ice walls, and waterfalls.

That's not a cloud in the peak of those mountain tops, that's a glacier on Crowfoot Mountain in Banff National Park.

hauling hundreds of thousands of tons of ore, that's like staring over the edge of a cliff. After many accidents, a pair of spiral tunnels were carved into the mountain to reduce the grade. It's a unique engineering feat that remains in use today, and there are several vantage points throughout Yoho.

About the same time the spiral tunnels were being built, self-taught paleontologist Charles Walcott was wandering along a trail across Mt. Stephen. It is said that his mule threw a shoe and when Walcott bent over to get it, his eye was drawn to an imprint in a chunk of shale lying on the trail. Walcott searched for the bedrock where the shale came from and found a vast pocket of fossils, the preserved remains of aquatic life from 500 million years ago. Experts think of this as a time that marked a departure from simple single-celled organisms to more complex life forms. The Burgess Shale Geoscience Foundation in Field continues to study and preserve the strange life forms found high in the Rockies (www.burgess-shale.bc.ca).

The entrance to Kootenay National Park begins by shimmying through a mountain ridge.

16

Segment Three
Prince George Loop

Once you start riding in British Columbia, folks at home may wonder if you're ever coming back. You see, when you get up to Kamloops and you're poring over the maps for the next day's ride, looking at all those great roads yet to cover, you start thinking on a bigger scale. Prince George doesn't look so far away, like it used to. Dawson Creek? That's just a little farther north. Coupla days. From there, why heck, you're

almost halfway to Alaska. And the Arctic Circle is just . . .

Don't say I didn't warn you.

The ride up to Prince George is laced with options that can extend your ride by an extra day beyond a one-day loop out of Kamloops if you have the time. For example, rolling up Route 5 to Little Fort, you can pick up the Interlakes Highway (Route 24) for a short and sweet 60 mile run to Route 97. Then

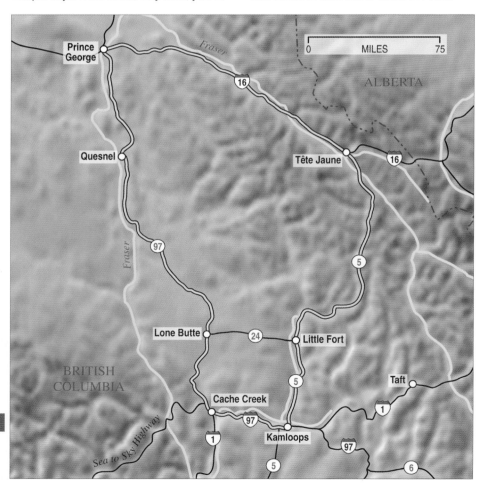

If you want to enter Hyder, Alaska, you'll have to fight your way through this gnarly gang of bikers. Or, you could just say "I'm buying the first round."

turn south to return to Kamloops. At 250 miles, that's an easy day's ride. The Interlakes is also known as the Fishing Highway. Many of the hundreds of lakes through the region are connected by remote gravel roads. If you're a dual-sport rider, I'm sure that got your attention.

But let's say you're going all the way to Prince George. In that case, follow the Southern Yellowhead Highway (Route 5) up to Tête Jaune. This puts you just two hours from Prince George. Prince George is the northernmost population center in British Columbia. The next town of any size is Whitehorse, up in Yukon Territory.

Let me just throw out a suggestion here. At this point, you are less than 450 miles from claiming bragging rights for riding to Alaska. Don't make a hasty decision, but if you were to do this, here's how it might work. Take out your now well-worn B.C. map and locate Prince George. Follow Route 16 west of town until it almost reaches the coast at Kitwanga (300 miles). See where it

bends to the north? Now, that road, Route 37, the Stewart-Cassiar Highway, is your ticket. Follow that to the Meziadin Junction and the route splits. Route 37 continues north where it intersects with the Alaska Highway. But Route 37A runs to Stewart, British Columbia, which is right across the border from Hyder, Alaska.

Invest just a couple more days, and you can ride out of Prince George for one more loop through the northern Rockies where you'll reach Dawson Creek and make a few miles on the Alaska Highway.

Like I said, when you start riding up here, your thinking gets bigger.

Route Details – 711 miles

➤ From Kamloops, British Columbia, take Rte 5 north to Tête Jaune. (212 mi.)

➤ Turn northwest on Rte 16 to Prince George. (171 mi.)

➤ Return to Kamloops via Rte 97 south. (328 mi.)

16

Segment Four
Dawson Creek Loop

The loop route to Dawson Creek is a 900-mile run, an easy three-day journey or a harder two-day run, depending on the forecast for both the weather and local butt conditions. If you thought lower British Columbia was remote, make this run and you'll be standing at the gateway to some of the most remote areas of the Earth where there are five square miles for each person. By the time you reach Dawson Creek, the distance you have ridden in British Columbia will equal the length of a ride through California, Oregon, and Washington combined.

When you finish the eastbound run on Route 16 from Prince George to Hinton, Alberta, you will have reached the edge of the Great Prairie on the western border of Alberta. If you're thinking about a three-day run, this would be a good place to stop. There are more than 20 motels here, including national chains. To make this a two-day run, turn north on Route 40 at Hinton. Route

40's broad shoulders and wide, high-speed sweepers will whisk you away to Grande Prairie, the logical half-way point in this loop. Even this far north, there are plenty of hotels in town to choose from.

When you're touring through the mountains, you often don't pay much attention to the vegetation. Out here in the prairie, it dominates the view. At any high spot, forests stretch as far as the eye can see. Most of inland Canada is dominated by boreal forest, the world's largest biome (major ecological community type). Twenty-seven percent of Earth's landmass is covered by this type of conifer forest, which in Canada extends well into the upper territories and above the Arctic Circle to where the treeless tundra takes over.

Dawson Creek marks the beginning of the fabled Alaska Highway, construction of which began in 1942 after the attack on Pearl Harbor raised fears that the western coast and Aleutian Islands might be vulnerable. Canada didn't have a pressing need to build a road through its vast wilderness, so the U.S. agreed to bear the full cost and turn over the Canadian portions at the conclusion of the war. Construction began on March 8, 1942; working from both ends, crews met up in September, just seven months later. The highway was dedicated November 20, 1942. Construction and maintenance have continued on the highway ever since, opening measureless stretches of wilderness to folks like you and me.

You'll find the famous MILE 0 signpost a block off the main road on 10 Street at the intersection of Route 2 and Route 49. An-

Road Tip – Ergonomics

Unless you're on an unlimited time budget, the scale of riding here usually means long days in the saddle. It's important to make sure the ergonomics of your bike will allow you to rack up 300-mile days regularly. Adding back support, highway pegs, handlebar risers, and seat supplements can go a long way toward increasing your comfortable riding range, but you want to have everything dialed in before you find yourself faced with a raw butt and 2,000 miles to get home.

16

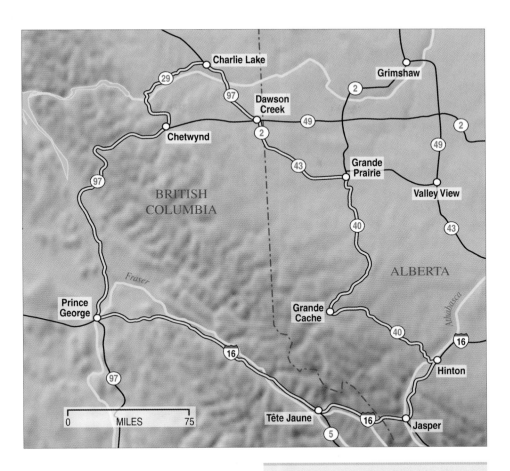

other MILE 0 sign had to be posted on the main road to accommodate the large numbers of folks in cars who stopped to commemorate the end or beginning of their journey. You can probably sneak a bike up to the original sign without blocking traffic.

Go ahead, try out a few miles of the Alaska Highway and see how it fits you. You can ride about fifty miles west to Charlie Lake, then turn south on Route 29 for 90 miles, reconnecting with Route 97 for the return run to Prince George.

Think you're ready for a run to Fairbanks? It's only another 1,500 miles. That's a stroll in the park.

Route Details – 898 miles

➤ From Prince George, British Columbia, take Rte 16 east to Hinton, Alberta. (283 mi.)

➤ Ride Rte 40 north to Grande Prairie. (207 mi.)

➤ Follow Rte 43 (becomes Rte 2 in B. C.) west to Dawson Creek, British Columbia. (81 mi.)

➤ Follow Rte 97 north to Charlie Lake. (51 mi.)

➤ Turn south on Rte 29 to Chetwynd. (89 mi.)

➤ Return to Prince George on Rte 97 south. (187 mi.)

16

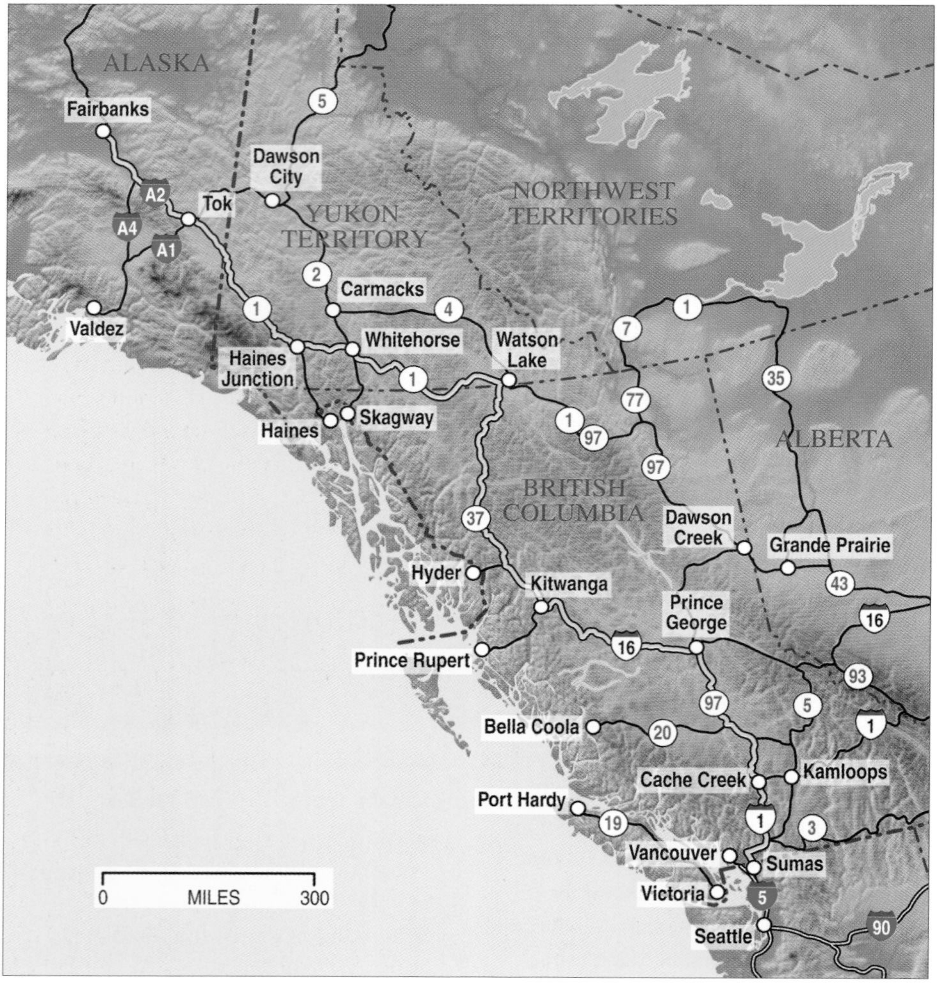

ALASKA

Fairbanks

Dawson City

Tok

YUKON TERRITORY

NORTHWEST TERRITORIES

5

A2

A4

A1

Valdez

2

Carmacks

Whitehorse

Watson Lake

4

7

1

Haines Junction

1

Skagway

Haines

1

97

77

35

ALBERTA

BRITISH COLUMBIA

Dawson Creek

97

37

Hyder

Kitwanga

Prince George

Grande Prairie

43

16

16

Prince Rupert

93

Bella Coola

20

97

5

1

Port Hardy

Cache Creek

Kamloops

19

1

3

Vancouver

Sumas

Victoria

5

Seattle

90

0 MILES 300

17

17 NORTH TO ALASKA

This tour presents a 3,100-mile all-paved one-way route from the US-Canadian border at Sumas, Washington, to Fairbanks, Alaska. This journey requires more planning than most. In return, you'll visit some of the most remote, wild and scenic portions of the world. And if you're lucky, you'll discover a bit of that pioneer spirit that lies dormant for so many. Finish this ride, and you'll accomplish a feat that only a small group of riders would ever contemplate. Expect the best, plan for the worst, and there's little doubt you'll enjoy the ride of a lifetime.

The ride to Alaska really is more than a motorcycle journey, it's an unforgettable adventure. The ride through western Canada and the northern Rockies is unmatched both for the roads and the scenery and wildlife.

Solitude—something that's rare at home—can be found in abundance here. You'll ride for hundreds of miles, keep company with nothing but your thoughts. If you can't get in touch with yourself on a ride like this, you're unreachable.

And even though this area is remote, there's an outstanding chance you'll meet folks here who will become friends for life. Riders from around the world are drawn to the beauty of this wild place, just like you. You'll find kindred spirits at every stop for gas or food. You'll have the chance most

Only a single road bisects Denali National Park's six million acres of wild land, but with views like this, one road is enough.

17

evenings to enjoy the tales of others who've encountered and overcome adversities on the journey and share a few of your own, too.

The beauty of British Columbia, Yukon, and Alaska is hard to express in words. Even pictures hardly do it justice. You'll follow roads for hundreds of miles that trace wild rivers and navigate deep canyons. Magnificent glaciers and mountain ranges will dominate the view for hours on end. From the top of a pass, you'll take in a view of clear lakes and pristine forests untouched by man.

If you think the ride to Alaska is beyond your reach or your capabilities, you'll be happy to know it's not. All the roads in this tour are paved but one, which includes just a few miles of dirt that is likely to be paved by the time you reach it. Any motorcycle in good mechanical condition can make this trip.

That said, don't take this trip too lightly. Most of the journeys presented in this book don't require much more advance preparation than checking your tires for air and your wallet for a credit card. Undertaking a ride to Alaska is quite a different matter. It has much more in common with an expedition than a weeklong fling through remote California canyons. It requires careful and thorough planning for a successful trip, as well as Plans B, C, and D for contingencies that may crop up along the way. And that's a big part of the thrill. It takes work to plan a ride to Alaska, and pulling it off is a testament to your careful forethought and your ability to execute a plan.

While the following list of special considerations is not exhaustive, it will alert you to some of the important issues to consider.

Special Considerations

This is a long ride, and it takes time. A round trip to Fairbanks and back from the U.S. following the shortest paved route is about 4,200 miles. At this high northern latitude, you'll have abundant daylight riding time, but with many long days in the saddle, you don't want to outride your comfort limits, even when there is a lot of daylight left. An average of 300 miles per day is a respectable pace for most folks; that works out to 14 days of riding. not including the time required to get to the starting point, days off for inclement weather, or time to do things other than ride every day. It can easily take a month to complete the journey to Alaska,

starting from the east coast. If you are tight on time, consider a shorter trip to Hyder, which is around 1,800 miles round trip from the border. At a reasonable 300 miles per day, that's six days of riding.

Expect any type of weather, any time. As the locals say, June is spring, July is summer and August is fall. Temperature and precipitation can vary to the extreme and often within the span of a single day's ride. Hit one of the higher passes along the way and temperatures can easily dip into the 20s with snow. A few hours down the road, it might be dry, sunny, and 90. It will not be uncommon for your trip to include days of overcast skies and rain. Summer is the rainy season in

Heading north to the Arctic Circle, you can easily see what's coming at you, and what lies ahead.

If you happen to ride north on a dual-sport, you'll have access to more out-of-the-way locations, like this view of Salmon Glacier 20 miles north of Hyder, Alaska. That's not to say the paved roads aren't also off the beaten path.

this part of the country. But that's part of the adventure, right? If you wanted an easy trip, you could have driven a car.

Accordingly, you should plan to carry gear that will keep you comfortable in a wide range of conditions. Multi-season gear with zip-in liners is handy, not only because you can change layers according to the weather, it also reduces the amount of overall gear you need to haul.

Outfitting your bike means ensuring that it is in peak mechanical condition. Tires are a special matter. If you're anywhere close to needing tires, reshoe your bike for this trip. And keep in mind that it's not abnormal to need a new set when you return home. Long segments of the road here are typically re-paired with chip seal. That, in combination

with the extra load your bike is carrying, will mean higher than normal tire wear. Replace the toolkit that came with your bike with a real set of tools and bring along a patch kit and some method of tire inflation (CO_2 or compressor). If you do plan to obtain routine maintenance on the road, schedule that well ahead of time.

Comfort and coverage are paramount. If you aren't comfortable on your bike for long stretches, you need to correct that or take a different bike. You may want to consider in-stalling a backrest, highway pegs, or handle-bar risers to maximize your comfort. If your bike doesn't have a windscreen, consider adding one, not so much for its weather pro-tection, although you'll appreciate that, but to protect you from the gravel that's flung by other vehicles. Another good idea is polycarbonate covers for glass lenses, such as your headlight and auxiliary lights.

You should have copies of paperwork for any trip longer than a weekender, but on this journey it's mandatory. Checking in at the Canadian border, you'll want to have a copy of your bike's title, registration, and proof of insurance that specifically includes coverage in Canada. You'll also need your passport. Bring along copies of any critical medical records and prescriptions. Keep a list of everything that's in your wallet, with contact numbers in case you need to replace them. Stow that list along with a duplicate drivers license, and zip-tie a spare key somewhere out of sight that you can reach easily.

What about gas, food, and lodging? Throughout all portions of this route, these essentials are readily available. Even in remote areas, gas can be found every 60 to 100 miles on average. Experienced riders recommend that you get gas whenever you see it because stations may close from year to year. It's best to make reservations for lodging well in advance. The travel season in Alaska is short, which means rooms are either booked well in advance or they sell out quickly. If you carry camping gear, your plans can be more flexible. If a motel room doesn't pan out, campsites are plentiful along the route.

When you're doing research for this journey, it's easy to become overwhelmed with the amount of information that's published. That's why I recommend you turn to a few select, authoritative resources for specific answers. The most detailed guide to services available along all roads leading to Alaska is *The Milepost* (www.milepost.com). This publication is updated annually and contains a mile-by-mile account of every road that runs through British Columbia and Alaska. It is indispensable. Greg Frazier's *Alaska by Motorcycle* offers you the sage advice of an experienced rider, discussing in greater detail the things you should plan for, as well as more information about side trips to the Arctic Circle, Deadhorse, Fairbanks, and more from a rider's perspective. Taken together, these two resources will help you concoct a successful venture to the Last Frontier.

Eat and Sleep

Refer to the Canadian Rockies tour for some lodging suggestions in Prince George and Dawson Creek. Your best bet is to obtain a copy of *The Milepost* and use that to help you identify lodging. This is not an area where you'll have many choices. Sometimes your only choice is a spendy 5-star lodge, other times it's a bed in a cinderblock room. Ya get what ya get. But in order to make sure you get something, plan your stops in advance, make reservations at those stops, and confirm them a week or two before you leave.

Connections

If you're primed for more riding after you've visited Alaska, there's plenty more to be found here. Continue your tour through the Rockies on the Canadian side, or drop down into the Lower 48 for the Coastal Cruise tour or Evergreens and Canyons tour.

17

Segment One
Sumas, Washington, to Prince George, British Columbia

So enough about logistics, you can think about all that later. Let's talk about the ride a bit and what you'll see along the way. This first segment leads to Prince George, British Columbia, the last large population area you'll find before turning toward Alaska.

The first long segment of road north of Hope runs through the Fraser Valley, a good mix of sweepers and straights for more than 100 miles along the river. Hells Gate is at the narrowest part of the river valley, where an aerial tram will take you down 500 feet to a café and shop complex overlooking the river.

Early settlers came to the region in pursuit of gold. The influx of immigrants leaving California's gold fields prompted the territory of New Caledonia to form a provincial govern-

Victoria, British Columbia marks the beginning, or the end, of the Trans-Canadian Highway.

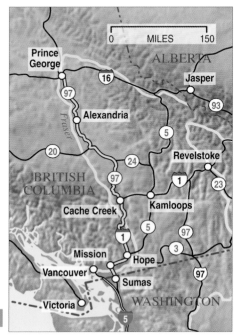

ment to handle the newcomers. In the years following the U.S. Civil War, some expected the region to be annexed by the United States because of a beef with Canada and discussions of reparations. The U.S. thought it would take British Columbia—and Nova Scotia, too—for compensation. Folks in the province, however, felt differently and elected to join Canada. Oh well, win some, lose some.

Cache Creek is about 200 miles from the border, and is where you'll turn north onto Route 97 for Prince George. Covering the 460 miles from the border to Prince George in unfamiliar territory may be more than you want to undertake, especially on the first day of your run. Cache Creek has multiple lodging and dining facilities and may make an attractive first stop. 100 Mile House at 260 miles north is another significant travel center, as is Williams Lake at 320. I'm not trying to talk you out of long days in the saddle, but you should know it isn't necessary; with all the things there are to see and do along the way, 250 miles may be all you want to ride in one day!

From the U.S. border you'll ride about 800 miles to get to this point. It's just 1,200 miles to Alaska from here. Chump change.

As you follow the map north toward Prince George, you've probably noticed a theme: 70 Mile House; 122 Mile House; 141 Mile House. What's up with that, you ask? These spots along Route 97 mark toll houses along the Old Cariboo Road, the original wagon road that began at Lillooet and ran to the Cariboo gold fields near Alexandria. Early in its history, camels purchased from the U.S. Camel Corps were used in an attempt to haul freight up the road. Apparently, camels and mules don't get along well and the rocky soil hurt the camels' soft feet. The experiment was quickly terminated and some of the camels escaped into the wild. Feral camels were spotted in the region until the 1930s.

Located at the junction of Route 97 and Route 16, Prince George (pop. 71,000) is the largest population area you'll encounter until you reach Fairbanks.

Route Details – 459 miles

➤ Enter British Columbia by way of Sumas, Washington.

➤ Follow Rte 11 north to Mission, British Columbia. (12 mi.)

➤ Take Rte 7 east to Hope. (51 mi.)

➤ Ride north on Rte 1 to Cache Creek. (120 mi.)

➤ Take Rte 97 north to Prince George. (276 mi.)

17

It's like this . . .

Segment Two

Prince George to Kitwanga, British Columbia

Route Details – 301 miles

➤ From Prince George, ride west on Rte 16 to Kitwanga, British Columbia (easy enough, eh?). (301 mi.)

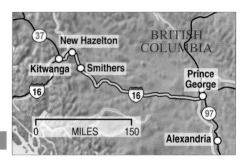

At Prince George you face a decision. Many travelers go to Alaska via Dawson Creek so they can begin at mile 0 of the Alaska Highway. If you want to take that traditional route, turn north out of Prince George on Route 97 to reach Dawson Creek and then continue on Route 97 (the Alaska Highway) to Watson Lake and beyond. The alternate route I'm describing here also originates in Prince George but it follows Route 16 to Kitwanga and then Route 37 to Watson Lake. It sounds kind of funny to say that this road to Alaska is more remote when by any stretch of the imagination the traditional

. . . and this . . . for a long, long time. Riding to Alaska requires as much mental preparation as physical.

route is not exactly like the Garden State Parkway. But for a growing number of riders, this alternate route is becoming more attractive. It is, in fact, more remote than the traditional route, features awesome scenery, and offers sufficient travel services. If you choose this route, you will pass within a short distance of Hyder, a popular rallying point for riders who want to make a quick run to Alaska.

At 235 miles from Prince George, Smithers offers the best selection of lodging. If you can eek out another forty miles to New Hazelton, you'll find lodging there too.

Here's where your research will be very important. If you want to optimize your travel days, you may find that you need to stop short some days and stretch longer than normal on others, in order to find lodging.

Located beside Kitwanga is the native village of Gitwangak, home to an impressive collection of totem poles. Totems tell the story of native families through symbols of nature and have been erected since area clans located here in 1835. For that reason, these totems represent the oldest collection to be found in their original village in British Columbia.

17

Segment Three
Kitwanga, British Columbia, to Watson Lake, Yukon Territory

Route 37 is the Stewart-Cassiar Highway (www.stewartcassiar.com) and it winds through the most remote western stretches of British Columbia. Fuel up before leaving Kitwanga for the next segment. Reliable gas stops include Bell II, 155 miles north of Kitwanga, Iskut at mile 255, and Dease Lake at 300. Route 37 has been upgraded in recent years and is paved its full length, save a couple of small stretches of hard packed high-speed gravel road totaling just a few miles. With plans to finish those final miles in the works, you may find even that has been completed.

Route 37 runs between the Skeena Mountains to the east and the Coast Range to the west, connecting the northwestern rain forest with Yukon forests dominated by spruce and jack pines. At Dease Lake you'll cross the continental divide that separates water flowing into the Pacific from water heading toward the Arctic.

The intersection with Route 37A at milepost 97 offers the time-pressed rider an opportunity to reach Alaska from the border in just a couple of days: Stewart, B.C. and Hyder, Alaska, are just forty short miles to the west. Tempting, eh? Stewart has a small

Highway 37 is the northernmost highway in British Columbia, traversing utterly remote and wild territory.

17

Many riders venture to Alaska to check out the extraordinary beauty of the mountains around Salmon Glacier.

Route Details – 447 miles

➤ From Kitwanga, British Columbia, ride north on Rte 37 to Watson Lake, Yukon Territory (this is a long haul). (447 mi.)

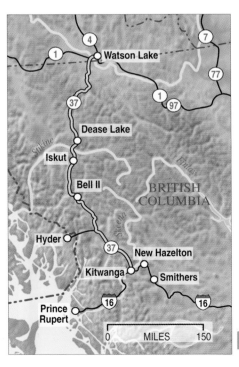

but full complement of travel services and is a popular site for bear-watching. Hyder is a frequent rallying point for motorcycle groups.

Just prior to reaching the Alaska Highway, a small sign signifies another achievement for you. You've just entered the Yukon Territory. Then after 450 memorable and solitary miles, you've arrived at the intersection with the Alaska Highway at milepost 626, a few miles west of Watson Lake. Congratulations, you're a little over halfway to Fairbanks!

There are probably more bears than people in Alaska. Certainly in these parts.

Segment Four
Watson Lake to Whitehorse, Yukon Territory

Watson Lake might be a good place to take a day off from riding and refill your mental gas tank. Check out the Alaska Highway Interpretive Center or a program at the Northern Lights Centre. Oh, and what did you do with that signpost you brought with you?

Route Details – 272 miles

➤ Ride west on Rte 1 from Watson Lake to Whitehorse, Yukon Territory. (272 mi.)

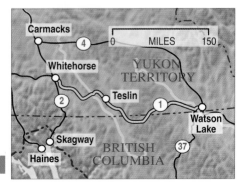

Watson Lake is home to the Signpost Forest, a collection of over 61,000 signs, and growing. You could easily while away an hour or more here, looking for familiar names and places.

Now that you're on the main road to Alaska, you'll notice a significant increase in traffic. It's not exactly the Garden State Parkway, but RVs, fifth-wheelers, and travel trailers are a common sight. Scenery, while still beautiful, won't be quite as arresting as in previous segments, but there will be exceptions. The 1,700-foot bridge crossing the Teslin River is an example. The bridge is the longest you'll encounter along the route. It's also an open grate bridge, so be careful as you cross.

Teslin also marks an important point in your journey, as you are leaving the Rocky Mountains behind. What looms ahead are the Cascades, a volcanic ring of mountains, including Mount St. Helens, that stretches into northern California.

17

Whitehorse is a fair-sized town and the capital of Yukon Territory. The 23,000 folks who live in or near Whitehorse represent three-quarters of the territory's population. You'll find anything you need here, including motorcycle service. But expect to pay a hefty premium for the convenience.

Located along the Yukon River, Whitehorse has a long history with miners and trappers, and the museums to prove it. Whether you're looking to while away a couple of hours on your arrival, or you plan to rest up here for a day, Whitehorse offers plenty of diversions. The MacBride Museum of Yukon History (www.macbridemuseum.com) offers the most comprehensive view of the characters and events that shaped early Yukon history. Another popular stop is a tour of the SS *Klondike,* a stern-wheel riverboat that served as the primary means for moving mail, freight, ore, and people along a 450-mile route between Whitehorse and Dawson City until the mid-1950s.

When you stop for gas and a night's rest, you're going to hear stories about bears. Bears chasing travelers. Bears catching travelers. Bears . . . well, you get the picture. For the most part, little of that is true, although funny stories do surface now and then. A riding buddy of mine once began the trip up the Haul Road (Dalton Highway) to Deadhorse, accompanied by his wife. They stopped at a pullout for a break, whereupon a mature grizzly appeared out of the brush and stood in the roadway, blocking their exit. My friend turned to his wife and whispered.

"I hear if you throw poop at them grizzlies, they'll turn and run away."

"Well where are we going to find poop to throw at a bear?" the wife asked.

"Just reach in my pants there and you'll find all you need."

At that, the bear sniffed the air, seemed to grimace, and ambled back into the woods. Or so I am told.

The Dalton Highway north of Fairbanks, on the way to Prudhoe Bay.

Segment Five
Whitehorse, Yukon Territory, to Tok, Alaska

Here's another way into Alaska. Top of the World Highway connects Dawson City, Yukon Territory, to Chicken, Alaska.

This segment between Whitehorse and Tok (pronounced like "toke," no joke) offers some of the most challenging road conditions on the trip with road repairs often creating long stretches of gravel-laced mud. Nonetheless, riders on all manner of bikes manage it, and you can too. Put a little more pressure on your footpegs and the bike will feel more stable crossing these stretches.

Despite advances in road building practices over the years, no one has yet found a process for paving over permafrost. Much of the soil underlying the northern portion of the Alaska Highway is of glacial origin, not well suited for building foundations. Higher summer temperatures cause the ice-rich per-

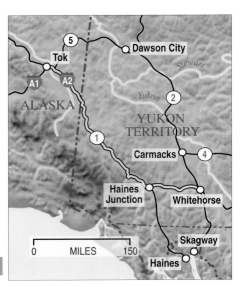

Route Details – 387 miles

➤ From Whitehorse, ride to the U.S.-Canada border on Rte 1. (297 mi.)

➤ Continue on Rte 2 to Tok, Alaska. (90 mi.)

17

You finished with that sandwich?

mafrost to melt, turning the soil to pudding; then lower temperatures in the fall (remember, that's August!) cause the soil to freeze and the pavement above it to buckle and heave. It's the primary reason the highway has needed, and will continue to require, ongoing reconstruction.

For good measure, this and other sections of the route include open range. Don't be surprised to find horses or other livestock grazing near the highway. Bison and bears are frequently spotted, too. Close as you are to the North Pole, heck, you might even spot a couple of Santa's reindeer fattening up for the Christmas Eve run.

Some 300 miles after Whitehorse and more than 1,700 miles from the border, a faint spot appears in the distance. As you draw closer, what could it be? Why it's the WELCOME TO ALASKA sign! Tok, Alaska is about

Road Tip – Bridge Crossings

Open grate and wooden deck bridges are common throughout this tour and some folks will find these difficult to navigate. Wooden decks get slick with the slightest bit of moisture, while open grate decks can weird you out with the way they make the bike twitch. If either makes you uncomfortable, the best approach is to maintain a slow but steady speed. On open decks, let the bike wander a bit. Too much overcorrection will result in a get-off.

80 miles to the west. Fairbanks is just 280 miles from this point. Tok has numerous hotels, so if you book far enough in advance you'll have no trouble getting a room.

17

Segment Six
Tok to Fairbanks, Alaska

In the final segment of this tour, you're on your way to Fairbanks via Route 2. Delta Junction is where you'll catch your first glimpse of the trans-Alaska pipeline. Built between 1975 and 1977, the 800-mile Alaska pipeline was the most expensive privately-funded project at the time, costing some $8 billion. The 48-inch pipe has carried more than 15 billion gallons of oil from the North Slope to Valdez, the northernmost ice-free port in Alaska.

Fairbanks' central location makes it a good base for exploring this land of the midnight sun (www.explorefairbanks.com). Flightseeing is both the most efficient and the most spectacular way to take in the full scope of the northern wilderness. For many, that includes a trip to Denali National Park, about 120 miles south of Fairbanks.

Denali's six million acres is larger than the state of Massachusetts and contains 20,320-foot Mount McKinley, North America's tallest peak. Denali is part of the Alaskan Range that runs some 600 miles in an arc between Alaska and British Columbia. One of the most adventuresome ways to see the park, and really appreciate it's size and scale, is by air. Fly Denali (www.flydenali.com) for example, offers flights over Denali. This tour also lands on a glacier and flies over the Great Gorge at Ruth Glacier, the world's deepest (www.nps.gov/dena).

Denali National Park is a popular destination, and a fitting reward for those who make the successful trek to Alaska.

This group has reached the Arctic Circle on the Haul Road north of Fairbanks. Above the Arctic Circle, the sun does not dip below the horizon on the summer solstice.

Route Details – 203 miles

➤ From Tok, Alaska, ride north on Rte 2 to Fairbanks, Alaska. (203 mi.)

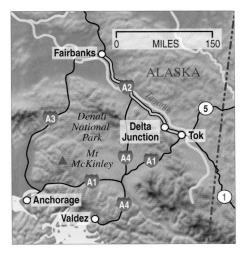

If you were thinking you could catch a glimpse of the Northern Lights, well, that'll have to wait for cold weather. This phenomenon is visible only in a dark sky and best in clear, cool conditions. The aurora borealis begins to appear in September as the skies begin to darken at night; it is in fullest form in mid-winter. Well, maybe if you put some knobbies on the bike, you could return then.

Have you been thinking about a run to Prudhoe Bay? Many riders launch from Fairbanks each year to make the 500-mile one-way run. Another popular ride is to the Arctic Circle, a round trip of about 400 miles from Fairbanks, a doable one-day ride out and back in good weather. Why not bag that at least, while you're here? The trip to Prudhoe requires an extra measure of

thought, research, and planning, so check out Frazier's book for more details.

Now that your Alaska journey has been completed successfully, where to next? I've heard the ride down to Tierra del Fuego is astounding, and I've been thinking . . .

17

PLANNING YOUR UNFORGETTABLE JOURNEY

Undertaking an extended journey begins way before you turn the key and ride out of the garage. Your trip begins the moment you get the itch to ride to the horizon and see what's around the curve.

You'll increase your chances of success if you make some preparations in advance. Although I've written about this extensively in *The Essential Guide to Motorcycle Travel*, this appendix contains an abbreviated version of the elements that I think are most critical.

Plan

The idea of planning a motorcycle trip is an anathema to some riders I talk to. "All I know is, I'm gonna get on the bike and ride." (This, in itself, is a plan.) I'm not saying that you need to spend all your free time poring over maps and travel sites, crafting an itinerary that specifies every stop and every turn. Overly complex plans are a recipe for creating unmet expectations.

When I talk about planning a trip, I'm referring to the steps you can take ahead of time that will help you get the most out of

your trip—things you can do that will minimize the hassles that crop up and give you more time to enjoy what interests you the most, whether that's visiting attractions on or off the beaten path, exploring small towns, or seeking out the best roads.

Research is key to good planning. Most folks do this whether they realize it or not and the resources available to you that can help you explore virtually have exploded in the last few years. Research tools include:

Books. By reading this book, you're doing research. You're getting ideas (I hope) that may lead to future rides. If you're interested in a particular region, there's a good chance Whitehorse publishes a more detailed book on that area. If you're planning a big adventure, a more detailed book on motorcycle travel (mine and certainly others) are worth reading. Chris Scott has authored the definitive title on world travel entitled *Adventure Motorcycling Handbook*.

Maps. Paper may be passé in many other forms, but old-fashioned maps are still awesome, especially for getting new ideas. I re-

You'll also encounter your share of the odd, unusual, and downright weird on your trips. They're especially delightful when you come upon them unexpectedly.

From points like this you can see into the future. And your future looks wet.

member how excited I was when DeLorme's Gazetteer series debuted, making it possible to explore back roads in my home state and beyond. I carry these maps with me as a backup to my GPS and as something to help me plan the next day's ride in my motel room at night.

Software. Planning software has come a long way. I use DeLorme's Street Atlas for most of my planning. Microsoft Streets and Trips is another popular package. These programs will help you lay out ideas for your trips and size them up before you commit to them on the road. I use Street Atlas in combination with Google to determine if an area I'm planning to stop at is a dusty crossroads with one fleabag motel or if it's large enough to have a selection of lodging and restaurants.

Forums. If you're short on ideas for your next trip, there are a few million riders in forums around the Internet willing to give you some ideas. Forums like Pashnit.com, ADVrider.com and HorizonsUnlimited.com are forums that welcome riders of all stripes united by a love of two-wheel travel. It's hard to imagine any situation you can conceive that someone hasn't already encountered and overcome.

Google. I mentioned sites, but I think Google belongs in a category of its own. Google Maps, Street View, and Google Earth in particular, are revolutionary, eye-opening tools that allow you to explore just about any road you might want to ride, anywhere in the country. When you explore with Google Maps, travel facilities like hotels and restaurants can be identified in context on the map. And, as you move the map, the listings change, allowing you to move around in a region to find a stopping point that has a good selection of services.

Google Earth allows you to travel roads throughout the world with an actual view of roads, cities, buildings, and other details, as though you were flying over it. Google Earth covers practically any road on Earth that you'd be inclined to follow.

Using any combination of those tools should be enough to yield a few hundred ideas. The tough part will be deciding where to ride first.

Inventory. If you already have some ideas of where you'd like to go, you'll naturally start taking inventory. Which journey do I have enough time to take? Will I need to outfit my bike differently? Is it the best bike for such a trip? Will I need a passport?

Here's where I start making lists. If I'm heading somewhere new, I'll come up with a list of questions, known issues, action items, anything I need to prepare for a trip. Doing this helps me identify issues that need to be handled well in advance. For example, if I were planning to stay at someplace unique like the Glacier Park Hotel, I'd need to make reservations at least a year in advance, especially for a date during the height of the riding season. Or if I planned to go into Canada, I might need to a) find and b) renew my passport.

The First Ultimate Motorcycle Journey

We tend to think of cross-country bikes as something big, faired, with neatly-arranged saddlebags and a top case. The first fellow to set out on a cross-country journey had none of that. George Wyman left San Francisco in May 1903, bound for New York on a 1.25 hp 90cc motorized bicycle. With few passable roads in that day, Wyman often found himself riding railroad tracks, and scaling passes by using the wooden train tunnels clinging to the mountain sides. When he became mired in mud, farmers would hitch up a team of horses to pull him out. Repairs were usually made roadside, using whatever materials could be improvised. By the time Wyman reached Albany, New York, the motor was unrepairable and Wyman pedaled the remaining 150 miles to his final destination. After 3,800 miles and 50 days, George Wyman was the first person to complete a transcontinental trip using any kind of motorized vehicle, and he did it on a motorcycle.

The farther you plan to roam from home, the more you need to think about your inventory list. Is it possible you might be riding dirt roads? Are you comfortable handling gravel or mud? Do you need to develop some new riding skills? Will your bike need to be serviced before or during your trip? Will you be tent camping or "credit card" camping? If you're motelling it, does the area you're riding into have many travel services, or do you need to plan ahead?

When you commit these things to a list, you can let them go and you don't have to keep turning them over in your head. You'll feel more confident when you're ready to leave that you haven't forgotten something important. And you'll have more fun on your journey.

Prepare

As you start ticking off stuff on your list, there are a couple of areas under preparation that I'd like to mention. Maybe this is just a personal preference but I hate, hate, hate scrambling around at the last minute preparing for a trip. Bending down to check tire pressures when I'm fully suited. Unpacking the tank bag to find my earplugs. Fiddling with that stupid Bluetooth headset,

There's something especially appealing about the notion of traveling by bike and sleeping under the stars.

The date for road openings through high mountain passes can vary widely from one year to the next. In 2009, Tioga Pass, a popular entrance to Yosemite, opened on May 19. The next year, it opened on June 5th.

trying to remember the right sequence of buttons to pair it up with my iPod. Dumb stuff that prevents me from just stepping over the bike and riding out on Day 1 with a clear mind and no agenda.

So, with that list of action items in hand, you should be able to start working that list, getting everything done months, weeks, and days in advance of your departure. If you've known a half year in advance you were planning a two-week trip, there's no reason you should have to scramble on the morning of the first day to get ready to leave.

One area that seems to give folks the most trouble is the idea of breaking in any new travel gear or gadgets they plan to take on their trip. Having spent some time in the powersports business, I can't tell you how often I've spoken to folks who want to, say, buy a motorcycle camper for a trip coming up in the next week. More commonly, how often have you spent the night before a big trip trying to get that GPS or radar detector or satellite radio dock wired up and working? Umm hmmm, I know you have (because I have, too).

It's important to tackle these items well in advance so that you can become comfortable with the changes these new accessories bring to your riding routine, and so you won't be tempted to slap them on any old way just to get the job done before you leave. Chances are you'll forget a safety pin, leaving your new GPS hanging by a thread. Or you'll wire up something that's gonna come loose and take out your lights on a moonless night in a Louisiana bayou.

Play

I'm going to admit right now that I am and have always been a goal-oriented person. It's hard for me to look at something and not consider how it can be optimized, organized, or turned into a business opportunity. That's just the kind of guy I am. So it's damned hard to undertake a motorcycle journey without some kind of agenda. I am currently involved in a twelve-step program to help me overcome this.

But seriously, I know there are riders like me who, intentionally or not, make too many plans and set goals too lofty for their journeys. When they find they're four days into a trip and five hundred miles behind,

Riders set off to tame a portion of US 212 through Beartooth Pass in the northwestern corner of Wyoming. This approach leads to the eastern entrance of Yellowstone.

frustration begins to mount. The habits of co-riders become noticeably more irritating. Your riding buddy seems to be moving slower instead of faster. A day of rain or a mechanical setback becomes calamity. The trip becomes much less fun.

Relax. Let it happen. This is what you're out here for. To roll with the punches. Take things as they come. If you did a little planning in advance and know you'll need new tires, that call you placed two months ago to the dealer to line up your service on the other side of the country will give you peace of mind. If you made a backup packet with credit card numbers and a duplicate license, losing your wallet will just be an inconvenience, not a disaster. Creating a rough itinerary with enough loops to cut out a day if bad weather prevails means you can unwind and spend time chatting with your riding buddy on the front porch of the lodge in-

stead of battling crappy weather to ride a hundred miserable miles. I don't mean to sound like a life coach, I'm just saying that if you've planned and prepared, let yourself go play. Stuff's gonna happen and the especially weird situations you encounter on the road make for a great stories around the campfire.

Or Pay . . .

An increasingly popular option for tackling big trips is to rely on the expertise of those who organize and conduct motorcycle tours for a living. This can be the best choice if you are limited on time. Heck, if you were planning to buy a dual-purpose bike and outfit it just for an occasional trip into the wild, beating the hell out of, I mean, renting someone else's equipment might be a less expensive option in the long run.

New tour operators spring up all the time.

Most are well-meaning, but only a few have the resources to build up a profitable touring company, so you'll want to do your homework before you put down your money for a trip deposit. Trip insurance isn't a bad idea.

If you are heading to the west coast and would prefer an organized visit of northern California, look no further than PashnitTours.com. Tim Mayhew has put in 20 years photographing and writing about California's roads. You've seen his published work in *Cycle World, City Bike,* and *Motorcycle Tour and Travel.* His partner Tim Regehr operates Sopiago Springs Resort (sopiago.com), the only moto-specific campground in California. These guys have logged hundreds of thousands of miles throughout California. Thirty-thousand riders a day check out www.pashnit.com to swap riding adventures. Must be something there worth checking out.

And then there's Ron Ayres. You may recognize Ron's name from some of the documented endurance rides he's done including setting the record for hitting the lower 48 states and Alaska within seven days. After Ron retired from the business world in 1999, he set out to create a motorcycle touring company that would offer a premium riding experience with adventures both in and out of the saddle. His company, Ayres Adventures (ayresadventures.com) offers motorcycle tours around the world including organized trips through western Canada and Alaska and the western states.

However You Choose to Ride, Ride!

It's a big world out there and there's a lot of twisty pavement that you need to carve. Go make some stories, with a group, or by yourself. And I'll see you—on the road!

Documented Rides and Tours

For goal-minded riders, the idea of achieving something adds to the appeal of a long journey. Displaying a certificate on your wall or adding a special patch can be a fun memento of your trip.

Documented tours are sponsored by local and national organizations with countless themes. The American Motorcyclist Association keeps track of many of the most prominent tours but they don't have a corner on the market.

One of the best known AMA tours is the Four Corners tour sponsored by the Southern California Motorcycling Association. Riders have 21 days in which to visit San Ysidro, California; Blaine, Washington; Madawaska, Maine; and Key West, Florida and return to their starting point (www.usa4corners.org).

Another class of documented endurance rides are sponsored by the Iron Butt Association (IBA), though these might not be for everyone. To qualify for membership in this august group, one must complete a 1000-mile ride in less than 24 hours, known as a Saddlesore 1000. The ride lengths escalate to greater heights of insanity after that, but it's all in good fun (www.ironbutt.com).

In recent years, states that encourage motorcycle travel, such as Virginia, have sponsored their own in-state tours to inspire local riders and to draw folks from outside as well (www.motorcycleva.com). This is a trend we can hope will continue as visitor bureaus around the country realize that riders like to spend money on vacation. And they need to eat and sleep, too!

INDEX

PHOTO CREDITS

Unless otherwise noted, all photos are by the author.

We gratefully acknowledge the following for photos used in this book:

Jeff Adams 49, 67; Nick Ares 297; Marshall Astor 168 lower; Bob Aylor 279, 299, 307, 337 lower, 341; AyresAdventures.com 169, 170, 171, 173, 174, 176, 177, 209, 228, 232 lower, 232 upper, 234 upper, 238 lower, 242, 351, 354 lower, 355, 359, 365, 370-371, 372, 380, 381, 382, 385, 389; Sam Bebee 277; Shane Becker 211 upper; Dave Bezaire and Susi Havens-Bezaire 376, 379; Matt Boulton 45; Vic Brincat 33 lower; Byways.org 126, 207, 216, 300; Phillip Capper 247; Martin Cathrae 25 upper; Scott Catron 239 upper; Charlottetown PEI 35; Andrea Church 205; Andy Clarke 44 lower; Diane Constable 87; Claye Curtis 101 lower, 127, 140 upper, 146, 182 upper, 183 upper, 212, 214, 219, 220-221, 225, 229, 230, 236, 244, 253 lower, 253 upper, 259, 260, 52 upper, 77, 83, 90, 94; Davebluedevil 157 lower; Richie Diesterheft 100, 241; Joshua Duggan 42; Eli Duke 89; Steve Dunleavy 258, 296 lower; Jamie Edmonds 268, 287 lower; Dawn Endico 265 upper; Tim Engleman 68-69; Environmental Protection Agency 101 upper; Marc Evans 362; Mark Flanagan 55; Eric Fredericks 296 upper; Leonard G 274 upper; Doug Gilmer 2-3, 313, 321, 322, 353, 354 upper, 358, 361, 363 upper; David Gluns 352; Chris Gushue 46; Billy Hathorn 185; HellsCanyonRally.com 334 upper, 344, 9; Robert Hilliard 179 upper; Tom Hiltz 15; H Matthew Howarth 261; Craig Howell 298, 305; Iron Horse Motorcycle Lodge 128; Dennis Jarvis 22, 25 lower, 27, 33 upper, 39 upper, 62, 63, 72-73; Doug Kerr 59; Frank Kovalchek 233, 335, 339, 384; Rachel Kramer 79 upper, 86; John Krieg 287 upper, 39 lower; Brett L. 291; Leaflet 155; Doug Letterman 265 lower; Matthew Lieber 323; Sean Loyless 160; Natalie Lucier 41, 43; Ken Lund 147, 250, 262, 269; Joe Mabel 348 upper; Bruce McKay 1, 378, 383; Nic McPhee 369; Dene Miles 233-234; Ian P. Miller 71; Roy Montgomery 189; Dana Moos 61 lower; National Park Service 1,vii?, 102, 103, 104, 141, 142, 150, 162, 166, 167, 168, 203, 210 lower, 210 upper, 223 lower, 223 upper, 224, 282, 293 lower, 293 upper, 301, 309, 316 upper, 317, 324, 331, 338, 50, 52 lower, 78 lower, 85; Chris Norrick 181; Deb Nystrom 96; Ky Olsen 91; Dzmitry Parul 124; Pashnit.com 274 lower, 292, 310; PDSPhil 152; Tim Pearce 202 upper; PedalFreak 79 lower; Randen Pederson 105; Greg Peterson 243; Joanna Poe 47; Public Domain 196 lower, 197, 263, 284, 357; Qyd 363 lower; Refractor 222; Ron Reiring 336; R. Robinson 319; Jason Rogers 240; Miles Sabin 295; Peter Schinkel 149; Reinhard Schon 226; Rob Shenk 56 upper; Shiny Things 314 lower, 315; Ed Siasoco 270 upper; Sierra Club 255; David Smith 270 lower; James Somers 36 lower; Michael Sprague 16; Wolfgang Staudt 13, 235 upper, 267; Stavkirke 97; Peter Stevens 6-7, 333; John Stracke 80 upper; DW Strucke 56-57 lower, 61 upper; US Army Corps of Engineers 106; USDA 99; USRiderNews.com 114 upper, 125, 140 lower, 143 lower, 143 upper, 144, 145, 151, 153; Miguel Vieria 266; Miguel Vieira 303; Mik Watson 276; Todd Wickersty 330; David Wilbanks 172; Chris Willis 283; Wonderland 337 upper; Snotty Wong 53; Woody 178; Roger Zender 80 lower; the following from iStockphoto: ACMPhoto 26 upper; Devin Allphin 281; Elvis Fontenot 164; fotogal 217; maomaotou 211 lower, 213; marekuliasz 215; Paul McKinnon 26 lower; Stephen Meese 27 lower; pchoui 36 upper; STA_C 128 lower; the following from Wikimedia: Aconcagua 17, 21; Adam Baker 156; Kimon Berlin 195, 202 lower, 206; ABoukai 273; Art Bromage 343; Chensiyuan 30, 31; CMBJ 175; Colonel47 159; Lee Coursey 65; Richie Diesterheft 201; Dori 93; J. Dykstra 163; Gregg M. Erickson 349 lower; Colin Faulkingham 198; HylgeriaK 360 lower; Ikiwaner 349 upper; Jorobeq 288 lower; Kelvin Kay 348 lower; Lars001 286; LoneStarMike 179 lower; Malber 69 upper; Ad Meskens 111, 182 lower; Nader Moussa 377; Mrhyak 334 lower; Nilfanion 44 upper; Omegatron 78 upper; P199 109; Plumbago 183 lower; Wing-Chi Poon 196 upper, 200; Sam 374; Daniel Schwen 285; Marc Shandro 345; Jason Sturner 275 upper; Taxiarchos 19; Mark A. Wilson 360 upper; Yufei Yuan 375; Zereshk 249;

Front cover photo by Steve Irby
Back cover photos (top to bottom) by chensiyuan/wikimedia; Ian P Miller; Ayres Adventures

Maps © Whitehorse Press

AUG 0 1 2012

ABOUT THE AUTHOR

Motojournalist Dale Coyner has long enjoyed discovering what's "around the bend" on his bike, an interest he credits to days spent roaming the countryside in his youth and the *On the Road* reports of legendary broadcast journalist Charles Kuralt.

On your next journey, you might pass him in some lonely spot, carving the curves on his Honda ST-1300. There's a better chance though you'll find him swinging on the front porch of a backcountry general store, chatting with folks over biscuits and gravy at the local diner, or peering through dusty glass at a thimble display in a one-room country museum.

Dale enjoys the fact that, contrary to popular belief, the people he encounters are equally curious about motorcycle travelers, viewing a rider with helmet in hand with less suspicion than someone in a four-wheeler.

Dale is the owner of OpenRoadOutfitters.com, an online store specializing in motorcycle cargo trailers, campers, and related accessories. Read more about his recent adventures and projects at DaleCoyner.com. He welcomes your e-mail at dale@coyner.com.